DATE DUE

DEMCO 38-296

AN INTRODUCTION TO
JAPANESE SOCIETY

CONTEMPORARY JAPANESE SOCIETY

Editor:
Yoshio Sugimoto, La Trobe University

Advisory Editors:
Harumi Befu, Kyoto Bunkyo University
Roger Goodman, Oxford University
Michio Muramatsu, Kyoto University
Wolfgang Seifert, Universität Heidelberg
Chizuko Ueno, University of Tokyo

This series will provide a comprehensive portrayal of contemporary Japan through analysis of key aspects of Japanese society and culture, ranging from work and gender politics to science and technology. The series endeavours to link the relative strengths of Japanese and English-speaking scholars through collaborative authorship. Each title will be a balanced investigation of the area under consideration, including a synthesis of competing views.

The series will appeal to a wide range of readers from undergraduate beginners in Japanese studies to professional scholars. It will enable readers to grasp the diversity of Japanese society as well as the variety of theories and approaches available to study it.

AN INTRODUCTION TO
JAPANESE SOCIETY

YOSHIO SUGIMOTO

La Trobe University

CAMBRIDGE
UNIVERSITY PRESS

VERSITY OF CAMBRIDGE
nbridge CB2 1RP, United Kingdom

The Edinburgh Building, Cambridge CB2 2RU, United Kingdom
40 West 20th Street, New York, NY 10011–4211, USA
10 Stamford Road, Oakleigh, Melbourne 3166, Australia

First published 1997

Printed in Hong Kong by Colorcraft

Typeset in Baskerville 10/12 pt

National Library of Australia Cataloguing in Publication data

Sugimoto, Yoshio, 1939–.
An introduction to Japanese society.
Bibliography.
Includes index.
ISBN 0 521 41692 2.
ISBN 0 521 42704 5 (pbk.).
1. Japan – Social life and customs – 1945–. 2. Japan –
Social conditions – 1945–. 3. Japan – Economic conditions –
1945–. I. Title. (Series: Contemporary Japanese society).

Library of Congress Cataloguing in Publication data

Sugimoto, Yoshio, 1939–.
An introduction to Japanese society / Yoshio Sugimoto.
    p.   cm. – (Contemporary Japanese society)
Includes bibliographical references and index.
ISBN 0-521-41692-2 (alk. paper). – ISBN 0-521-42704-5 (pbk. :
alk. paper)
1. Japan – Social conditions. 2. Japan – Social life and customs.
3. National characteristics, Japanese. I. Title. II. Series.
HN723.S7 1997
306'.0952–dc20   96-28229

A catalogue record for this book is available from the British Library

ISBN 0 521 41692 2 hardback
ISBN 0 521 42704 5 paperback

Contents

Figures

Tables

Preface

The images of Japanese society both in Japan and abroad have fluctuated over time under shifting intellectual contexts. Subjected to changes in Japan's political economy and international status, the portrait of Japan has swung back and forth like a pendulum between adoration and antipathy. The theoretical framework of Japan analysis has also fluctuated between two poles: particularistic characterizations and universalistic generalizations. Conscious of these competing perspectives, one inevitably has to be selective in producing a general textbook. In writing this book which delineates such a wide range of aspects of Japanese society as generation, occupation, education, gender, minority, and popular culture, I attempted to restore three balances in the study of contemporary Japan.

The first of these concerns the degree of homogeneity of Japanese society. The view that Japan comprises an extremely uniform culture continues to be both dominant and pervasive despite several studies which questioned and challenged this perspective in the 1980s and the early 1990s. The competing multicultural paradigm which highlights the internal variation and stratification of Japanese society remains peripheral and does not appear to have received the attention it deserves. This book makes a modest attempt to rectify this imbalance by focussing on subcultural diversity and class competition within Japanese society.

The second bias pertains to the continuing dominance of the so-called group model of Japanese society, which maintains that the Japanese are essentially faithful to their groups and uniquely oriented to their consensual integration. While the Japanese undoubtedly show group behavior in many situations, many questions remain unanswered as to whether Japanese groupism is uniquely high in comparison with other countries. It also continues to be debatable whether the Japanese act in a groupist way in all spheres of life, whether different social groups in Japan exhibit different levels of groupism, and whether the Japanese behave in groups on the basis of voluntary commitment or under the constraint of ideological manipulation. This text underscores the significance of these reservations and presents a countervailing perspective against the group model.

Finally, this book endeavors to strike a reasonable balance between Japanese- and English-language publications as sources of information and inspiration. Though designed as an introductory text, it invites readers to familiarize themselves with contemporary debates and controversies among Japanese analysts who write in Japanese. Many students in the English-language world would find it difficult to read Japanese publications in Japanese, though they can pursue their interests in reading books and articles in English. Students just beginning in Japanese studies will benefit greatly from having a balanced understanding of both insiders' and outsiders' views of Japanese society. For this purpose, I have introduced a number of Japanese *emic* concepts and propositions to demonstrate Japanese perceptions and self-images.

Financial support from the Australian Research Council enabled me to collect and examine data for this study. Thanks to the ARC grant, I have been able to travel several times between Melbourne and Tokyo, live in Japan for about half of the last three years and exchange views with Japanese academics on various issues. A fellowship from the Japan Foundation was also instrumental in implementing the initial phase of the study. I am grateful for the support of these organizations.

The multicultural environment in Australia where I have lived for nearly a quarter of a century has influenced my views of Japanese society. I am deeply indebted to the intellectual vitality of my colleagues in Melbourne and Canberra. My partner, Machiko Sato, who has published several books for the Japanese readership, has given me continuous encouragement, thoughtful criticism, and invaluable insight, for which I am most thankful. I have also benefitted from many lively discussions with my students at La Trobe University (Melbourne), Universität Heidelberg (Germany), and the University of Tsukuba (Japan) on the points contained in this study.

Writing a book is always a liberating experience for me. I hope that readers share some of my delight in treading the paths outlined in this text.

Yoshio Sugimoto
Hachioji, Tokyo

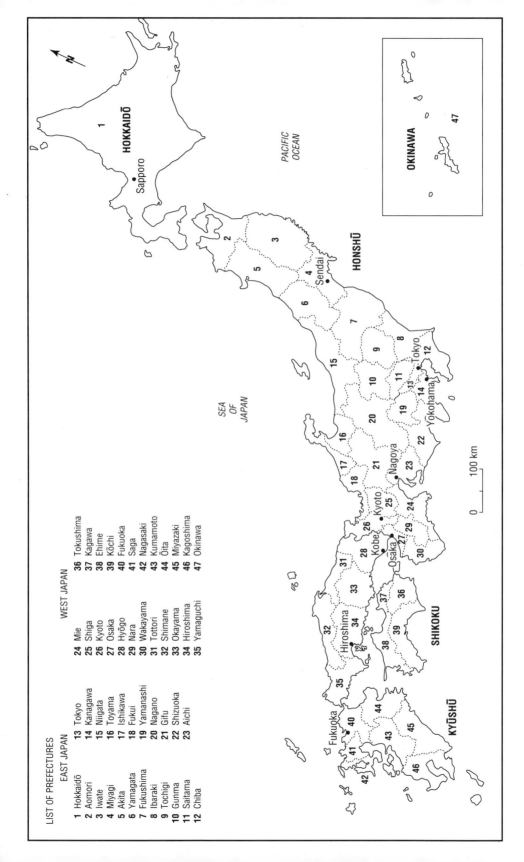

LIST OF PREFECTURES

EAST JAPAN

1 Hokkaidō
2 Aomori
3 Iwate
4 Miyagi
5 Akita
6 Yamagata
7 Fukushima
8 Ibaraki
9 Tochigi
10 Gunma
11 Saitama
12 Chiba
13 Tokyo
14 Kanagawa
15 Niigata
16 Toyama
17 Ishikawa
18 Fukui
19 Yamanashi
20 Nagano
21 Gifu
22 Shizuoka
23 Aichi

WEST JAPAN

24 Mie
25 Shiga
26 Kyoto
27 Osaka
28 Hyōgo
29 Nara
30 Wakayama
31 Tottori
32 Shimane
33 Okayama
34 Hiroshima
35 Yamaguchi
36 Tokushima
37 Kagawa
38 Ehime
39 Kōchi
40 Fukuoka
41 Saga
42 Nagasaki
43 Kumamoto
44 Ōita
45 Miyazaki
46 Kagoshima
47 Okinawa

HOKKAIDŌ

Sapporo

PACIFIC OCEAN

OKINAWA

47

HONSHŪ

Sendai

SEA OF JAPAN

Tokyo

Yokohama

Nagoya

Kyoto

Kobe

Osaka

Hiroshima

SHIKOKU

Fukuoka

KYŪSHŪ

0   100 km

1

The Japan Phenomenon
and the Social Sciences

I MULTICULTURAL JAPAN

1 Sampling Problem and the Question of Visibility

Hypothetical questions sometimes inspire the sociological imagination. Suppose that a being from a different planet arrived in Japan and wanted to meet a typical Japanese, one who best typified the Japanese adult population. Whom should the social scientists choose? To answer this question, several factors would have to be considered: gender, occupation, educational background, and so on.

To begin, the person chosen should be a female, because women outnumber men in Japan; the 1990 census shows that sixty-three million women and sixty million men live in the Japanese archipelago. With regard to occupation, she would definitely not be employed in a large corporation but would work in a small enterprise, since fewer than one in eight workers is employed in a company with three hundred or more employees. Nor would she be guaranteed life-time employment, since those who work under this arrangement amount at most to only a quarter of Japan's workforce. She would not belong to a labor union, because less than a quarter of Japanese workers are unionized. She would not be university-educated. Fewer than one in five Japanese have a university degree, and even among the younger generation today only about a quarter of the relevant age group advance to universities with four-year degree courses. Table 1.1 summarizes these demographic realities.

The identification of the average Japanese would certainly involve much more complicated quantitative analysis. But the alien would come closer to the "center" of the Japanese population by choosing a female, non-unionized and non-permanent employee in a small business without

1

Table 1.1 Japan's population distribution

Variables	Majority	Minority
Gender[a]	Female: 62.9 million (51%)	Male: 60.7 million (49%)
Employees by firm size[b]	Small firms – less than 300 employees: 48.4 million (88%)	Large firms – 300 or more: 6.6 million (12%)
Educational background[c]	Those without university education: 79.5 million (88%)	University graduates: 10.8 million (12%)
Union membership in labor force[d]	Non-unionists: 39.7 million (76%)	Unionists: 12.7 million (24%)

Sources:
[a] Population census conducted in 1990.
[b] The Establishment Census conducted by the Management and Coordination Agency in 1991. The data cover all private-sector establishments except individual proprietorship establishments in agriculture, forestry and fishery.
[c] Population census conducted in 1990. University graduates do not include those who have completed junior college and technical college.
[d] Labor Union Basic Survey, conducted by the Ministry of Labor in 1993.

university education than a male, unionized, permanent employee with a university degree working for a large company.

When outsiders visualize the Japanese, however, they tend to think of men rather than women, career employees in large companies rather than non-permanent workers in small firms, and university graduates rather than high-school leavers, for these are the images presented on television and in newspaper and magazine articles. Some academic studies have also attempted to generalize about Japanese society on the basis of observations of its male elite sector, and have thereby helped to reinforce this sampling bias.[1] Moreover, because a particular cluster of individuals who occupy high positions in a large company have greater access to mass media and publicity, the life-styles and value orientations of those in that cluster have acquired a disproportionately high level of visibility in the analysis of Japanese society at the expense of the wider cross-section of its population.

2 Homogeneity Assumptions

While every society is unique in some way, Japan is particularly unusual in having so many people who believe that their country is unique.[2] Regardless of whether Japan is "uniquely unique" in sociological and psychological reality, it is certainly unique for the number of Japanese publications which propagate the unique Japan argument. The so-called group model of Japanese society represents the most explicit and coherent formulation of this line of argument and remains the most influential framework for interpreting the Japanese and Japanese social structure. Put most succinctly, the model is based upon three lines of argument.

First, at the individual, psychological level, the Japanese are portrayed as having a personality which lacks a fully developed ego or independent self. The best-known example of this claim is Doi's notion of *amae* which refers to the allegedly unique psychological inclination among the Japanese to seek emotional satisfaction by prevailing upon and depending on their superiors.[3] They feel no need for any explicit demonstration of individuality. Loyalty to the group is a primary value. Giving oneself to the promotion and realization of the group's goals gives the Japanese a special psychological satisfaction.

Second, at the interpersonal, intragroup level, human interaction is depicted in terms of Japanese group orientation. According to Nakane, for example, the Japanese attach great importance to the maintenance of harmony *within* the group. To that end, relationships between superiors and inferiors are carefully cultivated and maintained. One's status within the group depends on the length of one's membership in the group. Furthermore, the Japanese maintain particularly strong interpersonal ties with those in the same hierarchical chain of command within their own organization. In other words, vertical loyalties are dominant. The vertically organized Japanese contrast sharply with Westerners, who tend to form horizontal groups which define their membership in terms of such criteria as class and stratification which cut across hierarchical organization lines.[4]

Finally, at the intergroup level, the literature has emphasized that integration and harmony are achieved effectively *between* Japanese groups, making Japan a "consensus society". This is said to account for the exceptionally high level of stability and cohesion in Japanese society, which has aided political and other leaders in their efforts to organize or mobilize the population efficiently. Moreover, the ease with which the energy of the Japanese can be focussed on a task has contributed in no small measure to Japan's remarkably rapid economic growth during the half-century since the war. From a slightly different angle, Ishida argues that intergroup competition in loyalty makes groups conform to national goals and facilitates the formation of national consensus.[5]

For decades, Japanese writers have debated on the essence of "Japaneseness." Numerous books have been written under such titles as *What are the Japanese?* and *What is Japan?*[6] Many volumes on *Nihon-rashisa* (Japanese-like qualities) have appeared.[7] Social science discourse in

Japan abounds with examinations of *Nihon-teki* (Japanese-style) tendencies in business, politics, social relations, psychology, and so on. Some researchers are preoccupied with inquiries into the "hidden shape,"[8] "basic layer," and "archetype"[9] of Japanese culture. These works portray Japanese society as highly homogeneous with only limited internal variation, and give it some all-embracing label. Hamaguchi, for example, who presents what he calls a contextual model of the Japanese, maintains that the concept of the individual is irrelevant in the study of the Japanese, who tend to see the interpersonal relationship itself (*kanjin*) – not the individuals involved in it – as the basic unit of action.[10] Amanuma argues that the Japanese core personality is based on the drive for *ganbari* (endurance and persistence), which accounts for every aspect of Japanese behavior.[11] Publishing in Japanese, a Korean writer, Lee, contends that the Japanese have a unique *chijimi shikō*, a miniaturizing orientation which has enabled them to skillfully miniaturize their environment and products, ranging from *bonsai* plants, small cars, and portable electronic appliances to computer chips.[12] The list of publications which aim to define Japanese society with just one key word could be expanded interminably, although the descriptive tag used may differ.

At least four underlying assumptions remain constant in these studies. First, it is presumed that *all* Japanese share the attribute in question – be it *amae* or miniature orientation – regardless of their class, gender, occupation, and other stratification variables. Second, it is also assumed that there is virtually no variation among the Japanese in the degree to which they possess the characteristic in question. Little attention is given to the possibility that some Japanese may have it in greater degree while others have very little of it. Third, the trait in question, be it group-orientation or *kanjin*, is supposed to exist only marginally in other societies, particularly in Western societies. That is, the feature is thought to be uniquely Japanese. Finally, the fourth presupposition is an ahistorical assumption that the trait has prevailed in Japan for an unspecified period of time, independently of historical circumstances. Writings based on some or all of these propositions have been published in Japan *ad nauseam* and have generated a genre referred to as *Nihonjinron* (which literally means theories on the Japanese). Although some analysts have challenged the validity of *Nihonjinron* assertions on methodological, empirical, and ideological grounds,[13] the discourse has retained its popular appeal, attracting many readers and maintaining a commercially viable publication industry.

The notion of Japan being homogeneous goes in tandem with the claim that it is an exceptionally egalitarian society with little class differentiation. This assertion is based on scattered observations of company life. Thus, with regard to resource distribution, some contrast the relatively modest salary gaps between Japanese executive managers and their employees with the marked discrepancy between the salaries of American business executives and their workers. Focussing on the alleged weakness of class consciousness, others point out that Japanese managers are prepared to get their hands dirty, wear the same blue overalls as assembly workers in factories and share elevators, toilets, and company restaurants with low-ranking employees.[14] Still others suggest that Japanese managers and rank-and-file employees work in large offices without status-based partition, sharing work in an egalitarian way. Furthermore, public opinion polls taken by the Prime Minister's Office have indicated that eight to nine out of ten Japanese classify themselves as middle class. While there is debate as to what all these figures mean, they have nevertheless strengthened the *images* of egalitarian Japan. A few observers have gone as far as to call Japan a "land of equality"[15] and a "one-class society."[16] Firmly entrenched in all these descriptions is the portrayal of the Japanese as identifying themselves primarily as members of a company, *alma mater*, faction, clique, or other functional group rather than as members of a class or social stratum.

3 Diversity and Stratification

The portrayal of Japan as a homogeneous and egalitarian society, however, contradicts many observations that it is more diversified, heterogeneous, and multicultural than is widely believed to be the case. This book presents these facets of Japanese society in some detail, examining the country's regional, generational, occupational, and educational varieties as well as gender and minority issues. It does not try to claim that Japan is unusually diversified or exceptionally stratified in comparison with other industrialized societies, but challenges the view that it is uniquely homogeneous and egalitarian. The central idea here is simple and modest: Japan does not differ fundamentally from other countries in its internal variation and stratification, though some of its specific manifestations and concrete forms may contrast with those in Western societies.

The image of multicultural Japan may sit uncomfortably with the relatively homogeneous racial makeup of Japanese society, yet subcultures do proliferate on a number of non-racial dimensions, such as region, gender, age, occupation, education, and so forth. To the extent that subculture is defined as a set of value expectations and life-styles shared by a section of a given population, Japanese society indeed reveals an abundance of subcultural groupings along these lines. As a conglomerate of subcultures, Japan may be viewed as a multicultural society, or a multi-subcultural society. Furthermore, most subcultural units are rank-ordered in terms of access to various resources including economic privilege, political power, social prestige, information, and knowledge. In this sense, Japan is a multistratified society as well. Let us now take a preliminary look at some concrete illustrations of these multicultural and multistratified features of Japanese society. Each point will be scrutinized in more detail in later chapters.

(a) Subcultural Diversity

Contrary to the widely held view, Japan has an extensive range of minority issues, ethnic and quasi-ethnic, which proponents of the homogeneous Japan thesis tend not to address. One can identify several minority groups in Japan even if one does so narrowly, referring only to groups subjected to discrimination and prejudice because of culturally generated ethnic myths, illusions, and fallacies.

In Hokkaidō, the northernmost island of the nation, over twenty thousand Ainu live as an indigenous minority. Their situation arose with the first attempts of Japan's central regime to unify the nation under its leadership around the sixth and seventh centuries and to conquer the Ainu territories in northern Japan. In addition, some three million burakumin are subjected to prejudice and many of them are forced to live in separate communities partly because of an unfounded myth that they are ethnically different.[17] Their ancestors' plight began in the feudal period under the Tokugawa shogunate which ruled the nation for two and a half centuries from the seventeenth century and institutionalized an outcast class at the bottom of a caste system. Though the class was legally abolished after the Meiji Restoration in 1868, discrimination and prejudice have persisted. Some seven hundred thousand Koreans form the biggest foreign minority group in Japan. Their problem originated from the Japanese colonization of Korea at the beginning of the twentieth century, and the Japanese importation of Koreans as cheap labor for industries. A similar number of foreign workers, both documented and undocumented, live in the country as a result of their influx into the Japanese labor market since the 1980s, mainly from Asia and the Middle East, in their attempt to earn quick cash in the appreciated Japanese yen. Finally, over 1.2 million Okinawans who live in the Ryukyu islands at the southern end of Japan face bigotry from time to time on the basis of the belief that they are ethnically different, and incur suspicion because of the islands' cultural autonomy over centuries.

The estimated total membership of these groups is about five million, which represents some 4 percent of the population of Japan.[18] If one includes those who marry into these minority groups and suffer the same kinds of prejudice, the number is greater. In the Kansai region where burakumin and Korean residents are concentrated, the proportion of the minority population exceeds 10 percent. These ratios may not be as high as those in migrant societies such as the United States, Canada and Australia,[19] but they seem inconsistent with the claim that Japan is a society uniquely lacking minority issues. These issues tend to be obfuscated, blurred, and even made invisible in Japan partly because the principal minority groups do not differ in skin color and other biological characteristics from the majority of Japanese.

In international comparison, Japan does not rank uniquely high in its composition of minority groups which exist because of their ethnicity or fabricated ethnic fictions about them. Table 1.2 lists some of the nations whose ethnic minority groups constitute less than 10 percent. Given that the Japanese figure is 4 percent, Japan's position would be somewhere in the second band; it is certainly difficult for it to be in the top band. To be sure, different societies define minority groups on the basis of different criteria, but that is exactly the point. Japan seems to be unique not in its absence of minority issues but in the decisiveness with which the government and other organizations attempt to ignore their existence.

Regional variation is perhaps the most obvious diversity in Japan. The nation is divided into two subcultural regions, eastern Japan with Tokyo and Yokohama as its center and western Japan with Osaka, Kyoto, and Kobe as its hub. The two regions differ in language, social relations, food, housing, and many other respects. The subcultural differences between the areas facing the Pacific and those facing the Sea of Japan are also well known. Japan has a wide variety of dialects. A Japanese from Aomori Prefecture, the northernmost area of Honshū Island, and one from Kagoshima, the southernmost district in Kyūshū Island, can scarcely comprehend each other's dialects. Different districts have different festivals, folk songs, and local dances. Customs governing birth, marriage, and death differ regionally so much that books explaining the differences are quite popular.[20] The exact degree of domestic regional variation is difficult to assess in quantitative terms and by internationally comparative standards, but there is no evidence to suggest that it is more limited in Japan.

Japanese language is a diversity-conscious tongue. Even if one does not assume any direct correlation between language and culture, one must acknowledge that Japanese, which is sensitive to diversity, reflects Japan's cultural patterns to a considerable extent. Japanese is a sexist language, differentiating between male and female vocabulary, expressions, and accents. The male language is supposed to be coarse, crude, and aggressive, while the female language is expected to be soft, polite, and submissive.[21] Even at the level of self-identification, the male expressions for "I", *boku, ore,* and *washi,* differ from their more formal and refined female

Table 1.2   Estimated proportions of ethnic and pseudo-ethnic minorities in selected countries

Level	Minority groups in the total population	Specific countries
Band 1	0–3 %	Austria, Bangladesh, Denmark, Dominican Republic, Greece, Iceland, Korea (North), Korea (South), Libya, Portugal
Band 2	3–6%	Czech, Finland, Germany, Haiti, Japan, Lebanon, Liberia, Netherlands
Band 3	6–11%	Albania, Cambodia, China, Egypt, Mongolia, Romania, Sweden

Note: Calculated from Famighetti (1994).

counterparts, *watashi* and *watakushi.* Japanese is also a hierarchy-oriented language. Honorific expressions are essential ingredients of everyday Japanese conversation, in which one must always be attentive to the social status of the person to whom one talks, noting whether the addressee is higher or lower in the social hierarchy. Without assuming that Japanese is exceptional in these regards, it can be postulated that the Japanese are at least heedful of a variety of status groups and their respective cultural orientations.

Conscious of the life-style differences of various groups, the Japanese often refer in everyday vocabulary to a variety of subcultural groupings using the term *zoku*, a suffix that literally means a tribe. Cases in point include *shayō-zoku*, those employees who have the privilege of using company expense accounts to enjoy drinking, eating, playing golf, and other entertainments with their clients after working hours; *madogiwa-zoku* (the window-gazing tribe), those company employees who have come to the end of their career in middle age, have few tasks to perform, and sit near the window away from the center of activity in a large, Japanese-style, non-partitioned office; and *bōsō-zoku*, the bikers who produce noise pollution in a quiet neighborhood.

In addition to these long-standing variations in Japanese society, there are strong indications that its degree of diversity is rapidly increasing in some areas. Specifically, the patterns of Japanese consumer behavior became diversified in a fundamental way in the 1980s. Previously, manu-facturers sold models standardized for mass consumption, successfully promoting them through sales campaigns and advertisements. Recently, however, this strategy has become ineffective because consumers have begun to take an interest in products in tune with their personal preferences. They have become more unpredictable, selective, and inquisitive. The notion of the Japanese as uniform mass consumers does not effectively account for their consumer behavior patterns today.

Numerous Japanese popular writings published in the 1980s and early 1990s paid attention to the variety and even stratification of Japanese lifestyles. Market analysts, for instance, were quick to point out the increasing diversity of the consumer market. A consumer behavior study[22] suggests the emergence of *shōshū* – individualized, divided, and small-unit masses – as opposed to *taishū*, the undifferentiated, uniform, and large-scale masses. The research institute of Hakuhōdō,[23] a leading advertising agency, also argued that the notion of *bunshū* (segmented masses) would account for the behavior of consumers more effectively than the conventional way of viewing them as a homogeneous entity. *Kinkonkan*, a best-seller produced by Kazuhiro Watanabe and Tarako Productions, classifies the everyday behavior of the Japanese as either *marukin* (the moneyed type) or *marubi* (the needy type), a caricaturized taxonomy which has attained a wide circulation. These concepts perhaps reflected some entrenched and emerging patterns of Japanese society, as the popularized notions, buzzwords, and catchphrases that they produced struck a responsive chord in the hearts of many readers who found they somehow represented reality.

Gender differences in value orientation are arguably more pronounced than ever with the gradual rise of feminist consciousness at various levels. Opinion surveys have consistently shown that more women than men disagree with the notion of home being the woman's place. The proportion of women who feel that marriage is not necessary if they can support themselves invariably outnumbers that of men.[24] Women show much more commitment than men to welfare, medical, educational, consumer, and other community activities.[25]

These observations of social diversification and segmentation, and of polarization of life-styles, imply that Japanese society is not as classless and egalitarian as the conventional theory of Japan suggests; it is not only diversified horizontally but also stratified vertically like other societies of advanced capitalism.

(b) Social Stratification and Class Reproduction

Comparative studies of income distribution[26] suggest that Japan cannot be regarded as uniquely egalitarian. On the contrary, it ranks as one of the advanced capitalist countries with the highest levels of unequal income distribution. Table 1.3 confirms this pattern, with the international comparative analysis of the Gini index which measures the degree to which a given distribution deviates from perfect equality (with larger

Table 1.3 Gini index of after-tax income distribution in some advanced capitalist countries

Japan		US		UK	
1980	0.330	1979	0.37	1981	0.28
1983	0.382	1989	0.40	1988	0.35
1986	0.388				
1989	0.421				
France		Norway		Finland	
1979	0.364	1979	0.346	1981	0.206
1984	0.372	1986	0.330	1985	0.200
Canada		Australia		New Zealand	
1981	0.395	1981	0.31	1981	0.29
1988	0.404	1985	0.32	1985	0.30

Source: Tachibanaki and Yagi 1994, p. 25.

figures indicating higher levels of inequality). The table also suggests that income inequality intensified during the 1980s.

Even to casual observers, the stratification of Japanese society is discernible in a variety of areas. Those who own or expect to inherit land and other assets have a considerable advantage over those who do not, and asset differentials are so wide that Japan is arguably a class society based upon land ownership.[27] In the area of consumer behavior, those who possess or expect to inherit properties such as houses and land spend lavishly on high-class, fashionable, and expensive goods, while those without such property assets are restricted to rather ordinary lifestyles to make ends meet.[28] The Social Stratification and Mobility (SSM) project of the Japanese Sociological Association identifies six distinct clusters in the Japanese male adult population on the basis of such major stratification variables as occupation, income, and education.[29] With regard to opportunities for education, students from families of high educational and occupational background have a much better chance of gaining admission to high-prestige universities, and this pattern has consolidated over time.[30] About three-quarters of the students of Tokyo University, the most prestigious university in Japan, are the sons and daughters of managers, bureaucrats, academics, teachers, and other professionals.[31] Since only about one-third of the relevant age group advance to four-year universities and two-year junior colleges, most Japanese students have little to do with the widely publicized "examination hell."[32]

Subcultural groups are reproduced intergenerationally through the inheritance of social and cultural resources.[33] Mindful of the intergenerational reproduction of social advantages and cultural prestige, the mass media have sarcastically used the term *nanahikari-zoku* in reference to those who have attained prominence thanks to the "seven colorful rays of influence emanating from their parents." Unlike company employees, professionals, and managers, small independent proprietors frequently hand over their family business to one of their children.[34] In the world of entertainment, numerous sons and daughters of established entertainers and television personalities have achieved their status with the aid of their parents' national celebrity. The SSM study also suggests that the class characteristics of parents significantly condition their children's choice of spouse.[35] Ostensibly spontaneous selections of partners are patterned in such a way that it is clear the class attributes of parents creep into the decision-making process, whether consciously or not.

Let us pose another hypothetical question. Suppose that a being from another planet has capped all adult Japanese with hats of different colors (visible only through special glasses) depending upon their educational background: blue hats for university graduates, yellow hats for those who have completed high school, and red hats for those who have completed middle school or less. The alien might also place invisible color marks on the foreheads of all working Japanese: white on employees in large corporations, gray on those in medium-sized firms, and black on those in small enterprises. If we wore glasses that made these colors visible, would we see different color combinations depending on where we observe Japanese? Would the color mixtures differ between an exclusive golf club in the outskirts of Tokyo, a meeting at a *buraku* community in Kyoto, a museum in Nara, a *karaoke* bar in a fishing village in Hokkaidō, a *pachinko* pinball parlor in Hiroshima, a PTA session at a prestigious private high school in Yokohama, and so on?

The alien could use many more invisible colors, denoting such things as the value of an individual's assets (such as properties and stocks), the individual's occupational position, region of residence or origin, and so forth. If we were to see these colors, how would they be distributed and in what patterns would they cluster? These are questions that a multicultural model of Japanese society attempts to address without assuming the thesis of a homogeneous Japan.

4 *Control of Ideological Capital*

Japanese culture, like the cultures of other complex societies, comprises a multitude of subcultures. Some are dominant, powerful, and controlling, and form core subcultures in given dimensions. Examples are the management subculture in the occupational dimension, the large corporation subculture in the firm-size dimension, the male subculture in the gender dimension, and the Tokyo subculture in the regional dimension. Other subcultures are more subordinate, subservient, or marginal, and may be called the peripheral subcultures. Some examples are the part-time worker subculture, the small business subculture, the female subculture, and the rural subculture.

Core subcultures have ideological capital to define the normative framework of society. Even though the life-time employment and the company-first dogma associated with the large corporation subculture apply to less than a quarter of the workforce, that part of the population has provided a role-model which all workers are expected to follow, putting their companies ahead of their individual interests. The language of residents in uptown Tokyo is regarded as standard Japanese not because of its linguistic superiority but because of those residents' social proximity to the national power center.

Dominating in the upper echelons of society, core subcultural groups are able to control the educational curriculum, influence the mass media, and prevail in the areas of publishing and publicity. They outshine their peripheral counterparts in establishing their modes of life and patterns of expectations in the national domain and presenting their subcultures as the national culture. The samurai spirit, the kamikaze vigor, and the soul of the Yamato race,[36] which some male groups may have as part of the dominant subculture of men, are promoted as representing Japan's national culture. And although the liberalization of the domestic agricultural market affects many consumers positively, producer groups that have vested interests in maintaining the status quo and are connected with the country's leadership have often succeeded in presenting their interests as those of the entire nation.

More generally, the slanted views of Japan's totality tend to reproduce because writers, readers, and editors of publications on the general characteristics of Japanese society belong to the core subcultural sphere. Sharing their subcultural base, they conceptualize and hypothesize in a similar way, confirm their portrayal of Japan between themselves, and rarely seek outside confirmation. In many *Nihonjinron* writings, most examples and illustrations are drawn from the elite sector, including male employees in managerial tracks of large corporations and high-ranking officials of the national bureaucracy.[37]

Core subcultural groups overshadow those on the periphery in inter-cultural transactions too. Foreign visitors to Japan who shape the images of Japan in their own countries interact more intensely with core sub-cultural groups than with peripheral ones. In cultural exchange programs, Japanese who have houses, good salaries, and university education predominate among the host families, language trainers, and intro-ducers of Japanese culture. Numerically small but ideologically domin-ant, core subcultural groups are the most noticeable to foreigners and are capable of presenting themselves to the outside world as representative of Japanese culture.

To recapitulate the major points: Japanese society embraces a significant degree of internal variation in both social and cultural senses. It comprises a variety of subcultures based upon occupation, education, asset holdings, gender, ethnicity, age, and so forth. In this sense, Japan is multicultural and far from being a homogeneous, monocultural entity. One can grasp the complexity and intricacy of Japanese society perhaps only when one begins to see it as a mosaic of rival groups, competing strata, and various subcultures.

II Multicultural Paradigm

1 Temporal Fluctuations in Understanding Japan

At a more conceptual and theoretical level, Japanese society has inspired social scientists over several decades to address a complex set of issues. For the last few decades, the pendulum of Japan's images overseas has swung back and forth between positive and negative poles, and between universalist and particularist approaches. As Table 1.4 displays, five distinctive phases are discernible during the postwar years.[38]

The first phase, immediately following the end of World War II and continuing through the 1950s, saw a flow of writings which characterized the defeated Japan as a backward, hierarchical, and rather exotic society which Western societies should educate. In particular, Benedict's *The Chrysanthemum and the Sword*[39] had a most significant impact on the postwar development of Japanese studies. Methodologically, she took a "patterns of culture" approach which assumed that Japanese society could best be understood as a social or cultural whole composed of a rather homogeneous set of individuals. She used anthropological techniques for describing small societies with relatively undifferentiated populations in her study of the complex society of Japan. Substantively, she highlighted what she regarded as the most common denominators in Japanese social organization which contrasted markedly with their counterparts in the West. The influence of the anthropological framework can be seen in *Village Japan*,[40] *Japanese Factory*,[41] and *Tokugawa Religion*.[42] This vein of literature set the stage for the persistent style of analysis in which Japanese society was portrayed as both monolithic and unique.

In the second phase, which dominated the 1960s, modernization theory provided a framework within which Japan was assessed in a more positive light. The mainstream of American scholarship began to regard Japan as a successful case of evolutionary transformation without

Table 1.4 Fluctuations in the frameworks and analytical tools of Japanese studies in English-language publications

Phase	US–Japan relationship	Evaluation of Japan	Possibility of convergence	Conceptual tools	Key words	Focus on internal variation
1945–60	Japan's total dependence on the US	Negative and positive	No	Particularistic	*on, giri, oyabun, kobun*	No
1955–70	Japan as the showcase of the US model	Positive	Yes/no (modernization)	Universalistic	Evolutionary change	No
1965–80	Japan's high economic growth and emerging competition with the US	Positive	No (unique Japan)	Particularistic	*amae, tate shakai,* groupism	No
1970–90	Japan out-performing the US in some areas of the economy and technology	Positive	Yes (reverse convergence)	Universalistic/ Particularistic	Japan as number one	No
1985–	Intense trade war between Japan and the US	Negative	No (different capitalism)	Universalistic	Enigma, threat	No

revolutionary disruption. In the context of the intense Cold War, the US establishment also began to see Japan as the showpiece of the non-communist model of development in Asia. The five-volume series on the modernization of Japan published by Princeton University Press represented the culmination of the collective efforts to examine Japan on the basis of a set of universalistic criteria. Using the yardstick of pattern variables developed by Parsons,[43] a leading sociological theorist of modernization, one of the most influential volumes, entitled *Social Change in Modern Japan*,[44] attempted to measure the degree to which Japan exemplified the expected changes from traditional to modern patterns. While using the universalistic model as its overall framework, however, the empirical findings of the series were equivocal, pointing out a number of distinctive features of Japan's modernization.

The third phase saw the revival of a more particularistic approach, lasting for about a decade from the late 1960s. Partly as a reaction to the universalistic modernization framework, there was emphasis on the supposed uniqueness of Japanese psychology, interpersonal relations, and social organization. The notion of *amae*, which Doi[45] spotlighted as the key to unlock the psychological traits of the Japanese, attracted much attention. Reischauer[46] contended that the Japanese were essentially group-oriented and differed fundamentally from individualistic Westerners. According to Nakane,[47] Japanese social organizations were vertically structured and apt to cut across class and occupational lines, unlike their Western counterparts which were horizontally connected and inclined to transcend company kinship lines. These writings were published when the Japanese economy began to make some inroad into the US market. To a considerable extent, they reflected increasing confidence in the Japanese way on the part of both Japanese and Western writers.

The fourth phase, which commenced toward the end of the 1970s and persisted for a decade or so, witnessed waves of "learn-from-Japan" campaigns. Japan's management practices, industrial relations, and education programs were praised as the most advanced on earth and endorsed as what other societies should emulate. Against the background of a gradual decline of American hegemony in the international economy and a visible ascendancy of Japanese economic performance, Vogel's *Japan as Number One*[48] was one of a number of works which championed what they regarded as the Japanese model. Many who wrote along these lines suggested the possibility of injecting some Japanese elements into the Western system to revitalize it. In the main, this argument emphasized transferable, transplantable, and therefore trans-cultural attributes of Japanese society.

The fifth phase, which started in the mid 1980s and has continued in the 1990s, witnessed the rise of the revisionists, who saw the Japanese social system in a much more critical light than previously. Johnson, the author of *MITI and the Japanese Miracle*,[49] argues that Japanese capitalism is a different kind of capitalism, based on the developmental state in which the national bureaucracy plays a pivotal role in shaping national policy for Japan's national interests only. He cautions that this structure poses an increasingly grave threat to the well-being of the international community. In a similar vein, Wolferen addresses *The Enigma of Japanese Power*[50] and maintains that the Japanese system, in which leaders lack accountability, makes each citizen unhappy. Against the background of Japan's economic superpower status, the intensification of trade friction between Japan and the West, and the rise of Japan-bashing, the revisionist writings point to the strategies with which Western societies may be able to contain the influence of Japan and make its social system more compatible with theirs. The revisionist analysis attaches importance to the institutional peculiarities of Japanese society and their consequences both at home and overseas.

Concomitantly with the fluctuation of these images of Japanese society, the changing political and economic relationships between Japan and the United States shaped the framework of analysis of Japan. Observed from outside, the analytical tools for assessing Japanese society have alternated between particularistic and universalistic types, while foreign evaluation of Japanese society has swung between positive and negative appraisals.

2 *The Convergence Debate*

At the highest level of abstraction, the so-called convergence debate has made Japan the focal point of analysis in recent years. The debate itself is as old as social sciences and has had many twists and turns. At one end of the continuum, convergence theorists have maintained that all industrial societies become akin in their structural arrangements and value orientations because the logic of industrialism entails a common batch of functional imperatives. At the other end, anti-convergence theorists have argued that the cultural background and historical tradition of each society are so firmly entrenched that the advent of industrialism cannot simply mold them into a uniform pattern; no convergence eventuates because each culture develops its own style of industrial development on the basis of its own momentum and dynamics. Japan provides a logical testing ground for this debate since it is the only nation outside the Western cultural tradition that has achieved a high level of industrialization. On balance, a majority of Japan specialists, be they culturologists or institutionalists, have tended to underscore the unique features of Japanese society, thereby siding either explicitly or implicitly with the anti-convergence stance. Yet this position has presupposed that the West continues to lead the direction of industrialism, though the Japanese pattern deviates from it.

Many convergence theorists see the so-called unique features of Japanese society mostly as the expression of the nation's late development, lagging behind the early-developer countries. Tominaga, for example, regards four patterns of transformation presently in progress in Japan as pointers that suggest that it is becoming increasingly like advanced Western societies.[51]

First, Japan's demographic composition is changing from one in which a young labor force comprises an overwhelming majority of the population to one in which the aged comprise the larger portion. The proportion of those who are sixty-five years of age or older exceeded the 10 percent mark in France in the 1930s, in Sweden and Britain in the 1940s, in Germany and Switzerland in the 1950s, and in the United States and Italy in the 1970s, while Japan arrived at this stage in the middle of the 1980s. This means that the comparative demographic advantage that Japan enjoyed in the past has begun to disappear. If the present trend continues, Japan will become the nation with the highest ratio of aged in its population in the early part of the twenty-first century, thus completing the catch-up cycle.

Second, Japan's family and kinship groups have dwindled and even disintegrated in a way similar to that familiar in Europe and the United States. Nuclear families are now the norm, and the percentage of singles has increased. While the anti-convergence theorists use the Japanese family system and kinship networks as a cornerstone of their argument for the distinctive character of Japanese society, Tominaga underscores their decline and suggests that the Japanese are undergoing a Western-type experience somewhat belatedly.

Third, so-called Japanese management is changing. There are many signs that the twin institutions of permanent employment and seniority-based wage structure cannot sustain themselves. Company loyalty is weakening among young employees. The ageing profile of the corporate demographic structure makes it difficult for starting workers to expect smooth and automatic promotions at the later stages of their career. Head-hunting is becoming rampant, and intercompany mobility is rising. In the long run, the convergence theory predicts, the Japanese employment structure and its concomitant management styles will more resemble Western patterns.

Fourth, the emphasis of the Japanese value system is gradually shifting from collectivism to individualism. The rising number of students

enrolled in universities and other institutions of higher education leads
to the mass production of citizens exposed and oriented to individualistic
and rational thinking. The disintegration of the family and kinship
systems, plus the gradual dissolution of the local community, tend to
liberate individuals from intense social constraints imposed by these
traditional structures. As Japanese workers become accustomed to
material affluence, their legendary work ethic tends to dissipate and
their life-styles become more hedonistic. In this process, the Japanese are
inclined to lose a sense of devotion to the groups and organizations to
which they belong and to experience the state of anomie much as do
citizens of advanced industrialized societies in the West.

Convergence theorists concede that these four transformations have
not yet run their courses, but maintain that they head undeniably in the
direction of convergence with advanced industrialized societies, contrary
to the view of unique-Japan theorists who frequently ignore the significance of different levels of development and make erroneous static comparisons between Japan and Western societies. It would be fair for social
scientists to compare Japan's present features with their counterparts in
Western countries several decades ago.

The convergence debate gained another twist with Dore's formulation
of the reverse convergence hypothesis.[52] According to his argument,
industrialized societies are converging on a set of patterns observed not
in Euro-American societies but in Japan. This proposition finds considerable support with the proliferation of the so-called Japanese-style
management around the world: an increasing number of industrial and
industrializing societies appear to have adopted the systems of multiskilling, just-in-time, and enterprise-based labor negotiations. In terms of
the role of the state in industrial policy implementation, many Western
analysts have made a positive assessment of the coordination and orches-
tration functions of national public bureaucracy à la the Japanese Ministry of International Trade and Industry.[53] In the sphere of education,
too, the Japanese-style structured and regimented mode of teaching has
attracted international attention and made inroads into some education
systems abroad. In the area of law enforcement, the Japanese *kōban*
police-box system is being instituted in many parts of the world.

The reverse convergence perspective signaled a new phase in the
debate in which the West was no longer regarded as the trailblazer in
industrial development. Advancing this line of thinking further, another
position which one may label the multiple convergence thesis has gained
ground in recent years. It postulates that two or more types of development are observable, depending upon when industrialization began or
the type of cultural background that predominated. The proposition
suggests that these types generate plural patterns of convergence in

structures and values. Table 1.5 maps the relative locations of the four perspectives under discussion.

The multiple convergence perspective has many versions. One of them is the so-called late-developer hypothesis that Anglo-American capitalism was a unique type of development of early industrializers, while late-developer societies such as Japan had to evolve different social config-urations to cope with different domestic and international constraints. Murakami,[54] for example, contends that, unlike Anglo-American soci-eties, Japan, Germany, Italy, and other late-developing countries could not achieve political integration suitable to industrialization at its initial phase. To cope, these countries had to devise a strategy of catch-up industrialization by preserving some elements of traditional heritage while establishing a powerful bureaucracy which steered the process of development.

Reflecting the swift rise of Asian economies since the 1980s, another version points to the possibility of "Confucian capitalism,"[55] in which the ethic of obedience to authorities and emphasis on selfless devotion to work leads to a path of development different from the Western type but conducive to rapid economic growth. Similar arguments have surfaced under the rubrics of the "East Asian model,"[56] "Oriental capitalism,"[57] the "Pacific Century,"[58] and so on. Japan's economic structure is re-garded as the most refined and polished of this type.

In a broader perspective, some theorists explore the ways in which different types of civilization take different routes of development. Civilization in this context includes not only culture but social organizations, structures and institutions. This approach attempts to place different civilizations in some evolutionary hierarchy in which Japan occupies a position near the top.[59] As early as the 1950s, Umesao[60] proposed an ecological model of the history of civilizations in which he attempted to demonstrate that Japan belonged to the same civilization zone as Western Europe in having an internally stimulated process of "autogenic succession" and attaining higher levels of development than continental Asia and Eastern Europe. In more recent years, Murakami, Kumon, and Satō[61] have argued that Japanese society is built upon what they call *ie* civilization, which emphasizes quasi-kinship lineage and functional hierarchy. They maintain that the *ie* principle permeates Japanese history as a "genotype," playing a central role in the formation of Japanese-style capitalism. They refute the assumption of unilinear development and argue for a model of multilinear development in which the Japanese pattern represents a distinctive type. Huntington[62] sees the fundamental division of the world in the clash of several civilizations, singling out Japan as the only non-Western civilization that has succeeded in the quest to become modern without becoming Western.

Table 1.5   Four positions in the convergence debate

The West is the dominant pattern	One point of convergence?	
	Yes	No
Yes	Convergence thesis	Anti-convergence thesis
No	Reverse convergence thesis	Multiple convergence thesis

All these generalizations use civilizations as the unit of analysis and explain multiple patterns of development in terms of macro-cultural variables. The multiple convergence thesis perhaps represents a return to emphasis on cultural variables in the convergence debate and reflects the fluctuations in the tone of another debate – that concerning cultural relativism.

3 The Cultural Relativism Debate

Given the multicultural features of Japanese society, can sociological analysis do justice to them by adopting a multicultural perspective? Can the analysis of societies be free from ethnocentric assumptions? These questions loom large against the backdrop of increasingly multicultural realities and rising tides of ethnic confidence around the world.

The Japan phenomenon poses a wide range of questions about the ethnocentric nature of Western sociology. The issue is looming large rather belatedly, partly because the founding fathers of sociology, and their followers, until very recently used Western Europe, the United States and a very limited number of non-Western societies as the empirical settings for the construction of theories of modernity and modernization. In the writings of Marx, Weber, and Durkheim, for instance, China, India, and Pacific islands are studied primarily as traditional societies for comparative purposes, but none of these scholars made any meaningful reference to Japan. Even today, Habermas, who talks much about the need to redefine the concept of modernity, makes little mention of Japan.

In anthropology, it is almost trite to distinguish two types of concepts. One type consists of *emic* concepts, which are specific and peculiar to a particular culture and meaningful only to its members. The other type consists of *etic* concepts, which are applicable to all cultures, transcending national and ethnic boundaries.[63] Most sociological concepts are assumed to be *etic*, but it can be argued that they were initially *emic* concepts of Euro-American societies which became *etic* notions because of the cultural hegemony of Western nations. Here one should not lose sight of the extent to which sociology contains elements of cultural imperialism, although this does not mean that proper research cannot often determine their applicability in diverse cultural settings. Cultural relativists would argue that the time is ripe for a wide range of Japanese *emic* concepts to be examined and used in comparative analysis of advanced capitalism.

At the conceptual level, the *Nihonjinron* literature provides a wide repertoire of *emic* notions that can be tested and scrutinized for cross-cultural studies. This may be an important contribution of this genre because, with some refinement and elaboration of conceptual boundary and substance, Japan-based notions can be developed as viable tools for sociological analysis. White[64] and others maintain, for example, that indigenous definitions of women's lives differ between Japan and the West. They also argue that feminism has different meanings depending on the cultural context, thereby making it impossible for a universally valid model of women's lives to be developed. Doi's notion of *amae*, which he regards as peculiar to the Japanese personality, may be used as a conceptual tool of comparative analysis. When these concepts are used as variables for cross-cultural studies, it may be that Japanese society does not always exhibit these characteristics in the highest possible degree. A quantitative comparative study of Australia, Hawaii, Japan, Korea, and the mainland United States, for example, shows that the level of *kanjin* contextual orientation, which Hamaguchi contends is *emic* to the Japanese, is lower in Japan than in any other country and lowest among Japanese men.[65]

At the theoretical level, some scholars, notably Befu and Deutschmann,[66] maintain that theories of bureaucracy as developed in the Western sociological tradition are "culture-bound." Large bureaucratic corporations in Japan tend to give priority to such paternalistic arrangements as company housing, company leisure facilities, and company excursions. At the level of interpersonal interaction, an elaborate system of particularistic arrangements enables superiors to maneuver their subordinates with great ease. In corporations, every supervisor spends an enormous amount of time paying personal attention to employees under his charge, beyond the call of his job specifications. He entertains his subordinates in pubs, bars, restaurants, and clubs after working hours, serves as a formal go-between in their wedding ceremonies, listens to personal problems of their families, and even attends the funerals of their grandparents. None of these activities is formally required yet no manager in Japanese firms could retain his position without them; the expectation is that his subordinates, in return, are willing to devote their time to work and to commit themselves to it beyond the call of their job specifications. This inordinate exchange of expressive resources between superiors and subordinates characterizes Japan's bureaucratic organizations. National time-series surveys have consistently shown that "a supervisor who is overly demanding at work but is willing to listen to personal problems and is concerned with the welfare of workers" is preferred to "one who is not so strict on the job but leaves the worker alone and does not involve himself with their personal matters."[67]

Befu and Deutschmann contend that the particularistic qualities of Japanese bureaucratic organization contradict the key thesis of Western theories of bureaucracy – that bureaucracy's most efficient mode is a legal-rational one. From Max Weber to Robert Merton, sociologists of modern bureaucratic organization have argued that its operation must be governed by universalistic law, formal criteria, and "functional specificity" and must transcend particularistic interactions, affective considerations, and "functional diffuseness." This is one of the reasons why nepotism is regarded as dysfunctional in formal organizations in the Western model of bureaucracy. Those researchers who find Japanese bureaucracy essentially non-Weberian suggest the possibility that the legal-rational approach may not be the only way of achieving bureaucratic efficiency; the opposite, which the Japanese pattern represents, may be another possible path.[68]

More broadly, there is every indication that the Japanese pattern of development may be the prototype of the social formation of rapidly developing capitalism in Asia, particularly in South Korea and Taiwan,[69] and to some extent in Singapore and Malaysia. These societies appear to share several attributes: a high degree of centralization of power, virtual one-party control of government over decades, a public bureaucracy with power to intervene in the activities of the private sector, widespread violations of individual human rights, enterprise unionism as a means to regulate labor, discipline-oriented regimented education, and so forth. These properties, finely tuned and blended, have conceivably contributed to the swift advancement of Asian capitalism. It would perhaps be fruitful to examine the patterns of sharp authority relations which newly emerging industrial economies of Asia share. These nations appear to be attaining measurable levels of industrialism and even post-industrialism without firmly establishing social arrangements and value orientations observable in major Western industrialized nations. It remains to be seen if the Japanese style of development can be classified as being closer to the Western mode or the Asian pattern when the latter economies become fully industrialized.

To the problem of possible bias built into theories of modernization and modernity, three solutions seem possible. The first is a Eurocentric solution based on the so-called convergence theory. According to this position, all industrial societies become increasingly alike in sharing the structural arrangements and value orientations observed in Euro-American societies. In showing patterns incompatible with these, Japan is simply lagging behind in institutional and orientational areas despite its indisputable technological advance, and will catch up over time.

The second possible solution is a Japanocentric approach. The reverse convergence thesis is the most sophisticated formulation of this position. This viewpoint presents a difficult dilemma. On the one hand, this approach has healthy implications in comparative sociology that tends to assume that Western countries are the unchallenged leaders of development. On the other hand, it leaves room for Japan's cultural imperialism being pursued in the name of cultural relativism. Explanations emphasizing the allegedly unique aspects of Japanese society have been used as a convenient negotiating tactic by Japanese in their dealings with people overseas. The Japanese are made to appear inscrutable, since decisions seem to be made by some distinctive process which foreigners cannot understand. Some Japanese negotiators suggest that it is contrary to the commonly accepted doctrine of cultural relativism to expect the Japanese to behave in a way predictable to foreigners. Such views of Japanese society create a mystique in which Japan is hidden as in a mist, making it easy for Japanese negotiators to outmaneuver their foreign counterparts.

The third solution would be to postulate a multilinear model of social change. According to this formulation, the Euro-American type is simply one of many modes of modernization. The Japanese model appears to represent another type, which latecomers to industrialization may follow. This perspective can lead to two opposing ways of conceptualization – a kind of mega-convergence model which encompasses at least these two patterns of development in a systematic manner, or a kind of infinite pluralism model which regards not only Western societies and Japan but also China, Malaysia, Indonesia, and other industrializing countries as taking distinct paths of development. Alternatively, one may be able to conceive of a model which stands somewhere in between.

4 Subcultural Relativism

Studies of development and social change certainly require comparative analyses of national averages. When carefully made, nation-level summaries and generalizations help one take a snapshot and global view of each society. One should not underestimate the importance of this approach, while avoiding the pitfall of stereotyping. A multicultural approach to Japanese society sensitizes one to such a danger and provides some guideposts to avoid it.

In addition to examining Japanese *emic* concepts at societal level, studies can probe the patterns of distribution of various *emic* notions of subcultural groups within Japan, for example, women's versus men's *emics*,[70] *emics* of inhabitants in the Kantō area versus those in the Kansai area, and elite *emics* versus mass *emics*. This approach implies that researchers can invoke the concept of cultural relativism not only cross-culturally between Japanese culture and other national cultures, but intraculturally, between subcultural groupings within Japan itself.

The multicultural framework will allow systematic comparative analysis of Japanese subcultures and their counterparts in other societies. One can compare, for example, the quality of life of small-shop owners in Japan and Britain, the life-styles of school dropouts in Japan and Germany, the life satisfaction of part-time female workers in Japan and France, and so on. One can also compare distributions of social resources and value orientations across different groups in Japan with those in other countries. Such analyses would spotlight some hitherto unanalyzed social groups and their subcultures, and rectify national stereotypical biases.

To highlight the point, we may think of another hypothetical situation where four individuals – two from Japan and two from Germany – get together, as shown in Table 1.6. Those from Japan are Mr Toyota, who is a business executive of a large corporation in Tokyo, and Ms Honda, a shop assistant in a small shop in a small town in Shikoku. Those from Germany are Mr Müller, who is an executive director of a large firm in Frankfurt, and Ms Schmitz, a clerk in a small firm in a small town in northern Germany. We assume that they can communicate in a common language. Which pair would be most similar in their thought and behavior patterns? According to the conventional national culture argument, Mr Toyota and Ms Honda would form one cluster and Mr Müller and Ms Schmitz the other, because the pairs would be based on shared national culture. The subcultural model suggests the possibility that the close pairs may be Mr Toyota and Mr Müller on the one hand and Ms Honda and Ms Schmitz on the other, membership of each pair being determined by similarities of gender, occupation, firm size, and place of residence.

5 *Desirability Debate*

In the current climate of ambivalence of Western nations toward Japan, analysts are often tempted to join either a "Japan-admiring camp" or a "Japan-bashing camp" and to portray Japanese society in simplistic black-and-white terms. Yet as Japan is a multifaceted, complex society, one would perhaps have to start with a kind of "trade-off" model which

Table 1.6 Similarities and differences in a four-person case

	Nations	
Subcultural dimensions	*Japan*	*Germany*
Business executive, large corporation, male, large city	Mr Toyota	Mr Müller
Worker, small firm, female, small town	Ms Honda	Ms Schmitz

focusses upon the ways in which both desirable and undesirable elements are interlinked. To the extent that Japanese society is an integrated system, its observers would be required to examine the processes in which its various parts depend on many others, and upon which the overall functioning of Japanese society depends. Pattern A may be an outcome of Pattern B, which may in turn be a consequence of Pattern C. From this perspective, every institutional sphere contains Janus-faced arrangements.

In work, for example, the permanent-employment system is regarded as a scheme which provides job stability, company loyalty, and job commitment. In exchange, however, most workers in this category find it difficult to disobey company orders which at times require great sacrifices. When married male employees are asked to transfer to a firm or a branch office distant from their place of residence, one out of four reluctantly chooses to live away from their families as so-called "company bachelors." In community life, low crime rates in cities are closely related to the costs of criminal activities: harsh prison conditions, merciless methods used to force suspects to confess, and the penetration of police into private lives of citizens.

With these trade-offs criss-crossing the Japanese social system, any simplistic argument for importing a particular element of that system into another country requires careful analysis; as long as that element depends on the operation of further elements, its transplantation would be ineffective unless the whole package were imported. The learn-from-Japan campaigners must be aware that in this process good things would be accompanied by bad.

6 Legitimation of Double Codes

In this context, one must be mindful that dominant subcultural groups rely heavily upon an ideology which discourages transparent and forth-right interactions between individuals. While indirectness, vagueness and ambiguity are facets of human behavior in any society, the Japanese norm explicitly encourages such orientations in a wide range of situations. Double codes are legitimized in many spheres of Japanese life, thereby creating a world behind the surface. The Japanese language has several concept pairs which distinguish between sanitized official appearance and hidden reality. The distinction is frequently invoked between the facade, which is normatively proper and correct, and the actuality, which may be publicly unacceptable but adopted privately or among insiders. In analyzing Japanese society, one should caution against confusing these two aspects, and pay special attention to at least three such pairs.[71]

One set is *tatemae* and *honne*. *Tatemae* refers to a formally established principle which is not necessarily accepted or practiced by the parties involved. *Honne* designates true feelings and desires which cannot be openly expressed because of the strength of *tatemae*. If *tatemae* corresponds to "political correctness," *honne* points to hidden, camouflaged, and authentic sentiment. Thus, an employee who expresses dedication to his company boss in accordance with the corporate *tatemae* of loyalty and harmony may do so because of his *honne* ambition for promotion and other personal gains. Or an advocate of the *tatemae* principle of the unique place of Japanese rice in Japanese culture may be a farmer whose *honne* may lie in the promotion of his agricultural interests.

Another pair is likened to two sides of a coin or any other flat object with *omote* (the face) and *ura* (back). The implication is that *omote* represents the correct surface or front which is openly permissible, whereas *ura* connotes the wrong, dark, concealed side which is publicly unacceptable or even illegal. Thus, in the business world, *ura* money flows with *ura* negotiations and *ura* transactions. Wheeler-dealers use various *ura* skills to promote their interests. At some educational institutions, students whose parents have paid *ura* fees to school authorities buy their way into the school through the "*ura* gate" (back door). In community life, *ura* stories (inside accounts) are more important than *omote* explanations.

The third pair consists of *soto* (outside or exterior) and *uchi* (inside or interior). When referring to individuals' group affiliation, the dichotomy is used to distinguish between outsiders and insiders, or between members of an out-group and those of an in-group. When talking to outsiders, company employees often refer to their firm as *uchi*, drawing a line between "them" and "us." One cannot candidly discuss sensitive matters in *soto* but can straightforwardly break confidentiality in *uchi* situations. In the context of human interaction, while *soto* aspects of individuals or groups represent their superficial outward appearances, their *uchi* facets account for their fundamental essence and real dispositions. For instance, a female worker may make a pretense of being obedient to her male supervisor in *soto* terms but may in fact be quite angry about his arrogant behavior in her *uchi*.

These dichotomies also exist in other cultures and languages. In Japanese society, however, these particular forms of duality are invoked in public discourse time and again to defend the publicly unacceptable sides of life as realities to be accepted. According to the dominant social code, the *honne* of the *uchi* members should be winked at, and the *ura* of their activities must be purposely overlooked. The legitimation of duality underlying the Japanese vocabulary provides a pretext for corrupt activities.

In the *ura* side of business transactions, for example, Japanese companies use the category of *shito fumei kin* (expenses unaccounted for) to conceal the identity of the recipient of the expenditure. They can do this as long as they declare those expenses to be subject to taxation. The corporate world uses this method extensively to hide secret payoffs, kickbacks, and political donations. About half the expenditures unaccounted for in the construction industry are thought to be undisclosed political donations of this nature.[72] The *honne* of the participants in these deals is to promote the mutual interests of *uchi* networks of business and politics.

The notion that the dual codes must be seen as facts of life is sometimes used to justify murky collusion known as *dangō*, the illegal practice most predominant in construction company tendering for public works projects. Companies which take part in *dangō* engage in artful pre-tender arrangements where they agree in advance among themselves on their bids and on which company will be the successful tenderer. In return, it is agreed that the unsuccessful companies are entitled to a certain share of the successful company's profits. The practice of *dangō* rests upon the prevailing "closed" tender system in which a government body designates several companies as entitled to tender. As the number of companies designated is normally limited to ten or so, they can easily engage in pre-tender negotiations and come to mutually agreed clandestine deals. To win designation, companies vie with each other for the arbitrary favor of bureaucrats and the influence of politicians, and this also tends to create an environment for corruption.[73] The practice rests upon the *ura* operations of *uchi* insiders attempting to materialize their *honne* of profit maximization among themselves.

To accomplish the *ura* part of their business exchanges, Japanese companies spend enormous amounts on entertainment expenses, the national total of which exceeds the entire government budget for primary schools throughout the country.[74] The *tatemae* and *omote* justifications of these expenses include the importance of informal contacts and communications. Many important political policy decisions are made by politicians who wine and dine in high-class Japanese-style restaurants (called *ryōtei*) where *ura*-type trading is done behind closed doors. Similarly, local government officials often entertain their national counterparts in these and other restaurants in order to secure high allocations of national government subsidies, a *ura* practice which citizens' groups have criticized as illegitimate use of taxpayers' money.

In the sphere of law, the Japanese are said to be reluctant to sue. In *tatemae* and *omote* terms, this is often attributed to a peculiarly Japanese cultural aversion to litigation. In *ura* reality, however, suing does not pay in Japan because the cost of taking a dispute to trial is high and pay-off is low for a number of reasons:[75] the utility of judiciary solutions is reduced by bond-posting requirements, the limited dissemination of information about the court, the relatively small numbers of lawyers, and delays in court proceedings. Because the *honne* of Japan's potential litigants is no different from their counterparts in Western countries, they do take legal action once the availability of judiciary relief and the effectiveness of litigation become known. This was the case with lawsuits by feminist groups, environmental organizations, and other citizens' movements in the 1980s and 1990s.

Studies of Japanese society are incomplete if researchers examine only its *tatemae, omote,* and *soto* aspects. Only when they scrutinize the *honne, ura,* and *uchi* sides of Japanese society can they grasp its full picture. To be Japan-literate, they should not confuse outward appearances with inside realities when examining a society in which double codes play significant roles.

III Towards a Multicultural Analysis

To reiterate the main points of the discussion: this book attempts to take issue with two types of monoculturalism which have long pervaded studies of Japanese society. First, it explicitly challenges descriptions of Japan as a culturally homogeneous society with little internal variation, and contests the view that Japan is "uniquely unique" among advanced industrial societies in being uniform, classless, egalitarian, and harmonious, with little domestic variety and diversity. Second, it wishes to be sensitive to Japanese *emic* concepts as well as established *etic* notions of the social sciences, and to avoid the pitfall of two types of conceptual monoculturalism. On one hand, it seeks to avoid the assumptions of those who claim that Japan can be understood fully only with the application of Japan-specific conceptual yardsticks, as seen in the influential so-called *Nihonjinron* writings, the discourse which tries to highlight the presumably unique aspects of Japan and the Japanese. On the other hand, it does not follow those social scientists who have sought to investigate the Japanese situation exclusively in terms of the concepts and rhetoric of Western social sciences. It intends to be pluralistic regarding the use of *emic* and *etic* concepts and to count on many fine published studies which have been based upon such pluralism.

Seeking to avoid these two sorts of monoculturalism, the book suggests that two types of multicultural approaches would allow the sociological pulse of contemporary Japan to be taken in a realistic way. One is a multicultural research focus that spotlights the domestic stratification and subcultural differentiation of Japanese society; the other is an international, multicultural conceptual paradigm for the understanding of Japan.

This book consists of four major themes. The first (chapters 2 and 3) presents an overview of class and stratification in Japan, and of Japan's demographic variation, preparatory to depicting Japanese society. The second (chapters 4 and 5) addresses stratification based upon achievement criteria such as occupation and education, and investigates the degree of class reproduction in these spheres. The third theme (chapters 6 and 7) is the way in which Japanese society is stratified on the basis of gender and ethnicity, two ascriptive criteria that are determined at birth and are generally unalterable thereafter. The fourth (chapters 8, 9 and 10) explores the patterns of trade-off and tug-of-war between forces of control and dissent in the Japanese social system.

Students of Japanese society must be mindful of the complex patterns of diversity in Japanese society and sensitive to the types of devices used to monitor its functioning. By attending closely to Japan's intrasocietal multicultural reality and adopting a perspective of intersocietal conceptual multiculturalism in cross-cultural analysis, we may perhaps be able to see a new horizon in our endeavor to understand Japanese society in an international perspective.

While politicians and economists speak of the Japanese economic, financial, and technological challenge, the challenge which the Japanese model presents to the sociological paradigm appears to be far less recognized. The sooner we realize the implications of this challenge, the better equipped our sociological theories of industrialization, modernization, and development will be.

Notes

1 See Mouer and Sugimoto 1986, p.150.
2 Befu 1990a, pp. 145–7; Mouer and Sugimoto 1987, p. 12.
3 Doi 1971 and 1973.
4 Nakane 1967, 1970, and 1978.
5 Ishida 1983, pp. 23–47.
6 For example, Umesao 1986; Yamamoto 1989; Sakaiya 1991 and 1993; Umehara 1990.
7 For instance, Hamaguchi 1988; Watanabe 1989; Kusayanagi 1990.
8 Maruyama, Katō, and Kinoshita 1991.
9 For instance, Takatori 1975.
10 Hamaguchi 1985 and 1988. For a debate on this model, see Mouer and Sugimoto 1987, pp. 12–63.
11 Amanuma 1987.
12 Lee 1984.
13 Befu 1980; Mouer and Sugimoto 1980 and 1986; Dale 1986; McCormack and Sugimoto 1986; Sugimoto and Mouer 1989; Yoshino 1992. See also Neustupný 1980.
14 White and Trevor 1984.
15 Tominaga 1982.
16 De Roy 1979.
17 This is why some observers called them "Japan's invisible race" (De Vos and Wagatsuma 1966).
18 De Vos and Wetherall 1983, p. 3, provide a similar estimate. Nakano and Imazu 1993 also provide an analogous perspective.
19 These societies are perhaps "unique" in their high levels of ethnic and racial diversity.
20 For example, Shufu to Seikatsusha 1992.
21 Ide 1979; Shibamoto 1985; Takahara 1991.
22 Fujita 1984.
23 Hakuhōdō 1985.
24 See, for example, the Management and Coordination Agency's surveys on women in 1987 and 1990.
25 See, for instance, the Economic Planning Agency 1985.
26 Ishikawa 1994; Tachibanaki 1989 and 1992; Tachibanaki and Yagi 1994.
27 Shimono 1991 and 1992.
28 Ozawa 1989.
29 Tominaga 1979; Imada 1989; Tomoeda 1989.
30 SSM III.
31 Tokyo Daigaku 1991.
32 Inui 1990.
33 Miyajima and Fujita 1991.
34 Shimizu 1991.
35 Kobayashi et al. 1990.
36 The Japanese phrase for this is *Yamato damashii*. Most Japanese are popularly presumed to belong to the Yamato race.
37 Kawamura 1980; Sugimoto and Mouer 1995, pp. 187–8.
38 See Kawamura 1980, pp. 56–7; Mouer and Sugimoto 1986, pp. 57–8.
39 Benedict 1946.
40 Beardsley, Hall, and Ward 1959.

41 Abegglen 1958.
42 Bellah 1957.
43 Parsons 1951.
44 Dore 1967.
45 Doi 1973.
46 Reischauer 1978.
47 Nakane 1967, 1970, and 1978.
48 Vogel 1979.
49 Johnson 1982.
50 Wolferen 1990.
51 The description below follows Tominaga 1988, pp. 2–50.
52 Dore 1973.
53 Johnson 1982 and 1990.
54 Murakami 1984a.
55 Dore 1987.
56 Berger and Hsiao 1988.
57 Twu 1990.
58 Burenstam Linder 1986; Borthwick 1992.
59 For instance, Itō 1985.
60 Umesao 1967.
61 Murakami, Kumon, and Satō 1979; Murakami 1984b.
62 Huntington 1993.
63 See Befu 1989 for a discussion of these two types of concepts in the context
    of Japanese studies.
64 White 1987b.
65 Kashima et al. 1996. The same study also demonstrates that the level of *kanjin*
    orientation is consistently higher among females than among males in all the
    societies under analysis. See also Hofstede 1984.
66 Befu 1990b; Deutschmann 1987. The discussion below follows Befu's
    argument.
67 Tōkei Sūri Kenkyūsho 1994, p. 68. Also discussed in Befu 1990b, p. 179.
68 The Befu–Deutschmann argument is possibly subject to debate on two
    grounds: many analysts of Western bureaucratic organization have pointed
    out a number of informal and non-rational elements in it, and the Japanese
    bureaucracy is basically a highly formalistic system and expressive ties may be
    a matter of nuance. The exact opposite of legal-rational bureaucracy would
    be pure nepotism or patrimonialism.
69 For example, Nester 1990; Chan 1990.
70 Duran 1990.
71 See, for example, Shibata 1983; Nitoda 1987.
72 MM June 29 1993, p. 26.
73 To eliminate these practices, a handful of municipalities and prefectures
    have adopted the "open" tender system where any company is qualified to
    put in a bid. This scheme enables any number of companies to submit a
    tender and makes it difficult for a small number of companies to seal *dangō*
    deals. The open competition also encourages small subsidiary companies to
    place tenders on their own initiative; they have virtually no chance of being
    included in the list of designated companies in the closed system. Despite the
    obviously fair and impartial qualities of the open method, both national and
    local bureaucracies have resisted calls for reform on the grounds that it
    would escalate the amount of paperwork and office chores involved. Some
    dangō players go as far as to advocate that the existing, illegal convention

lessens the possibility of contract-winning companies engaging in intentional negligence to cut costs so that they can achieve the unrealistically low figures of successful tenderers in open tendering competition. There is little question that these claims seek to justify the vested interests of the beneficiaries of the status quo.

74 Based upon comparisons between National Tax Administration Agency statistics and Ministry of Education statistics.
75 Haley 1978; Ramseyer 1988.

2

Class and Stratification:
an Overview

There is a considerable amount of literature which suggests that the basic cleavages in Japan are not between social classes but between corporate groups.[1] It has been argued that in Japan "it is not really a matter of workers struggling against capitalists or managers but of Company A ranged against Company B."[2] Some go as far as to claim that the Western notions of class and stratification do not find expression in the daily realities of the Japanese. Others contend that class consciousness is weaker in Japan than in Western countries.[3] Often-publicized government statistics which show that some 90 percent of Japanese regard themselves as belonging to the "middle class" appear to bear out this line of thinking.

However, an increasing number of studies appear to demonstrate that these claims may represent only the *tatemae* side of Japanese society. Some comparative quantitative studies suggest that Japanese patterns of socioeconomic inequality show no systematic deviance from those of other countries of advanced capitalism. Income inequality is higher in Japan than in Western countries (see Table 1.3). The overall social mobility rate in Japan is basically similar to patterns observed in other industrialized societies, as Table 2.1 shows.[4] Stratification analysts break the observed gross mobility from one generation to another into two parts: forced mobility, which is engendered by changes in the structural distributions of occupational positions, and pure or net mobility, which reflects the degree to which individuals are able to move from one occupational category to another, controlling for structural changes.[5] Table 2.1 shows that Japan experienced a higher degree of structural transformation than the United States and the United Kingdom, presumably because of Japan's extremely rapid tempo of industrialization and urbanization – a larger proportion of people were "forced" to change their occupation from their fathers' by shifting from farming to manual work, from blue-collar to white-collar occupations, and so on. However, the pure mobility rate, which reflects the degree of net circulation from one generation to another, after removing the impact of structural mobility, is low in Japan in comparison with the United States and the United Kingdom. In other words, the opportunity for intergenerational mobility (net of structural changes) appears to be more closed and less fluid in Japan than in the other two countries.

The sense of inequality is quite marked in many dimensions of stratification, including those of income, assets, education, gender, and ethnicity. While the nation and companies may be rich, many individual Japanese do not feel that they themselves are, suspecting that a privileged fraction must be reaping the increasing wealth. Reliable nationwide surveys indicate that significant proportions of respondents regard "inequity" (*fukōhei*) and "selfishness" (*migatte*) as the attributes that best characterize contemporary Japanese society.[6] The widespread notion that Japan is *gakureki shakai* (a society oriented inordinately to educational credentialism) testifies to the popular belief that it is unfairly stratified on the basis of educational achievement. Moreover, unlike the United States and the United Kingdom, Japan has a relatively strong Communist party which constantly polls about 10 percent of total votes in national elections and 20–30 percent in its strongholds like Kyoto, suggesting that some sections of the community harbor a strong sense of class inequality. These observations suggest that the "90 percent middle class" thesis may be losing sight of the *honne* side of Japan's social stratification structure. The notion of Japan being a highly egalitarian society is useful for overseas *soto* consumption but may not reflect the *uchi* reality of material and cultural inequality.

There is an abundance of data on class in Japan. The Japan Sociological Association has conducted a Social Stratification and Mobility (SSM) Survey every ten years since 1955 and amassed systematic time-series data over four decades.[7] Government agencies, newspaper organizations, and private research institutions have also published a large amount of quantitative data on the ways in which resources, values, and behavior patterns are distributed among different strata in Japanese society. They provide ample material for understanding internal stratification in Japanese society.

Studies of class and stratification have long been a battleground between those who follow Marx and various non-Marxists and anti-Marxists, most notably those who favor a framework which originates in the work of Max Weber. The Marxian tradition tends to define social class as a grouping of people who share a common situation in the organization of economic production. Those who disagree with this framework are

Table 2.1 Comparison of social mobility rates among Japan, the United States and the United Kingdom

Mobility type	I			II		III	
	Japan (1975)	US (1980)	UK (1972)	Japan (1985)	US (1973)	Japan (1985)	UK (1972)
Gross (total) mobility	67.6	67.8	66.8	63.8	70.7	63.4	62.7
Forced (structural) mobility	33.9	13.7	13.6	25.9	20.3	18.7	13.9
Pure (net) mobility	33.8	54.1	53.1	38.0	50.4	44.7	48.8

Notes
1 Column I was adapted from Ishida 1993, p. 177.
2 Columns II and III were adapted from Seiyama 1994, pp. 71 and 75. The Japanese figures are different in two columns because they were adjusted to be comparable to the US and the UK data: Japanese scores were recalculated in accordance with the methods of computation used in the US and the UK figures respectively.
3 Gross mobility = forced mobility + pure mobility.

inclined to take the structural-functional approach and to classify individuals into statistically defined strata according to income, power, and prestige.

This chapter tries to provide preliminary signposts to issues covered in subsequent chapters. To these ends, the chapter will:

1 present some quantitative studies by Japanese sociologists of the ways in which classes and strata are formed;
2 schematize the ways in which economic and cultural resources are distributed;
3 discuss whether levels of inequality and stratification are increasing or decreasing;
4 examine the extent to which inequality is reproduced from one generation to another; and
5 investigate a number of Japan-specific concepts related to class and stratification.

1 Classification of Classes and Strata

Exactly how many classes or strata are there in contemporary Japan? Researchers on social stratification have failed to come up with a definitive answer to this elementary question. Marxian analysts apply conventional class categories to the Japanese situation, but sometimes do so dogmatically, while non-Marxists tend to rely mainly on standard occupational classifications and engage in highly sophisticated statistical analysis without producing a clear overall portrayal of the class situation. In both camps, analysts tend to borrow, and sometimes refine, Western concepts and theories, and methodological techniques first developed in the United States and Europe.

Researchers who prefer to use Marxian categories have produced empirical portrayals of class distribution in contemporary Japan.[8] For example, using SSM data, Hashimoto estimates Japan's changing class composition as displayed in Table 2.2. The four classes have different characteristics.

The capitalist class consists of corporate executives and managers. They have high incomes, considerable assets, and many durable consumer goods. Their political orientation is conservative and, by and large, they regard the status quo as impartial and fair.

The working class is comprised mainly of blue-collar workers, both skilled and unskilled, plus temporary and part-time workers. This is by far the largest class in Japan today. A majority of the working class have only the lowest levels of education and income and express the highest level of discontent with the existing situation. However, they remain apathetic and pessimistic about political change.

The middle class is divided into two groups: the old middle class composed mainly of farmers and self-employed independent business people, and the new middle class made up of white-collar employees including middle managers, professionals, and clerical office workers.

1 The old middle class comprises two groups: the farming population whose numbers have consistently declined as a consequence of industrialization and urbanization, and independent small proprietors, classified as *jieigyō*, whose numbers have not significantly changed over time. Many of the latter run the small and medium-sized stores that line the streets of shopping areas (called *shōten-gai*) throughout the country. Running greengroceries, liquor stores, barber shops, pharmacies, fish shops, confectioneries, and so on, within or adjacent to residential communities, these small, independent business people form a formal association in each shopping area, with executives and other office-holders, and play lively and leading roles in community affairs. Owners of small family factories and backstreet workshops comprise another important group of independent proprietors. Some with highly specialized manufacturing skills and others serving as subcontractors, they buttress Japan's economy and technology. The old middle class, some members of which are cash-rich, is generally conservative both politically and socially, low in educational credentials, and not inclined to engage much in cultural or leisure activities.

2 The model figure in Japan's new middle class is (in the Japanese English phrase) a "salaryman," a white-collar, male company employee

Table 2.2 Class distribution based on Marxian categories

Class	1955 (%)	1965 (%)	1975 (%)	1985 (%)
Capitalist	5.5	8.4	6.2	6.3
New middle	17.0	23.1	25.9	32.0
Working	19.5	34.4	36.2	37.2
Old middle	58.0	34.1	31.7	24.5
Farming	39.3	18.0	14.3	6.6
Self-employed	18.7	16.1	17.4	17.9

Source: Hashimoto 1990, p. 55.

in the private sector. He embodies all the stereotypical images associated with the Japanese corporate employee: loyalty to his company, subservience to the hierarchical order of his enterprise, devotion to his work, a long and industrious working life, and job security in his career. The new middle class which salarymen typify constitutes only a third of the labor force, but is an ideological reference group for the working population. In literature, the genre of "salaryman novels" focusses on the joys and sorrows of Japanese organization men. In housing, "salaryman dwellings" are simple units with three small rooms and a kitchen. In money management, the "salaryman finance" system enables financially ambitious corporate employees to borrow substantial amounts at high interest rates without the need to mortgage property. In psychoanalysis, "salaryman apathy" refers to white-collar employees' psychological state of work rejection, in which they display psychosomatic symptoms every morning when they have to leave for work. In politics, the New Salaryman Party was once formed as a minor political party which campaigned primarily for reduction of taxes on salary incomes. Members of the new middle class are generally well educated but dissatisfied with their income.

Non-Marxian sociologists take a different approach, positing a more multidimensional framework and attempting to identify several "clusters" using the concept of status inconsistency. They define an individual as status-inconsistent when he or she ranks high on one ladder of social stratification (for example, occupation) but low in another (for instance, school background). A Korean, female doctor in Japan, for example, would be a status-inconsistent person in the sense that she is high on the ladders of income and educational qualifications but low on those of gender and ethnicity because of prevailing prejudice and discrimination. Using the notion of status inconsistency and the 1975 SSM data, Imada and Hara measure the distribution of income, knowledge, status, assets, life-style, and power, identifying six different clusters and providing detailed descriptions of each.[9] Two of these are the upper and lower clusters of Japan. Respectively, they consistently show high or low scores on all measures. Four other groups are status-inconsistent, exhibiting different patterns of incongruence across the ladders of stratification, as shown in Figure 2.1.

The upper cluster is comprised mainly of highly educated managers and professionals with incomes more than twice the national average and with assets including high-class consumer durables, stocks, bonds, debentures, loan trusts, and membership rights in exclusive sports clubs. With regard to leisure activities, their resources allow them to play golf and tennis, enjoy sailing, and go to theaters, concerts, and exhibitions. Most people in this cluster are middle aged.

The lower cluster consists chiefly of blue-collar workers and farmers. With compulsory education only, their incomes are nearly half the national average. They have limited opportunity for leisure activities and little influence over the political process. This group's share of the population has declined,[10] because Japan's rapid economic growth shifted a sizeable proportion of this cluster to higher levels.

Between the two status-consistent clusters at the top and bottom of the social hierarchy are four status-inconsistent groups.

1 The first cluster consists chiefly of elite white-collar university graduates in clerical, professional, or managerial occupations. They are ranked high in occupational status, educational background, life-styles and leisure activities, but have relatively low incomes and limited political influence in their community.

2 The second cluster is composed mainly of non-managerial employees – blue-collar and low-level white-collar workers who have completed high school and tend to enjoy leisure and sporting activities. These individuals rank high on the life-style dimension and at middle levels on the others. There are signs that this cluster, which was clearly status-inconsistent in the 1950s and 1960s, became increasingly status-consistent in the 1970s and 1980s.

3 The third, and largest, status-inconsistent cluster mainly comprises self-employed and manual workers who have completed either middle school or high school but earn handsome incomes that do not correspond with their educational background. Despite their high earnings, these individuals do not have much leisure, nor do they have high life-styles. However, they are capable of influencing the decision-making processes of community organizations.

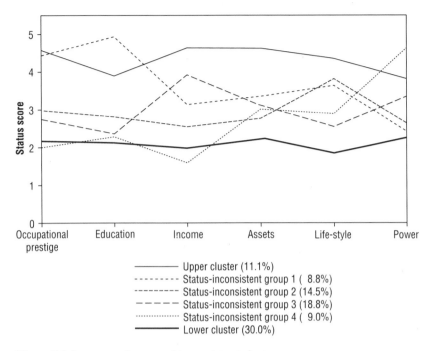

Figure 2.1 Status-consistent and inconsistent clusters
Source: Imada 1989, pp. 175–6. Some 8 percent of the sample did not belong in any of the six clusters.

4 The fourth cluster shows the highest range of status inconsistency – low on the income dimension and high on the power dimension. Those in this cluster are predominantly middle-aged and senior citizens influential in local communities. They are farmers, shop owners, and self-employed individuals, some of whom have yielded their business responsibilities to their sons.

While the above analysis relies upon 1975 SSM data, Tomoeda uses more restricted data limited to three variables – education, income, and occupational prestige – but examines the trend from 1955 to 1985, confirming that six clusters remain robust though the proportion and internal composition of each cluster changes from time to time. Notably, the share of status-inconsistent individuals steadily increased from 48 percent in 1955, to 59 percent in 1965, 65 percent in 1975 and 70 percent in 1985.[11] The speed of change has declined but the trend has remained unidirectional. Boundaries between classes have become blurred, as at least seven of every ten persons lead a split-level existence, high in one dimension of social stratification and low in another. Status-inconsistent individuals tend to find it difficult to share coherent class-based interests and class solidarity. Accordingly, the growth of status-inconsistent conditions has led to the decline of clearly demarcated class lines. Based upon the 1985 SSM data, Tomoeda also identifies six clusters.[12]

2 Distribution of Economic and Cultural Resources

The foregoing studies make no analytical distinction between two aspects of social stratification. The first concerns various societal resources that one acquires as a consequence of occupying a position in a stratification hierarchy. They include economic, political, and cultural resources. The other relates to the agents of stratification, those variables which determine individuals' differential access to societal resources. These agents include occupation, education, gender, ethnicity, and place of residence.[13] While chapters 3 to 7 are organized around different agents of stratification, it might be helpful to draw here a schematic picture of how two key types of resources – economic and cultural – are distributed among the Japanese.

Economic resources can be classified into two types. On one hand, income such as salaries and wages constitute flow-type resources.[14] On the other hand, a variety of assets form stock-type resources, including immovable assets such as houses and land and movable assets such as shares, bonds, and golf club membership rights.

Cultural resources cover knowledge- and information-based prerogatives which some sociologists call cultural capital.[15] These resources in Japan tend to derive from educational credentials and overwhelmingly are determined in teenage years according to whether youngsters win or lose what Japanese media call the "education war." In a finely graded rank-ordered system of high schools and universities, the amount of prestige that they earn derives from the status of the school or university they attended and graduated from. Japanese leaders in bureaucracies and large firms tend to place excessive emphasis upon their members' schooling backgrounds, and this pattern has filtered through other social strata. The dominant definition of cultural resources in Japan is extremely education-based in this sense. One can also enhance one's cultural resources through receipt of honors, awards, and titles from established institutions, by winning popularity as a sportsperson or entertainer, and by acquiring fame through the mass media.

As the status-inconsistency model suggests, the levels of one's economic and cultural resources do not necessarily coincide. A rich store owner might not be a graduate of a prestigious university. A well-educated female graduate might not have a high-paying job. Academics at universities of low standing tend to receive higher salaries than those in high-ranking institutions. The very notion of status inconsistency points to such incongruity.

Cross-tabulation of the dimensions of economic and cultural resources produces a four-fold conceptual chart like Table 2.3.

Cell A represents the upper class that possesses great quantities of both resources: executive managers of big corporations, high-ranking officials in the public bureaucracy, large landowners and real-estate proprietors, and those who own large amounts of movable assets. Generally, they have university degrees, usually from top institutions.

Some of these people may not have education-based cultural resources but acquire functional substitutes by obtaining some honor or decoration for distinguished services, for establishing and managing a school or university, or starting an endowment or foundation in their name for charitable work or to support various cultural activities.

Cell B comprises those who have considerable economic resources but not a commensurate level of cultural assets. Many belong to the above-mentioned old middle class, including independent farmers and petty-scale manufacturers and shop owners.

The self-employed business class has remained a self-perpetuating stratum which is more or less free of the influence of educational qualifications. These self-employed business owners tend to hold both traditional and authoritarian views and, in this respect, resemble farmers in their value orientations. They generally find it desirable to follow a conventional way of life and look askance at those who question existing traditions and practices.[16] Many well-educated children of these independent people who succeed to their parents' businesses move into the upper class in Cell A with relative ease.

A television drama heroine of the 1980s, called *Oshin*, a figure who moved many Japanese to tears, arrived at Cell B in the later phase of her life. Born in an impoverished family, she worked as a live-in baby carer, maid and in many other jobs in her childhood and adolescence with remarkable patience and perseverance. Without formal education, she

Table 2.3   Cross-tabulation of economic and cultural resources

Cultural resources	Economic resources	
	High	Low
High	A	C
Low	B	D

succeeded as a business woman in establishing and managing a chain of supermarkets.

Given that educational credentials are the most significant cultural resource for upward social mobility, one should not lose sight of the fact that the majority of high-school students do not advance to university and have little choice but to establish themselves through the acquisition of economic resources, abandoning cultural prestige.

Cell C consists of those with high cultural credentials, who lack corresponding income and wealth. The major group in this category comprises well-educated salaried employees, "organization men" who include administrative, clerical, sales, and non-manual employees as well as corporate professionals. High-circulation weekly magazines which target this group have many stories of their discontent and disillusion. Many Japanese organization men with good cultural resources feel frustrated by the present institutional order precisely because their earnings do not appear to match their cultural privilege; it seems to them that more uneducated people, such as those in Cell B, lead more monetarily rewarding lives. A newspaper reporter who has much leverage in conditioning public opinion may lead a financially mediocre life. People in the higher substratum of this category eventually move up to Cell A as they climb to the top of their occupational pyramid, becoming directors of large companies, high-ranking officials of the public bureaucracy, or professionals with handsome earnings.

Cell D represents the underclass that lacks both economic and cultural capital. Most blue-collar workers, female workers in the external market, minority workers, and immigrant foreign workers fall into this category. This group is numerically quite large and will be the focus of analysis in subsequent chapters.

3 Direction of Social Inequality

Is Japanese society becoming more egalitarian? The balance of evidence suggests that the answer to this question was generally affirmative up to the end of the high-growth economy and the oil crisis in the early 1970s, but negative thereafter, with escalating income differences, widening disparity of purchasing power among different strata, and emerging "restratification."[17]

There is no doubt that the high-growth economy of postwar Japan led to changes in the occupational composition of the population and shifted large numbers from agriculture to manufacturing, from blue-collar to white-collar, from manual to non-manual, and from low-level to high-level education.[18] However, this transfiguration left a false impression – as though industrialization were conducive to a high measure of upward social mobility. In reality, the relative positions of various strata in the hierarchy remained unaltered. For example, the educational system which produced an increasing number of university graduates cheapened the relative value of degrees and qualifications. To put it differently, when everyone stands still on an ascending escalator, their relative positions remain unaltered even though they all go up. A sense of upward relative mobility in this case is simply an illusion. When the escalator stops or slows down, it becomes difficult for the illusion to be sustained. The occupational system then cannot continue to provide ostensibly high-status positions, thereby revealing that part of the apparent social mobility in the past was attributable to the inflationary supply of positions.

Since the mid 1970s, the rich appear to have become increasingly affluent and the poor more and more deprived, thereby widening the status discrepancy. One indication of this trend is that the Gini coefficient of income distribution, which measures the overall level of inequality, has increased its value during this period, suggesting that income disparity in the population has grown.[19] Another is that the correlations between education, occupation, and income all increased during this period, as Table 2.4 indicates;[20] those who have high income are increasingly among those who have high education and high occupational prestige. Low-income earners tend to be those with limited education and low-ranking jobs.

This trend stems from three sources.[21] First, overall disparities of wages have grown as variations have increased between age groups, between workers in large and in small firms, and between different industrial sectors. The reform of the wage system along lines emphasizing merit-based evaluation also contributes to wage differences among workers.

Second, Japan's tax system has decreased the rate of progressive taxation with the result that its redistribution functions have been weakened. The revenue trade-off between the decreasing share of income tax and the introduction of consumption tax has exacerbated this tendency.

Third, differences in incomes derived from assets have widened. Assets

Table 2.4 Changes in correlations between three status variables

Variables correlated	1955	1965	1975	1985
Education and income	.198	.125	.213	.256
Occupation and income	.305	.232	.393	.419
Education and occupation	.517	.461	.419	.467

Source: Imada 1989, p. 182. The higher the correlation coefficient, the stronger the connection.

here refer both to land, houses, and other real estate, and to financial holdings such as interest-bearing deposits, bonds, and stocks. The current situation derives from corporate manipulation of land and share prices. This is attributable to the cessation of Japan's high-growth economy, which reduced the level of corporate demand for investment in plant and equipment. With large amounts of surplus funds in hand, banks financed corporate speculation in real estate and securities on a massive scale. This "money glut" phenomenon during the bubble economy period of the 1980s made their values skyrocket. As a consequence, the owners of properties, particularly land, came to hold assets of enormous value; those without land became unable to purchase a house. The recession in the 1990s reversed this trend to some extent, lowering land and stock prices.[22] But the after-effects of the bubble economy are still firmly entrenched, sustaining the fundamental pattern. The following section provides further discussion of this tendency.

4 Reproduction of Inequality

How are economic and cultural resources transmitted from one generation to another? Occupation and education are the most visible factors that perpetuate inequality intergenerationally across social classes. Chapters 4 and 5 deal with these areas in some detail, but here we will briefly look at two processes. On the economic side, the degree to which assets are handed down from one generation to another has consequences for the continuity of interclass barriers. Furthermore, the cultural continuity of different class groups is affected by the ways in which people are socialized into certain values and whether marriage partners come from a similar class background. Though often less conspicuous and more latent, these variables are fundamental to the processes of intergenerational economic and cultural reproduction of classes.

(a) Asset Inheritance

Focussing on the rising prices of city properties, Ozawa[23] demonstrates that purchasing power and consumption capacity are determined chiefly by the size of property assets rather than wage income. Contrary to the trend in the preceding high-growth period, she argues, the rate of increase in property income has outpaced that in wage income since the mid 1970s. Consequently, in the 1980s, the differentials of net financial assets in the population remained greater than income differentials.[24] To examine inequalities in contemporary Japan, therefore, one must investigate its land ownership pattern, in view of the fact that land assets constitute about 60 percent of national wealth.[25]

These asset disparities have led to the formation of two distinct subcultural groups in the consumer market: a small number of spenders who have resources to pay for costly *de luxe* commodities, and a large group of those who cannot afford to do so. Those who have considerable financial assets and large property incomes form a minority stratum at the top, and only they can enjoy an extravagant life-style, purchasing expensive houses, bearing inordinate social expenses, and spending lavishly on fashion goods. The remaining majority, whose livelihood is constrained by housing mortgages and bank loans, must carefully calculate their expenditure and cannot assume such profligate life-styles.[26] However, there is very little difference between the asset "haves" and "have nots" in their purchasing of more ordinary commodities, including cars, bicycles, medical services, musical instruments, sports goods, audio equipment, and education.

Shimono[27] estimates that about 70 percent of household asset holdings of workers between forty-five and fifty-nine years of age were inherited. This means that the asset owners of Japan have largely sustained and even expanded their holdings intergenerationally through inheritance. Asset disparities have not only produced, but also *reproduced*, two subcultural groups which show distinctly different consumer behavior patterns in Japan today.

The excessive increase in land prices, in particular, has given rise to a situation where the level of inequality between property owners and renters is so stupendous and so predetermined that those without properties to inherit cannot catch up with those with inheritable assets simply by working hard and attempting to save.[28] One's income as measured in terms of salary and wage levels does not directly represent one's power to purchase commodities. The point is obvious when one compares, for instance, two company employees (Yamada and Suzuki) who have the same annual net salary of five million yen. Yamada inherited his parents' house and flat, and leases the apartment at two million yen a year, thereby enjoying a net annual disposable income of seven million yen. Suzuki has not yet been able to purchase a house and rents a condominium at two million yen a year, having therefore a net yearly disposable income of three million yen. One can imagine that though their corporate salaries are identical, their purchasing power is substantially different.[29]

(b) Socialization and Marriage

More broadly, cultural capital appears to be transmitted through highly stratified channels. In her study of residents of Kobe in 1989 and 1990, Kataoka[30] explores the extent to which the amount of inherited cultural capital of individuals in their childhood affects the amount of cultural capital that they possess in adulthood. To generate a quantitative indicator of cultural capital in childhood, she examines the cultural environment of individuals in their primary school and preschool days and uses a combined index which takes into account how frequently they listened to classical music at home, made family trips to art galleries and museums, had family members read books for them, and whether they had collections of children's literature at home, and played with building blocks. She also looks at the types of cultural activities of individuals in their adulthood and classifies them into "orthodox" culture and "mass" culture. "Orthodox" cultural activities include writing poems, visiting art galleries, museums, and exhibitions, and appreciating classical music, while "mass" cultural activities include going to concerts of popular music, rock-and-roll, and jazz, singing *karaoke* songs, and playing *pachinko* pinball. For both males and females, the study demonstrates very significant connections between cultural environment in childhood and participation in "high" cultural activities in adulthood. The cultural capital available before one's teenage years influences one's style of cultural activity more strongly than do other variables as one's occupational prestige, household income, and even educational background. The cultural resources of a family condition and even determine its children's cultural lives after they reach adulthood.

In an empirical study of family socialization in Osaka, Kataoka[31] observes that parents of high social standing tend to inculcate the values of social conformity in their children, while those of low social status generally attempt to orient their children to individual integrity and family obligations. Specifically, fathers of high occupational position and mothers of high educational background are inclined to train their children to acquire proper etiquette and language, and well-educated mothers in particular try to discipline their daughters to behave decorously. The children of parents (especially mothers) of high educational background feel burdened by intense parental expectations of conformity.

In contrast, fathers with less education place more emphasis on the honesty of their children than do university-educated fathers. Compared with children from wealthy families, those from poor backgrounds are taught to refrain from being dishonest, and daughters of worse-off families are instructed not to break their promises. Parents with only compulsory education try to educate their daughters to avoid disgracing family members and to attend to family chores.

In the main, families of higher status appear to concern themselves with the outward appearance of their children's behavior. In contrast, parents of low status tend to stress internal probity and family responsibilities. These findings appear to run counter to the observations of Western studies[32] which suggest that middle-class socialization stresses the formation of a non-conformist, individualistic self while working-class families socialize their children into collective values.

The process of choosing marriage partners is neither random nor unstructured. The extent to which people find partners from the same occupational and educational background has always been great.[33] Intra-class marriages within identical occupational and educational categories remain predominant, and in that sense "ascriptive homogamy" persists as an entrenched pattern. This is most robust in the professional and managerial class,[34] and intergenerational class continuity endures most firmly in the highest strata of Japanese society.

On the basis of data from the SSM study, Table 2.5 shows the most frequent combination of educational backgrounds between married couples who are classified according to their respective fathers' occupations. Suppose, for example, a married couple come from a background where either the husband's father was self-employed and the wife's father was white-collar, or the wife's father was self-employed and the husband's father was white-collar. In this category of marriages, the most typical cases (38 percent) are those where both the husband and the wife have completed middle-level education. In the marriages in which both of the fathers occupied professional or managerial positions, the most typical couple have both completed university or junior college (45 percent). Among all fifteen cells, only two have different educational background combinations, confirming the extent to which both intraclass and inter-class marriages involve similarities in partners' educational backgrounds. Relatively independently of parental occupational background, the educational environment appears to influence the choice of marriage partners. In this qualified sense, the popular perception that Japan is a society based on educational credentialism seems correct in the marriage market.

5 *Japanese* Emic *Concepts of Class*

How do the Japanese conceptualize dimensions of social stratification? The Japanese equivalents of class and stratum, *kaikyū* and *kaisō*, are both terms translated from English. As such, they do not constitute part of the everyday folk vocabulary of most ordinary citizens in Japan. Yet anyone familiar with the Japanese language would attest to the wide circulation of such Japanese terms as *jōryū kaikyū* (upper class), *chūsan kaikyū* (middle class), *kasō shakai* (lower-stratum society), and *shakai no teihen*

Table 2.5 Affinity in educational backgrounds among intraclass and interclass marriages

Father's occupation	Professional and managerial	White-collar	Blue-collar	Self-employed	Agricultural
Professional and managerial	H – H (45%)				
White-collar	H – M (37%)	H – M (47%)			
Blue-collar	M – M (32%)	M – M (41%)	M – M (47%)		
Self-employed	H – H or M (28%)	M – M (38%)	M – M (39%)	M – M (30%)	
Agricultural	M – M (49%)	M – M (36%)	L – L (32%)	M – M (31%)	L – L (51%)

Notes

1 H stands for higher education, including universities and junior colleges. M means middle-level education, namely, completion of high-school education. L indicates low-level education, meaning compulsory education at middle and primary school. The categories for those who have gone through the prewar education systems are adjusted.

2 Percentage figures in parentheses indicate the proportion of modal couples in the total number of cases in each class-background combination. Only modal categories are listed in this table.

Source: Adapted from SSM III, p. 114.

(bottom of society); the Japanese have a clear conception of stratification in their society even if their notions may not be conceptually identical to their Western counterparts.[35]

One can easily list several Japanese *emic* terms that describe the dimensions of stratification. *Kaku* denotes a finite series of ranks. As a generic term, it can be applied to a wide range of ranking systems. *Mibun* implies a status position into which one is born. Though used more loosely at times, the term connotes ascriptive characteristics and points to caste-like features. In feudal times, a samurai's *mibun* clearly differed from a peasant's *mibun*. Even today, "blue-blood" families are supposed to have higher *mibun* than that of the masses. The term *kakei* (family line) has a similar connotation, with a more explicit emphasis upon lineage and pedigree. In contrast, *chii* means a status position which one achieves over time. One's *chii* moves up or down in an occupational hierarchy. A company president occupies a higher *chii* than a section chief of the company. The most common word for rapid social mobility is *shusse*. It applies to successful promotion to high positions accompanied by wide social recognition. When one moves from a low *chii* to a high *chii*, one would achieve an appreciable level of *shusse*.

With regard to the concept of the middle class, different imagery underlies each of the three terms used by survey analysts to indicate a middle position in a pyramid of ranks.[36] The first of these, *chūsan*, tends to point to the dimensions of property and income and to the middle to upper positions in the economic hierarchy. The second category, *chūryū*, has connotations of a middle domain of social status, respect, and prestige, rather than straight economic capacity. In interpreting this term, respondents primarily think of their occupational ranking and of such things as their family status, educational background, and friendship network, situating themselves in the middle on the basis of a combination of these criteria. A white-collar company employee might see himself as located below small-business owners and skilled blue-collar workers economically, but would still describe himself as middle with regard to educational qualifications and occupational prestige. In contrast to the first two concepts, the third yardstick, *chūkan*, carries somewhat negative implications and suggests a middle location of insecurity, uncertainty, instability, and ambivalence between high and low positions. Survey results have shown that the largest percentage of the population classifies itself as *chūryū*, followed by a considerable proportion assessing itself as *chūsan*. The smallest segment identifies itself as *chūkan*.

While the Japanese may not define stratification in precisely the same way as do other nationalities, there is little doubt that people in one of the most competitive capitalist economies on earth live with their own sense of class and inequality, as subsequent chapters will reveal in greater depth. Chapter 3 examines geographical and generational variations and inequalities as two basic sets of demographic diversities. Chapters 4 and 5 investigate the worlds of work and education in which people compete in an attempt to optimize their resources and rewards through achievement. Chapters 6 and 7 shift the focus onto such ascriptive modes of stratification as gender and ethnicity, attributes which are determined at birth and determine one's life opportunities and life-style in a fundamental way. The four chapters also probe the institutional and ideological apparatuses which sustain and reproduce the patterns of inequality and stratification.

Notes

1 The most influential books which take this line are Nakane 1967, 1970, and 1978.
2 Nakane 1970, p. 87.
3 Reischauer 1977, pp. 161–2.
4 See also Ishida, Goldthorpe, and Erikson 1991.
5 See Seiyama 1994, pp. 54–60 for the details of these and other concepts of social mobility.
6 AM January 1996, pp. 16–17. The largest number of respondents in 1988 and 1991 saw "inequality" as the term that best describes Japanese society. The ratio of people who believe that the term "confusion" depicts Japanese society most accurately has dramatically increased in the 1990s.
7 See Kosaka 1994 for the summary of the 1985 survey.
8 Ōhashi 1971; Steven 1983; Hashimoto 1990.
9 Imada 1989, pp. 164–84; Tomoeda 1989; Tominaga and Tomoeda 1986; Imada and Hara 1979, pp. 161–97.
10 Tomoeda 1989, p. 156.
11 Tomoeda 1989, p. 152. See also Kosaka 1994, p. 51.
12 Tomoeda 1989. This analysis is based upon only three variables: occupational prestige, income, and education. Therefore, the cluster patterns identified are somewhat different from Figure 2.1. See also Kosaka 1994, pp. 50–2.
13 For more details, see Mouer and Sugimoto 1986, part 4.
14 "Incomes" in this chapter refers to flow-type resources, not stock-type resources.
15 Bourdieu 1986.
16 SSM I, p. 57.
17 See Naoi 1989.
18 The total index of structural mobility records a consistent upward trend throughout the postwar years. The agricultural population provides the only exception to this propensity, showing a consistent downward trend. The total index arrived at its peak in 1975, reflecting a massive structural trans-

formation which transpired during the so-called high-growth period starting in the mid 1960s.

19 SSM I, p. 18; Kosaka 1994, p. 36. See also Table 1.3.
20 Imada 1989, pp. 181–2.
21 Tachibanaki 1989, 1992, and 1994, p. 75.
22 Asset differentials and wage disparities change in opposite directions, depending on the economic cycle. Income disparity declines during high economic growth when the supply of labor does not meet demand, so that companies must pay high salaries and wages to recruit and maintain their employees. An economic boom increases asset disparity because land and commodity prices rise, owing to brisk corporate investments in plant and equipment and soaring individual investments in housing in anticipation of continuous inflation in the market. In contrast, when the economy slows down, prospects for large capital gains decline and land transactions become sluggish, thereby inhibiting the increase of property values and curbing asset differentials. The low-growth recession phase produces a labor surplus, lowering the wage levels of workers in weak positions. Elite employees who are protected by the system of life-time employment enjoy a steady increase in their salaries, thereby expanding wage differences in the workforce. See Ozawa 1989, pp. 180–1.
23 Ozawa 1989.
24 Some figures speak for themselves. The metropolitan survey conducted in Tokyo, Osaka, and Nagoya by the Ministry of Labor in 1990 (Rōdōshō Kanbo 1991a, p. 35) shows that, on average, the net total asset value of house owners is about seventy-one million yen, and that of non-owners is about eight million yen. The difference between haves and have-nots is nearly nine times the asset value of the latter. The top 20 percent of the sample own 161 million yen, and the bottom 20 percent only one million. This means that the disparity between them corresponds to the total life-time income of the average worker.
25 Shimono 1992.
26 The Hakuhōdō Advertising Corporation calls these two groups the "new rich" and the "new poor," an attempt to pinpoint the polarization of the middle class into two groups which show distinctly contrasting patterns of consumer behavior. The "new rich" can buy high-class, fashionable, and expensive goods because they have a good quantity of properties and stocks or expect to have them through inheritance. In contrast, the "new poor" have difficulty in satisfying their swelling consumer desires because of the slow increase in their income and their increasing expenditure on housing, education, and leisure activities. Though they have such basic middle-class commodities as electric appliances, television sets, and cars, they still feel poor because they cannot keep up with and purchase ever-diversifying consumer goods.
27 Shimono 1992.
28 The *Economic White Paper* of 1990 points out that "the proportion of the households that own no housing and cannot expect to inherit any exceeds thirty percent" and goes as far as to suggest that "the level of (latent) asset disparity at the start of one's life has widened so much that equality of opportunities has been considerably eroded."
29 For a similar illustration, see Ozawa 1989, p. 177.

30 Kataoka 1992 sustains the claims of Bourdieu and Passeron developed in the
    French context.
31 Kataoka 1987.
32 Kohn 1977. See also Kohn and Schooler 1983.
33 SSM IV, pp. 131–43.
34 SSM IV, pp. 142–43.
35 Befu 1980, p. 34.
36 Odaka 1961.

3

Geographical and Generational Variations

The Japanese have different life-styles depending on their place of residence and their age or generation. Their eating habits, type of housing, language, style of thinking, and many other aspects of their everyday life hinge upon where they live and how old they are. This chapter examines both geographical and generational variations in Japanese society with a view to assessing the ways in which these demographic characteristics condition the options and preferences of each Japanese.

I Geographical Variations

1 Japan as a Conglomerate of Subnations

A total of about 125 million Japanese live in the 378 thousand square kilometer Japanese archipelago. In terms of territorial size, Japan is larger than Great Britain, similar in size to unified Germany, and considerably smaller than France and Italy. But being mountainous and hilly, with only about one-third of its land being inhabitable,[1] Japan is more densely populated than any of those countries.[2] Not surprisingly, the strain of population density affects the life-styles of the Japanese. In a crowded environment, urban dwellers in Japan learn early in life how to cope with the pressure of many people living in limited space. On station platforms in urban centers, passengers line up in two or three rows in an orderly manner. During rush hours, Tokyo subways and railways use "pushers" to push workers into overpacked trains. Most city dwellers live in small houses, tiny condominiums and meager flats, a situation that is the source of widespread dissatisfaction among urban residents. Though the housing and furnishing qualities have greatly improved and are

53

generally better than those in other Asian countries, many city dwellers justifiably feel that their houses are not commensurate with the nation's status as an economic superpower. In the narrow streets of Japanese cities, drivers and pedestrians struggle to make their way.

The Japanese archipelago comprises four major islands. The largest, Honshū, which stretches from Aomori prefecture in the north to Yamaguchi prefecture in the southeast, has the principal metropolitan centers. The four largest Japanese cities – Tokyo, Yokohama, Osaka, and Nagoya – are all on this island, as are other well-known cities such as Kobe, Kyoto, and Hiroshima. Hokkaidō, the second largest island, lies in the north and has the lowest population density. Traditionally the territory of the Ainu, this island came under the full jurisdiction of the Japanese government only in 1879. In the southwest is Kyūshū island, which used to serve as the corridor of contact with the Korean peninsula, the Asian continent, and the southern Pacific islands. Shikoku, the smallest of the four major islands, has been closely connected with the Kyoto–Osaka–Kobe nexus in the western regions of Honshū and served as its hinterland for centuries.[3]

In addition, Japan has nearly seven thousand small isles. The Ryūkyū islands in the southernmost prefecture of Okinawa maintain a distinctive regional culture. Near Hokkaidō, a group of four islands under Russian occupation – Habomai, Shikotan, Kunashiri, and Etorofu – has been subject to territorial dispute between Japan and Russia for decades. The Sea of Japan is studded with such sizeable isles as Okushiri, Sado, Iki, and Tsushima. The Inland Sea area between Honshū and Shikoku is also dotted with numerous tiny isles and the sizeable island of Awaji. Even Tokyo is comprised not only of urban centers and suburban communities but of many small inhabited islands in the Pacific, including Ōshima, Toshima, Niijima, Shikinejima, Kōzushima, Aogashima, Miyakejima, Mikurashima, Hachijōjima, and the group of Ogasawara isles. The total number of people who live outside the four major islands is close to two million. Though numerically few, these islanders maintain life-styles that are dominated by the marine environment, a reminder that the population of nation's rural areas is by no means restricted to rice-growing farmers.

Japan is conventionally divided into eight regional blocs according to climatic, geographical, and cultural differences. These eight are Hokkaidō, Tōhoku, Kantō, Chūbu, Kinki, Chūgoku, Shikoku, and Kyūshū. The nation is divided into forty-seven prefectures, the largest government units below the national level. Within each prefecture are numerous municipalities – cities, towns, and villages – which form local governmental units each with a government office and a legislative body. Prefectures were first established in 1871, corresponding to several dozen regional units called *kuni* (nations) which had existed for more than ten centuries. Throughout Japanese history, these subnations were the sources of regional identity and local distinctness. Even today in major cities there exist prefectural associations (*kenjin-kai*) organized by emigrants from each prefecture who wish to maintain social ties among themselves. Some observers[4] find it profitable to examine prefectural character (*kenmin-sei*) rather than Japanese national character. They maintain, for example, that people in Kyūshū and Shikoku are generally stubborn, authoritarian, and uncompromising. Residents of Kyoto are regarded as schizophrenic in sticking to traditional norms while introducing radical reforms. Inhabitants in Hokkaidō are said to enjoy relaxed life-styles, take an open-minded attitude towards outsiders, and have a sense of independence of other areas of the nation. While these descriptions may be speculative, impressionistic, and stereotypical, the point remains that these prefectural character-types are so diverse, and often contradictory, that one can hardly speak of the national character of the Japanese as though it were cast from a single mold.

While Japan is often described as an internally homogeneous island nation, it has never been a stable territorial unit with consistent cultural uniformity. In reality, Japan has had fluctuating national boundaries and changing constituent regions. The territorial boundary of Japan as we see it today is a post-World War II concept. Even in the early twentieth century, it colonized Korea, Taiwan, northeast China, and Saghalien, with their population constituting about 30 percent of "imperial Japan."[5]

For centuries, Hokkaidō remained outside the jurisdiction of the central Japanese regimes until its formal incorporation into Japan as a prefecture in the second half of the nineteenth century. The Ainu, who were its inhabitants, did not consider themselves to belong to the Japanese nation. In northern Honshū and southern Hokkaidō, an autonomous area had long existed in which the Ainu and the Honshū islanders enjoyed unique life-styles. As a legacy of World War II, four small islands off the east coast of Hokkaidō have been under Russian occupation since the end of the war, and have been the subject of dispute between the two governments.

Similarly, the independent Ryūkyū kingdom endured in Okinawa for about four centuries during Japan's feudal period until the central government formally absorbed it as a prefecture only a little over a century ago. Before its full incorporation into Japan, Ryūkyū enjoyed close trade relationships with China and South-east Asia, maintained its own autonomous culture, and identified only to a limited extent with main-island Japan. After the end of the Allied occupation of Japan which followed its defeat in World War II, Okinawa remained under the occupation of the United States to serve as the American bulwark against communist nations, and was not part of Japan until 1972 when the United States returned it to Japan. This is why about three-quarters of American military bases in Japan are in Okinawa, a situation which Okinawans regard as unfair and which, the national government admits, must be rectified.

As a geographical unit, Japan should thus be seen as a variable, not as a constant. Furthermore, throughout Japanese history many living in the area which is now known as Japan did not have the consciousness that they were "Japanese" (*Nihonjin*). Even in Honshū this consciousness has fluctuated. At the time of the establishment of the Japanese state in the late seventh century, the term *Nihon* (Japan) emerged as a description. Yet the concept then covered mainly the Kinki region, as evidenced by the fact that nobles and officials sent outside it regarded their assignment as a posting to a foreign area or a land of foreigners.[6] At the time, ordinary people dwelling outside the Kinki region hardly conceived of themselves as belonging to the nation of Japan.

Several territorial blocs, which initially were almost nations in themselves,[7] were identifiable during the formation of the Japanese state. Far from being a uniform nation, Japan has developed as a nation with multiple internal subnations. From the establishment of imperial rule based in Nara and Kyoto in the seventh century until the Meiji period in the nineteenth century, these subnations engaged in bitter warfare in a bid to defend or expand their respective hegemony. In the initial phase, the Kinki subnation gradually conquered other blocs, placing them under its control. The feudal period from the end of the twelfth century to the middle of the nineteenth century eventually shifted the seat of real power to the samurai class of the Kantō subnation, but the Kinki area remained the seat of imperial power and the most dynamic hub of Japan's commercial activity.

These spatial variations of Japanese society have crystallized into two major dichotomies: competition between eastern and western Japan, and domination of the center over the periphery.

2 Eastern Versus Western Japan

The cultural styles of residents in the Kinki area are distinctively different from those in the Kantō area.[8] During the feudal period, Edo (present-day Tokyo and the heart of eastern regional culture) was the seat of samurai regimes, and Osaka was the center of commercial activities. The vestiges of their different pasts are still pervasive. Comparatively, Tokyo maintains a warrior-style local culture with the marks of formality, hierarchy, and face-saving, while Osaka retains a merchant life-style with an emphasis on practicality, informality, and pragmatism.

Community studies have found that vertical authoritarian relationships between landlords and tenants prevailed in eastern Japan, while egalitarian horizontal networks among rural households were stronger in western Japan.[9] On the whole, the family and kinship structures were more patriarchal and less democratic in the eastern region than in the western region. Comparatively, the status of women was higher in western Japan than in eastern Japan. Each household had a higher degree of independence in the village community in the west than in the east. These and other differences in village structures between east and west Japan are displayed in Table 3.1. Some analysts[10] suggest that the widely held view that Japan is a "vertically structured society"[11] derives more from observations of eastern Japan than from western Japan, which is more horizontally organized.

Kyoto, the capital of nation for more than ten centuries until 1868, represents the culture of western Japan in an acute way: the interpersonal relationships of Kyotoites are based upon the principles of non-intervention, partial commitment, and mutual freedom rather than those of total loyalty and obligation.[12] In this sense, Kyoto has developed a more refined and "modern" style of group dynamics than those in Tokyo and eastern Japan. This is why some observers contend that Japan is divided into two areas: Kyoto, and the rest, which adores and hates it.

Table 3.1   Differences in village structures between eastern and western Japan

Dimensions	East	West
Relationship among households	Vertical	Horizontal
Relationship of branch family to parent family	Subordinate	Independent
Inheritance	First son (or first daughter)	First son (or last son)
Retirement of house head	Absent	Present
Rank difference between first son and other sons	Strong	Weak
Relationship among relatives	Patriarchal	Matriarchal
Status of bride	Low	High
Control of hamlet community on households	Strong	Weak
Family lineage	Broadly defined kinship groups	Direct lineal descendants

Source: Summarized from Izumi and Gamō 1952, Table 21.

From Kyotoites' point of view, Tokyo is simply a local city which embodies the deep-seated inferiority complex of all non-Kyoto areas towards Kyoto.[13]

The regional distributions of minority groups display a pattern. Buraku communities are concentrated in the western region, which contains nearly 80 percent of the burakumin population. In particular, the Kansai district (Hyōgo, Osaka, Kyoto, Nara, Wakayama, and Mie prefectures in particular), the Chūgoku area (Okayama and Hiroshima), the Shikoku region (Kōchi and Ehime), and Fukuoka prefecture all have large urban buraku communities. In eastern Japan, buraku communities are generally small and scattered in agricultural and mountain villages. This distribution reflects the historical background. Western Japan differed from eastern Japan in its attitude to animal slaughter. In the east, where hunting and fishing played significant roles, the killing of animals and fish was accepted as a routine part of life. In the west, where farming was more important, there developed a tradition in which blood-related trades and activities were held in abhorrence.[14] To the extent that discrimination against buraku communities originated from attitudes to ancestors' alleged engagement in animal slaughter, butchery, and tanning, this divergence sheds some light upon the comparative abundance of buraku communities in western Japan and their relative absence in eastern Japan.

Permanent Korean residents in Japan are also more concentrated in the western region than in the eastern areas, though major eastern cities like Tokyo and Yokohama have large numbers. Osaka is the population center of resident Koreans, with about a quarter of them residing in this prefecture. Other areas of concentration include Hyōgo, Kyoto, Fukuoka, and Hiroshima prefectures. This geographical distribution reflects the fact that Koreans came, or were brought, to Japan during the colonial period as cheap labor to work for the construction, mining, and shipbuilding industries which flourished during the prewar and war years.

The two regions differ even in food taste. While Tokyoites use heavily colored, strong soy sauce, Kansai residents prefer a lighter-colored and weaker one. *Soba* noodles in Tokyo are generally more salty than *udon* noodles in Osaka. The patterns of health and illness are also regionally diverse. The adjusted prefectural death rates calculated for 1990 data by the Ministry of Health and Welfare[15] suggest that, with regard to the three major causes of death in Japan, western Japan records more cancer deaths, eastern Japan more deaths caused by stroke (cerebral apoplexy), and central Japan shows the highest concentration of deaths by heart attack. Traditional methods of pain relief and alleviation of stiffness are more popular in the west than in the east. On a per capita basis, prefectures in western Japan have larger numbers of acupuncturists, masseurs, and moxa treatment specialists.[16]

The life-styles of the aged also show regional variation. Though a high proportion of older people live with one of their children, this tendency is stronger in eastern Japan. Those in western Japan, particularly in Kyūshū, prove more independent, leading lives of their own and living alone after the death of their spouse.[17] The proportion of married couples living independently of their children is also higher in the west than in the east.

Many new businesses were first established in Osaka. For example, a variety of distribution stores originated from that city and spread across the nation. They include department stores attached to private railway terminals, public and private retail markets, consumers' cooperatives, and supermarkets. Some major media organizations also began in the Kansai area. Three of the five national dailies, *Asahi*, *Mainichi*, and *Sankei*, originated in Osaka. The first commercial radio station, Shin-Nippon Hōsō, commenced its broadcasting in 1951 in Osaka.

Osaka is also the breeding ground of popular culture. On national television, comedians who speak the Osaka dialect dominate entertainment programs. *Manzai*, dialogue shows in which two comedians exchange a series of uproarious jokes, are a form of entertainment in which performers from Osaka overshadow those from Tokyo. Yoshimoto Kōgyō, the entertainment production house which established itself in the 1910s in Osaka, has continued to produce the nation's most popular comedians, who have introduced a fresh current into this hilarious comic genre. *Karaoke*, do-it-yourself vocals which spread across the nation and became popular overseas, started in Kobe, adjacent to Osaka.

The residents of the Kansai region, which includes Osaka, Kyoto, and Kobe, do not hesitate to speak openly and publicly in their own language, and Kansai is the only language-region which challenges the monopoly of the Tokyo dialect in the electronic media. This contrasts with the linguistic behavior of other non-Tokyo Japanese, who attempt to hide their accents when outside their own dialect area. Whereas the status of western Japan has declined in the postwar years, Osaka remains the most vibrant counterpoint to the dominance of Tokyo.

3 Center Versus Periphery

There is a clear center of power in Japan, lying in a region of Honshū. Within this region, the long-standing contest between the Tokyo–Yokohama metropolitan area and the Osaka–Kyoto–Kobe metropolitan area is a competition between the two major centers of the nation. A third center, the Chūkyō metropolitan area, whose focus is the city of

Nagoya, sits between these complexes. Economic, political, and cultural power concentrate in the industrial belt that stretches along the Pacific coast between these three key areas. The world-famous bullet train line (*Shinkansen*) commenced its operation along this route in 1964, consolidating the region's position as the nucleus of Japan's economic development. Nearly half of Japan's population reside in these three urban centers. But more than half of the population live in the peripheries which depend very much upon the activities of the central region.

The process of population concentration was expedited by the national bureaucracy, which sought to make Tokyo the center of centers. If Tokyo were a nation, its gross national product would be larger than that of China and Korea and comparable to that of Canada.[18] Under ministerial instructions, each industrial sector established its national headquarters in the capital. Numerous industrial associations mushroomed in Tokyo, ranging from the Japan Automobile Manufacturers Association to the Japan Iron and Steel Federation. Other professional groups, such as the Japan Medical Association and the Japan Writers Association, also operate in the capital. High-ranking officials of the national bureaucracy are given executive positions in these industrial and professional federations after their career in the public sector. With the intention that governmental programs and policies should be transmitted from these national associations to every member firm in Japan, the national bureaucracy has succeeded in establishing a government-controlled, Tokyo-centered industrial hierarchy. Large companies which previously had their headquarters in Osaka have gradually shifted them to Tokyo, thereby accelerating the concentration of economic power in the capital. Demographically, some thirty-two million people, or about a quarter of the national population, reside in Tokyo and three surrounding prefectures, Kanagawa, Saitama, and Chiba. Yokohama, the prefectural capital of Kanagawa, has a population greater than Osaka's and has become the second most populous city in Japan.

Individuals move to these centers mainly because they provide more job opportunities, higher incomes, and more entertainment venues. As people continuously migrate into Tokyo with such motives, the capital has become the largest megalopolis, with accompanying functions and dysfunctions. On the positive side, the concentration of offices, firms, and stores makes communication between organizations less costly and time-consuming, and promotes efficiency in interorganizational networking and coordination. For corporate negotiations, business people from various companies can organize meetings without needing to travel far. Government officials and company managers can meet face-to-face at short notice. However, organizational productivity and efficiency of this kind is accompanied by negative effects on individual life: poor housing conditions, congested environment, and extended commuting time. The weekday commuting time of the average employee in the Tokyo area, for instance, exceeds one hour, with many travelling more than one hour each way.[19] For those who choose to live near their workplace, a well-equipped but small condominium is an option, a situation which prompted Western observers to describe the Japanese as "workaholics living in rabbit hutches."[20]

While Japanese industrialization since the middle of the nineteenth century consistently absorbed the rural population into city areas, the high-growth economy from the 1960s onward accelerated the tempo of urbanization, giving rise to extreme population congestion in some urban centers and depopulation in some rural villages. Japan's complications lie not so much in the ratio of the total population to the amount of inhabitable land, as in the skewed demographic distribution across regions.

Residents in depopulated areas are alienated both economically and culturally. With youngsters leaving their villages for work in cities, older people find it difficult to sustain the agricultural, forestry, and fishery economies of those areas. With the liberalization of the agricultural market, the farming population has gradually lost government protection and competitive morale. Negative images of agricultural work make it difficult for young male farmers to attract spouses; an increasing number of them resort to arranged marriages with women from the Philippines, Sri Lanka, and other Asian countries.

At the national level, a series of legal measures have been introduced to promote public works projects such as road construction and resort development in the depopulated areas to stem the tide of rural emigration. At the provincial level, such localities have taken initiatives to organize the so-called village revitalization movement (*mura okoshi*) to develop agricultural products unique to each village, form networks for their nationwide distribution, and organize events and resorts attractive to city dwellers.

Admittedly, the per capita prefectural income (*kenmin shotoku*) measured by the Economic Planning Agency indicates that Tokyo, Osaka, Kanagawa, and Aichi, the central regions of the nation, top the list while peripheral areas score lower.[21] However, on statistical quality-of-life measures, such rural prefectures as Yamanashi, Nagano, Toyama, and Fukui are ranked high, and Chiba, Saitama, and Kanagawa prefectures (adjacent to Tokyo) are graded at the bottom of the ladder.[22]

On the whole, residents in peripheral areas enjoy a higher quality of life in many ways: they live in more spacious houses, commute to work in less time, and dwell in a more natural environment with fresher air and more trees. On the whole, in peripheral areas goods are cheaper and residents enjoy more free time. These are among the factors which have brought some emigrants back to their home towns and villages, the so-called U-turn phenomenon of the 1980s and 1990s.

4 Other Dimensions of Regional Variation

The plurality of Japan's domestic geo-political structure gave rise to various dimensions of internal variation in the nation. Three of these are described below.

(a) Local Industries

In the economic sphere, each locality in Japan has *jiba sangyō*, unique local industries which use local resources and merchandise their products nationally or even internationally. These commodities range from ceramic ware, handicrafts, and special produce to luxury cloths. Many of these goods have a history of several centuries. *Yūzen-zome*, silk kimonos printed with colorful and gorgeous patterns, have long been known as Kyoto's refined local product, manufactured with sophisticated dyeing techniques developed in the seventeenth century. Hakata textiles in northern Kyūshū, which originated in the thirteenth century, made much progress during the feudal period. Other well-known examples of local industries with long histories include: Arita ware in Saga, Aizu lacquerware in Fukushima, Ōshima pongee on Amami island, and family Buddhist altars in Kyoto. Many regions produce unique kinds of *sake* rice wine (*jizake*) which are marketed across the nation. Small-scale but often innovative in product marketing, *jiba sangyō* enterprises have survived the challenges of megacorporations based in Tokyo and other major metropolitan centers and have established themselves as the bastions of their regional economies.

(b) Popular Culture

Popular culture is also regionally diversified. Local folk songs called *min'yō* are distinctively provincial in their content and tunes, which have developed over time. Among the best known nationally, "Tankō-bushi," a coal-miners' song, originated in the coal mining region of Fukuoka prefecture in northern Kyūshū . "Yasugi-bushi" is a song from Shimane prefecture on the coast of the Japan Sea; it is accompanied by the loach-scooping dance, which imitates the scooping up of iron-rich sand in the area. A type of song called *oiwake* derives from travellers' chants in Nagano and Niigata prefectures in north-central Japan. In the Ryūkyū islands at the southern end of the Japanese archipelago, folk songs accompanied by the long lute called the *jabisen* have a special scale structure. Northern Japan abounds with such unique regional songs as the *obako* of Akita prefecture and the *okesa* of Niigata prefecture.

Traditional local festivals are also rich in regional variation, with sharp differences between village and city areas. In rural communities, festivals are generally linked with agricultural rites held in connection with spring seeding and autumn harvesting, and orientated to the communion between gods and humans. In urban localities, festivals take place mostly in summer and emphasize human bonding.

Grassroots sports culture also appears to differ regionally. Traditional sumo wrestling is popular in relatively peripheral areas like Tōhoku, Hokkaidō, and Kyūshū regions, which produce the top-rated wrestlers. In contrast, most well-known baseball players come from more urban districts such as the Kantō, Tōkai, Kansai, and Seto Inland Sea areas. Most teams that win the All Japan National High-school Baseball Tournament also come from these districts, reflecting the popularity of baseball at the community level there.[23]

(c) Language

While the Japanese language is divided broadly into the eastern type and the western type with regard to both accent and vocabulary, such a complex variety of dialects exists that a person from Iwate prefecture, the northernmost area of Honshū island would not be able to communicate with someone from Okinawa prefecture, the southernmost district of the nation, if they spoke in their respective dialects. Since the vocabulary, pronunciation, and accent of radio and television announcers reflect those of middle-class Tokyoites, those who live outside the Tokyo metropolitan area hear so-called standard Japanese, but speak among themselves in their own dialect. Those raised outside the Tokyo region are thus bilingual, being competent in two types of Japanese. Most Japanese lead a dual life with regard to language.

5 Ideological Centralization

The concentration of the information industry in Tokyo lessens the visibility of the extensive regional diversity of Japanese society. In the world of electronic media, both the public broadcaster NHK (Japan Broadcasting Corporation) and commercial TV networks televise an overwhelming majority of programs from Tokyo, transmitting them through local stations. Throughout Japan, most commercial television stations are associated with one of the five "key stations" in Tokyo, and relay the programs made in the capital. Very few locally produced programs have a chance of being broadcast nationally. In the print media, three major national dailies have a total circulation exceeding twenty million, and most pages of national dailies are edited in Tokyo. Since two major book distributors in Tokyo control most of the distribution of books and magazines, bookshops around the country rely almost exclusively on them. As a result, publishers in Kyoto, for instance, must send their publications to the Tokyo distributors or their regional headquarters for distribution to bookshops in adjacent Shiga prefecture. Because of this system, it is virtually impossible for local publishers to publish current affairs magazines bound by deadlines. Thus the Japanese public is constantly fed views of the world and the nation that are constructed, interpreted, and edited in Tokyo. Outside the capital, local situations draw attention only as sensational news stories, or as provincial items satisfying the "exotic curiosity" of the Tokyo media establishment.

The centralization of the dissemination of information is accompanied by Tokyo control of Japanese "language correctness." The curriculum set by the Ministry of Education dictates that pupils should be taught to speak standard Japanese. Dialects of the periphery are often disparaged. For example, the dialect spoken in the Tōhoku district is regarded as rustic, and some schools in the region go as far as to force pupils to speak standard Japanese at school and to avoid using the Tōhoku dialect in the classroom. Thus, the dominance of the Tokyo subculture in media and language often obscures the reality of regional diversity in Japan.

In socio-geographic terms, Japanese society can perhaps be seen as being subjected to both the forces of centralization and the persistence of decentralized cultural order. While there is little doubt that the ruling power of Tokyo has homogenized the nation, distinctive local cultural configurations have also endured. In many ways, this tug-of-war between the centralizing and decentralizing dynamics ends up making various areas similar in many ways. At the same time, it frustrates the domestic process of convergence of practices and values across regions. In this respect, Japanese society appears to be neither peculiar nor exceptional among advanced capitalist societies.

II Generational Variations

The rapidity of change in Japanese social structure has produced distinct generational subcultural groupings. Different age groups underwent different family socialization and educational training. They also encountered different social and political circumstances in their childhood, adolescence, and early adulthood. Accordingly, the outlooks of contemporary Japanese differ depending upon whether they experienced in their youth the two fundamental phases of Japan's recent history. The first of these was World War II and its aftermath during the 1940s and 1950s; the second was the relative stability and affluence of the 1960s and after, consequent on the nation's rapid economic growth.

In relation to these two stages of history, the Japanese may be classified into three generations. The oldest of these is the wartime generation comprised of those born in or before the early 1930s, who grew up before and during wartime and who are now in their sixties or older. Next is the postwar generation, born between the late 1930s and early 1950s, whose childhood occurred during the nation's recovery from postwar devastation and impoverishment through the rapid economic growth of the 1950s and early 1960s. They are now in their forties and fifties, and many are at the peak of their careers. The youngest group is the prosperity generation, born in or after the late 1950s, which has no recollection of Japan's wartime activity or postwar poverty, and which grew up during the period when Japan achieved economic prosperity and high status in the international community. Members are now in their twenties and thirties and will lead Japan in the near future.

The socialization experiences of these three generations reflect the changing patterns of social constraint on the everyday life of the Japanese. Over the decades, disciplinarian, repressive, and stoic styles of sanctions and control have given way to manipulative and permissive forms. Concurrently, the key elements of generational subculture have shifted away from perseverance, patience, and diligence towards indulgence, relaxation, and an orientation valuing leisure. Viewed in the light of postmodernist theories, the wartime generation perhaps embodies premodern elements most extensively, the postwar generation exemplifies predominantly modern ingredients, and the prosperity generation increasingly shows postmodern tendencies. Table 3.2 presents the characteristics of the three generations.

1 The Wartime and Postwar Generations

The wartime generation went to school under the prewar and wartime education system which placed an emphasis upon emperor worship, jingoism, and austerity. Many men in this group fought in battle and still justify aspects of Japan's wartime aggression. Others carry feelings of remorse, guilt, and shame for their actions, and have committed themselves to pacifism. While politically split, however, the wartime generation has little choice but to face collectively the realities of post-retirement life.

Those of the postwar generation had their childhood in the most turbulent years of change in this century. In their primary- and middle-

Table 3.2   Some attributes of three generations

Characteristics	Wartime generation	Postwar generation	Prosperity generation
Date of birth	The early 1930s and before	The late 1930s to the early 1950s	The late 1950s and thereafter
General life-style aspirations	Premodern	Modern	Postmodern
Experience of postwar hardship	As adults	As children	None (born into an affluent society)
School life experience	Breakdown of the wartime value system	Social anarchy; emphasis on democracy and freedom	Growing control and regulation
Work ethic	High	High	Low (emphasis on a playful life)
Environment of social movements in early adulthood	Rise of labor movements	Rise of citizens' movements	Rise of environmental movements
Attitude to the monarchy	Respectful	Ambivalent	Indifferent
Attitude to sexuality	Closed and strict	Relatively open	Permissive

school years they witnessed the breakdown of their value system and became skeptical of the war generation and the insecurity and inconsistency of its militaristic philosophy.

The oldest of the postwar generation began school life during the war. City pupils in this group were evacuated to the countryside under the supervision of their teachers, grew up separated from their parents, and at the end of the war were primary-school children. They remember a time when their teachers, who previously had preached imperialistic, militaristic, and totalitarian values, suddenly began to lecture on the importance of democracy, equality, and freedom. The middle group of the postwar generation comprises those who were born in 1939 and commenced their primary schooling in April 1946 as the first batch of pupils to receive postwar education without exposure to wartime state propaganda. These children have memories of their teachers telling them to blot out militaristic and nationalistic sentences from their textbooks.

The final group of the postwar generation are those born in the so-called baby boom period of the late 1940s. They faced intense competition at all stages of their lives – entrance examinations to schools and universities, job applications, and promotions – because of sheer numbers. The media have popularized the phrase "clod and lump generation" to describe the great size of this group.[24] Following the social anarchy that prevailed immediately after the war, this age-group grew up in a milieu of reaction, when school life began to show signs of increasing rigidity and control.

The postwar generation grew up in an environment in which every traditional value was questioned, liberal values were encouraged, and democratic principles were inspired. When members of this generation reached their late teens and early twenties, they spearheaded the nationwide protests against ratification of the US–Japan security treaty in the late 1950s and 1960 and social movements of the late 1960s and early 1970s against the Vietnam War. The baby boomers also led campus protests around the country, which challenged all forms of academic and cultural authority.

When the tide of these movements subsided, however, most of the activists became company employees and public bureaucrats seeking to climb the occupational ladder, with some turning into "corporate soldiers" devoted to the dictates of their firms. With regard to their internal value system, those of the postwar generation are skeptical of collective dedication to organizational norms and bureaucratic mandates. In their actual behavior, however, they have inherited the style of the wartime generation and worked hard as "working ants," "workaholics," and "economic animals" who toil for their organizations at the cost of personal pursuits. This discrepancy is perhaps partly attributable to a variety of powerful sanctions imposed upon individual employees against lazy work styles, as delineated in chapter 4: employers and managers tightened control over workers under devastated conditions in postwar years. Employees also had strong incentives to work hard because Japan's economy could provide tangible rewards in return for their toil during the high-growth period until the early 1970s and during the bubble economy period in the 1980s.

These wartime and postwar generations remember how penurious the whole country was during and immediately after the war. Some experienced food shortages, even acute hunger, and shortages of cloth and other basic daily necessities. Others recall the days when people burned wood to cook rice and heat baths, warmed their hands and rooms in winter with charcoal braziers, and used newspapers as toilet paper. These generations witnessed – and were themselves the engine of – the spectacular transformation of Japanese life into the one in which satiation, oversupply of automobiles, and overconsumption of paper pose national problems.

2 The Prosperity Generation

The Japanese economy recovered fully in the 1960s from wartime and postwar destruction, bringing new affluence to the young. The prosperity generation that emerged in this economic environment has become increasingly open in expressing self-interest and defending private life. This generation has been brought up in the context of three trends resulting from Japanese economic success: information revolution, consumerism, and postmodern value orientation.

First, the prosperity generation has grown up in the middle of the information revolution. The Japanese now live in a highly advanced information environment, which is dominated by such electronic devices as car telephones, vending machines for food and tickets, satellite and cable television networks, compact disk stereos, fax machines, and word-processors. With Japanese electronics companies dominating international and domestic markets, the life-style of the Japanese is increasingly automated, their social relations being influenced by electronic media, and their mass culture being presented through the medium of electronic devices. As high-tech manufacturing and knowledge-intensive industry have come to occupy a central position in Japan, the prosperity generation has taken it for granted that incessant innovations in the information environment constitute part and parcel of their daily reality. These youngsters diversify their approach to media. Television plays a major role in their lives as a means of acquiring news and assessing social issues. This generation has not abandoned print media in general but gives attention to a wide range of publications other than established newspapers and magazines.[25]

Second, the prosperity generation has matured after Japanese society underwent a fundamental change of economic motives from production orientation to consumerism. Sociological analysts maintain that what drives young, affluent Japanese is not the deprivation motive of people who are working to free themselves from economic hardship, but the "difference motive" which prompts them to purchase luxury goods and services that give them a sense of being different from other people.[26] In this respect, Japan has attained a level beyond the stage of development in which consumer conformism dominated. In post-postwar Japan, it is argued, consumer preference is diversified, and the distribution market is segmented in such a way that a wide range of individual consumer choices can be met. The consumer conformity of industrial Japan has been transformed into consumer diversity in postindustrial Japan.

A third aspect of the subculture of the prosperity generation concerns a decline in both progress orientation and political radicalism, a trend which is said to characterize postmodern societies. Unlike older generations, the prosperity generation is not interested in pursuing knowledge for the progress of society or in succeeding in the corporate world. Nor is it interested in organizing a revolutionary movement to fight the injustice of the existing order. For these youngsters, the dominant themes are playfulness, gaming, escape, tentativeness, anarchy, and schizophrenic differentiation, in contradistinction to the rigidity, calculation, loyalty, fixity, hierarchy, and paranoic integration of modern society.[27]

The prosperity generation shows a marked departure from the work ethic of the preceding generations, the cornerstone of Japan's economic "miracle." The new generation has the luxury of being able to be choosy in the job market. Far from being loyal to corporate imperatives, those who belong to the prosperity generation are willing to change from one job to another.[28] Studies of these youngsters classify them into four types according to their motivations.[29] The first are those who favor occupations whose titles are phrased in English or some other European language and which carry professional status, such as graphic designers, illustrators, coordinators, counsellors, editors, colorists, and stylists. Because these occupations have titles which are given in *katakana* characters used for foreign words in Japanese, they somehow sound modern, international, and independently minded and thereby attract youngsters with little interest in "organization man" careers in large organizations. The second type comprises those who are willing to work for corporations only if they provide not only good salaries but sufficiently long paid holidays. Though these youngsters are prepared to work in established organizations, their priority is not devotion to the company but having leisure time outside the work setting. The third type comprises "free casuals" who work at a specified task for a short period, moving from one temporary job to another. Their primary aim is to lead a playful life (travelling abroad, climbing mountains, enjoying marine sports, and so forth) after saving a certain amount of money. They regard work as a way of achieving such a fun-loving existence outside the world of production and service. The fourth type is composed of daily casual workers who stick to this life-style on a long-term basis. They float from one workplace to another every day or every week with no clear direction in life and with a strong sense of tentativeness and uncertainty.

Observers of the prosperity generation have characterized it as the "new race" (*shin jinrui*), which has qualitatively different values and lifestyles from the old, or as the "moratorium" generation that hesitates to make long-term decisions or life-plans. The wartime and postwar generations followed the traditional principle of neglecting the self in support of the public. With the emergence of the prosperity generation came the advent of what a perceptive observer has termed the "neglect of the public and indulgence of the self."[30]

Table 3.3 Changing value orientations of the Japanese: the most congenial life-style (%)

	1930	1940	1953	1958	1963	1968	1973	1978	1983	1988	1993
To do what you find interesting, regardless of money or honor (interests)	12	5	21	27	30	32	39	39	38	41	40
To lead an easy life in a happy-go-lucky fashion (comfort)	4	1	11	18	19	20	23	22	23	23	26
To work hard and make money (wealth)	19	9	15	17	17	17	14	14	18	15	17
To lead a pure and upright life, resisting the injustices of the world (propriety)	33	41	29	23	18	17	11	11	9	9	6
To live a life devoted entirely to society without thought of self (civic spirit)	24	30	10	6	6	6	5	7	5	4	4
To study seriously and establish a reputation (honor)	9	5	6	3	4	3	3	2	2	3	3

Note: Columns may not add to 100% due to other answers and "do not know" cases.
Source: Adapted from Tōkei Sūri Kenkyūsho 1994, p. 39, and Hidaka 1984.

Table 3.3, which shows changing value orientations of the Japanese at different points of time, indicates an almost unidirectional trend in which priority is given by an increasing proportion of Japanese to private interests and individual comfort, while less and less importance is attached to such public commitments as propriety and civic spirit. The work ethic and wealth orientation fluctuate slightly but remain more or less constant.

3 Other Dimensions of Age-based Differentiation

Some studies schematize differences in life-styles and value orientations between generations typologically. A few examples will be helpful.

1 *Money and time:* One can develop a four-fold classification of age groups by combining the two dimensions of availability of money and time, as Table 3.4 demonstrates. This shows that those in their thirties and forties have neither money nor time to spare, while those in their twenties and in their sixties or above have much more of both. Those in their fifties have reasonable amounts of money but insufficient time for free activities. Teenagers show the opposite pattern, having much free time but little money to spend.

2 *Monarchy:* Attitudes towards the Japanese monarchy differ sharply according to generation (Figure 3.1). According to time-series surveys by NHK on attitudes toward the Shōwa emperor, older Japanese are apt to show respect toward him while youngsters tend to have no feelings. For the generations who received prewar education, the emperor is a positive symbol deserving deference and esteem. The prosperity generation is indifferent and impassive toward the monarch and sees him simply as a figure whose images they happen to see on television, in weekly magazines and other mass media. Those who were

Table 3.4: Availability of money and time among different age groups

	Spending money	
Free time	*Plenty*	*Limited*
Plenty	Twenties Sixties and above	Teens
Limited	Fifties	Thirties and forties

Source: Adapted from Minami 1989, p. 149. The original figure was constructed by Toshio Sakimura.

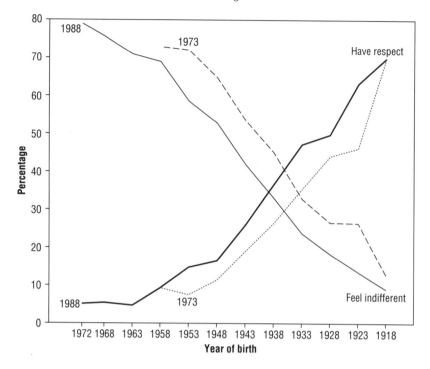

Figure 3.1 Attitude to the Shōwa Emperor in 1973 and 1988 surveys
Source: NHK 1991, p. 105.

born between 1933 and 1938 express mixed views and form a water-shed between the two contrasting groups.[31]

3 *Religious beliefs:* Age-based differences manifest themselves markedly in religious orientation. The older Japanese become the more they tend to engage in praying, sutra chanting, ascetic training, and other forms of spiritual training. Young people relate to temples and shrines in expectation of secular returns; they visit them to pray for success in examinations, success in business, or safety in life. They have amulets and charms and consult fortune-tellers. The proportion of people who get involved in semi-religious activities to procure worldly benefits declines with age. Even though Japanese religious behavior often derives from earthly motivations, spheres of religious interest change during life. Chapter 9 discusses religion in Japan in some detail.

4 *Attitude to premarital sex:* The sexual norm that operated in one's adolescence conditions one's moral standards about sexual behavior. With regard to premarital sex, for instance, the proportion of those

who find it acceptable, even if the couple are not engaged, increases with age, as Figure 3.2 suggests. Sexual liberation appears to have progressed most dramatically in the 1960s for men and in the 1970s for women. Gender differences in sexual liberalism became minimal among youngsters in the 1990s.[32]

5. *Popular songs:* Popular songs have generational diversity. The songs that are called *enka* are popular among middle-aged and older persons. Sharing basic tunes with some Korean popular songs, *enka* rely upon Japanese traditional melodies and use song lyrics centering upon the symbolism of ports, tears, and rain, and themes of unrequited love, sad parting, and sentimental nostalgia. Western-style pop and rock music attract younger generations. Teenage singers appear on television screens as cute and attractive idols for youth and make the visual elements of their performance central to their popularity.

One could add many items to this short list of varying characteristics across age groups. In combining the regional and generational dimensions, it may be useful to visualize two Japanese: a retired farmer in a village in eastern Japan and a young casual worker in the city of Osaka, the center of western Japan. With a matrix of demographic variables affecting their life patterns, it is only natural for their value orientations and behavior patterns to display many differences.

III Demographic Crisis

The age profile of the Japanese population is rapidly changing because of the declining birth rate and increasing life expectancy. The changing demography of age distribution in Japan has brought about crises both in the labor market and in the social welfare sector.

1 Ageing of the Population

The life-cycle of the Japanese has changed dramatically during the twentieth century. In prewar Japan, the average life expectancy was less than fifty years and each family produced a number of children. In 1994, the average life span was eighty-three years for women and seventy-seven for men, both the longest in the world.[33] The size of the average household was a little over five persons between 1920 and 1950, but began to decline sharply from around 1955. It was about three in 1990.

Japan has become an ageing society with an increasing aged population and decreasing numbers in the active workforce. An official estimate made by the Ministry of Health in 1991 is that the number of senior citizens over sixty-four years of age will exceed that of children

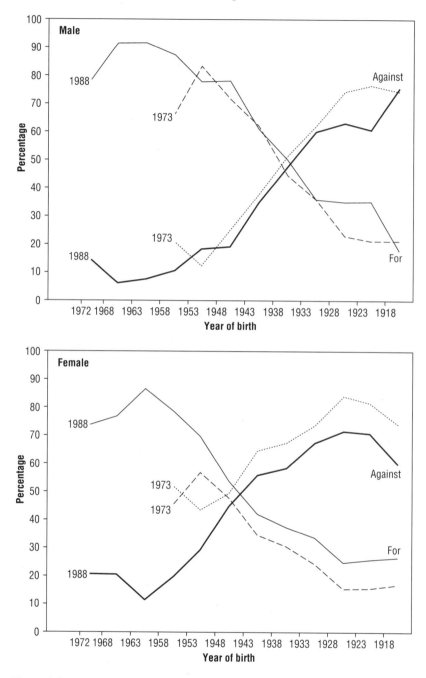

Figure 3.2 Attitude to premarital sex
Source: NHK 1991, p. 85.

below fifteen before the end of the twentieth century. If one defines those between sixty-four and fifteen as the active population and those outside this range as the inactive population, whereas five actives support two inactives in the early 1990s, by around 2020 two actives will have to sustain one inactive. While a continuous supply of young active labor has previously underpinned the expansion of Japan's economy, this situation no longer exists. This is also the case with Western European countries. According to the most pessimistic estimate of the Ministry of Health, if the present trend continues the population of Japan will be only half that at present in about one hundred years.[34]

The increasing life expectancy of the Japanese has altered the retirement age of workers and the job market for the aged. The retirement system in Japan, which started in large firms at around the turn of the century and became widespread in small businesses after World War II, used to set the mandatory retirement age at fifty-five, but with the advent of an ageing society many firms have raised the age limit to sixty. Implementation of the new practice varies greatly depending upon firm size. A greater proportion of larger companies has instituted the practice of raising the retirement age, while smaller enterprises generally lag behind.

After leaving employment in their late fifties, however, most workers choose to continue work until their mid sixties by finding jobs in subsidiary companies or through personal networks, with reduced earnings and shorter working hours.

2 Declining Birthrate

The statistics of population dynamics that the Ministry of Health compiles annually show that the average number of children that a woman bears declined to 1.46 in 1993, the lowest figure ever recorded in Japan and one which gives it the third-lowest birthrate in the world after Italy (1.29) and Germany (1.39). The birthrates of Sweden and the United States hover around two. Since the rate needs to be at least 2.1 to maintain the present population level, this trend heralds a long-term decline in Japan's population.

The dwindling birthrate is attributable to the changing attitudes of women to marriage and family life. There appear to be at least two factors underlying the transformation. First, an increasing number of women feel that they cannot afford to raise many children when education costs are an immense burden. Second, women increasingly prefer to marry later, as more and more job opportunities become available to them. In 1990, the average age of first marriage for women was twenty-six,[35] which contrasts sharply with previous decades when women married much younger. In 1950, for instance, women were an average age of twenty-three years when embarking upon their first marriage.

3 Pressure on the Welfare Structure

The pension system in Japan consists of eight different schemes. The two largest are Welfare Pension Insurance and National Pension, state-administered programs that cover some 90 percent of pension policy-holders.

Welfare Pension Insurance is designed to cover company employees in the private sector. The National Pension scheme, started in 1961, is intended to look after individuals not covered under any other pension program, and to provide a system in which all persons in the workforce, particularly those in agriculture, forestry, and fishery as well as independent proprietors and their families, can expect to receive pensions. Full-time housewives of company employees can join the scheme provided their husbands arrange to have the required contribution deducted from their salaries. It is compulsory for students aged twenty or older to join the National Pension scheme. Generally, members of this program start receiving pensions at sixty-five years of age.

Additionally, five mutual benefit associations administer pension programs for national bureaucrats, local public servants, employees of public corporations, staff of agricultural, forestry, and fishery organizations, and teachers and staff of private schools. There is also a special pension program for sailors.

Since many find the pension insufficient to cover the cost of living after retirement, some contribute to additional pension funds during their working lives so as to have a larger pension income during retirement. For this purpose, Welfare Pension Foundations operate for private-sector employees and National Pension Foundations for the self-employed. Many large corporations have their own enterprise pension schemes which provide participating employees with handsome sums after retirement. In addition, post offices and life insurance companies sell personalized pension plans on an individual basis; installments to these plans are tax-deductible.

Recipients of pensions in Japan are only those who have contributed to a pension insurance program during their working life. Their monthly entitlement after retirement depends upon the sum of their contributions. Because of the shifting demographic situation, the government has tightened its belt by introducing legislation in 1994 which gradually increases the entitlement threshold age of the Welfare Pension scheme from sixty for men and fifty-eight for women to sixty-five for both sexes. To conserve funds, pension entitlement is now adjusted in accordance with increases in net salary, whereas previously it rose with gross salary.

Together with savings amassed through the Postal Savings system, the interest from investment of pension funds provides an important source of support for the Financial Investments and Loans Program. These funds are deposited with the Ministry of Finance, and interest from them is used to support a wide range of national projects not only in welfare-related areas but in housing and road construction. The ageing of Japanese society, however, is likely to curtail the size of funds available for the Financial Investments and Loans Program and bring pressure to bear on its viability.

To cope with the labor crisis caused by the ageing of the workforce, the Japanese establishment has two options to bring cheap labor into the job market. One of these solutions focusses upon women as the chief source of additional labor. An alternative strategy involves using foreign workers to resolve the problem. Though these solutions are not mutually exclusive, the predicament must inevitably force the Japanese leadership to abandon the predominantly male and Japanese-only labor market and to manage the labor system on the basis of a more heterogeneous working population. Chapters 6 and 7 discuss these tendencies at some length.

Notes

1   According to the estimate of the Bureau of Statistics of the Management and Coordination Agency in 1996, the proportion of inhabitable land (*kajū-chi*) in Japan is 32.2 percent. Mountains, forests, and wilderness constitute 66.1 percent. See Sōrifu 1996, p. 3.

2   Even in terms of conventional measures of population density, Japan (320 persons per square kilometer) is ahead of Germany (258), the United Kingdom (258), Italy (189), and France (103).

3   The archipelago's climate differs greatly from region to region. While southernmost Okinawa is semi-tropical, northernmost Hokkaidō is snow-covered in winter and cool even in summer.

4   Sofue 1971; Toneri 1980.

5   Oguma 1995, pp. 4 and 161–6. Prewar school textbooks published by the Ministry of Education stated unequivocally that the Japanese nation is multi-ethnic.

6   Ōtsu 1985.

7   Amino 1990, pp. 59–69.

8   Tanigawa 1961.

9   Fukutake 1949, pp. 34–48 and 69–115.

10   For example, Yoneyama 1971.

11   Nakane 1967 and 1970.

12   See Nagashima 1977, pp. 199–211; Yoneyama 1976.

13   For instance, Umesao 1987, pp. 252–5.

14   Amino 1990, p. 61.

15   See the population dynamics survey of the Ministry of Health and Welfare.

16 Toneri 1980, pp. 15–16 and 43–4. Moxa treatment is a traditional pain-relieving method in which moxa is burned on the skin of the painful part of the body.

17 Analysis of 1980 census data as reported in Eijingu 1993, pp. 249–50.

18 Gaimushō 1995.

19 NHK 1992, pp. 276–7.

20 This comment, made by an OECD observer, has attracted much media attention in Japan, together with the phrase "the Japanese economic animals," which Asian leaders attached to Japanese business activities in the region in the 1970s and 1980s.

21 See, for example, AM, April 10 1992, p. 3.

22 Economic Planning Agency 1991.

23 AM, July 19 1992, p. 1.

24 Sakaiya 1980.

25 NHK 1992, pp. 244–7.

26 Imada 1987.

27 Asada 1983.

28 A survey conducted by the Japan Labor Research Institute reveals that one out of three male graduates who have worked for ten years up to March 1992 has left the company he joined upon graduation. See AM, December 11 1993, p. 1.

29 Sengoku 1991, pp. 181–96, which relies in part upon the survey results of the Tokyo metropolitan government.

30 Hidaka 1984, pp. 63–78.

31 NHK 1991, pp. 104–5.

32 NHK 1991, p. 85.

33 The population dynamics survey of the Ministry of Health and Welfare.

34 An estimate made by Kōseishō in 1991.

35 The male age was twenty-eight years.

4

Varieties in Work
and Labour

I The Numerical Dominance of Small Businesses

1 Small Businesses as Majority Culture

Popular overseas *soto* images of Japanese society are colored by the notion that it is a country of megacorporations. These perceptions have been engendered by Japanese products and associated with such household names as Toyota, Mitsubishi, and NEC. However, the *uchi* reality is that, though powerful and influential, large corporations constitute a very small minority of businesses in Japan, both in terms of the number of establishments and the size of their workforce. An overwhelming majority of Japanese enterprises are small or medium in size, and it is these which employ the bulk of the workforce. While small may or may not be beautiful, "it certainly is bountiful, and thereby deserving of its fair share of attention."[1] Small and medium-sized companies are the mainstay of the Japanese economy.[2]

In the Japanese business world they are known as *chūshō kigyō*, medium- and small-sized firms. For brevity, one may lump both types together and call them small businesses. The Small Business Standard Law defines *chūshō kigyō* as those companies which employ not more than three hundred persons or whose capital does not exceed one hundred million yen.[3]

As Table 4.1 shows, nearly nine out of ten employees work in businesses with fewer than three hundred workers. Furthermore, more than half of private-sector workers are employed by establishments with fewer than thirty workers. Large corporations with three hundred or more workers employ less than one-eighth of the labor force in the private sector.[4]

79

Table 4.1   Distribution of establishments and employees in the private sector by firm size (1991)

Firm size (employees)	Establishments (%)	Employees (%)
1–4	64	17
5–9	19	14
10–29	13	24
30–99	2	21
100–299	2	12
300 >	0.1	12
Total	100	100

Source: Calculated from the Establishment Census conducted by the Statistics Bureau of the Management and Coordination Agency.

Even in the manufacturing sector, small businesses employ three-quarters of workers and are overwhelmingly in the majority in the textile, furniture, ceramics, and fittings industries. Numerically, small businesses also dominate the parts-production sectors of the export-orientated car and electronics industries. In the construction industry, 95 percent of employees work in small businesses.[5] Since large firms and their employees occupy only a small segment, the so-called "Japanese management theories" based on *omote* observations of this minority section lose sight of the *ura* dynamics of the great majority of Japanese enterprises.

Macroscopic data analysis shows that the most fundamental division of stratification in the male population of Japan lies between those employed in large corporations and those in small ones.[6] Table 4.2 shows key differences between large and small businesses. Notably, the so-called lifetime-employment system does not operate in the small-business sector. This is the system under which employees are expected to remain with the same company or enterprise group for their entire career; the enterprise in return provides a wide range of fringe benefits. The system applies only to regular employees in large companies,[7] though there are signs that it has weakened due to the prolonged recession during the 1990s. In general, job mobility between firms is considerably higher in small enterprises. It is often claimed that Japanese companies have accomplished the managerial revolution so fully that their top managers are usually not their owners. This generalization holds true for large companies, but owner-managers abound in small businesses.

Table 4.2   Relative characteristics of large and small firms

Dimensions	Firm size	
	Large	Small
Intercompany mobility	Low	High
Separation of corporate ownership from management	Sharp	Weak
Labor union organization ratio (proportion of unionists as employees)	High	Low
Working hours	Short	Long
Educational background of employees	High	Low
Salary levels	High	Low
Employees' involvement in community affairs	Low	High
Decision-making style	Bureaucratic	Entrepreneurial

2 Plurality of Small Businesses

Japanese economists who have debated the nature of Japan's small enterprises fall into two broad categories. The first group expands on the dual-structure thesis which holds that big businesses accumulate their capital by exploiting and controlling small businesses which have little choice but to offer workers low pay under inferior working conditions.[8] The second position emphasizes the vitality, dynamism, and innovativeness of small businesses that have responded flexibly to the needs of clients and markets: small firms have adapted themselves effectively to the changing environment by developing their own technology, know-how, and service methods, thereby playing the key role in the Japanese economic "miracle."[9] The phenomena identified by both positions do exist in the world of Japanese small businesses. Its internal variation is partly determined by the extent to which small businesses are controlled by large companies at the top of the corporate hierarchy.

At the highest level, Japan has six major industrial conglomerates: Fuyō, Sanwa, Daiichi Kangin, Sumitomo, Mitsui, and Mitsubishi. With a major bank at its center, each of these groups includes diverse large-scale companies ranging from manufacturing to trading. The Sumitomo group, for example, has twenty-one major companies specializing in banking, the chemical industry, the metal industry, construction, real estate, life insurance, the electrical industry, forestry, warehousing, aluminum refining, and a number of other areas; most of them have a company name starting with "Sumitomo." In addition to those six conglomerates, one can list some eighteen big business combines in particular industrial areas.[10] These include the Toyota, Toshiba, Daiei, Nippon Steel, and Kintetsu groups, among others. Positioned at the helm of the business community, these groups each have a string of subsidiary companies and subcontracting firms organized hierarchically in a structure known as *keiretsu* (enterprise grouping). Within each group, subsidiary companies offer mutual support, arranging reciprocally profitable finances, cross-ownership of stocks, and long-term business transactions. This formation is based on a family and normally requires each company to belong to a single *keiretsu* group. In a sequence of subcontracting arrangements, higher-level companies give contract jobs to companies lower in the chain, who may in turn give contracts to still lower companies. Generally, the lower the subcontractor the smaller its size.

A significant part of the small business community remains reasonably free of the intervention and influence of the *keiretsu* network. While these relatively independent small firms differ in size, they are comparatively autonomous, self-reliant, and maverick in their behavior. Cross-tabulation of the two dimensions – firm size and the extent of *keiretsu* intervention by large companies – is shown in Table 4.3, which represents four kinds of small businesses.

(a) Medium-sized Subsidiaries in Keiretsu Networks

Type A comprises medium-sized firms belonging to a grouping of enterprises under the immediate direction of large companies. These *keiretsu* companies can rely upon finance, expertise, and other support from their parent companies. In return, parent companies appoint their own employees as directors, managers, and executives of the main businesses under their direct control in the *keiretsu* network. Large companies regard these positions as suitable postings for management staff who are close to retirement age.

(b) Low-level Subcontractors under Keiretsu Control

Many of the small businesses that fall into Type B are petty subcontracting factories. At the bottom rungs of the subcontract hierarchy are ultra-small enterprises called *reisai kigyō*, which employ fewer than ten workers. This type includes firms run by self-employed individuals with the assistance of family members. Vulnerable to the manipulations of large corporations, this group is the most deprived zone of Japan's economy.[11]

In particular, the working hours of those employed in small businesses contrast markedly with those of workers in large enterprises. While a

Table 4.3 Types of small businesses

| Company size | Keiretsu intervention | |
	High	Low
Medium	(A) Subsidiary companies	(C) Venture businesses; maverick high-tech firms; entertainment promoters
Small to petty	(B) Low-ranking subcontractors; franchise shops	(D) Independent proprietors; neighborhood retail shops; professional offices

Table 4.4 Employees who work five days a week, by firm size (1990)

Firm size	Proportion (%)
10	24
10–49	38
50–299	56
300–999	73
> 1,000	84

Source: NHK 1991, p. 72.

majority of the latter, particularly in companies employing one thousand workers or more, take two days off every week, only a tiny fraction of small businesses have achieved a five-day working week. The working week remains long in independent enterprises which count on the supporting work of family members and in petty companies employing fewer than ten workers (see Table 4.4).

Subcontracting companies find it difficult to reduce the working hours of their employees since these companies operate at the whim of their parent corporations. A government survey of about ten thousand sub-contractors in 1991[12] found that 41.2 percent either occasionally or frequently receive orders immediately before a weekend or a holiday and must deliver goods immediately following it. To meet this requirement, subcontractors have little choice but to operate throughout weekends and holidays. The same survey revealed that 18.7 percent of the subcontractors received orders from their parent companies after normal working hours with the requirement that the goods be delivered the following morning. For these subcontractors, overtime remains the norm, and as long as parent companies wield such power their working conditions are unlikely to change.[13] Because of the power relationship between the two layers of enterprises, the reduction of working hours in parent corporations tends to increase those in subcontracting companies. Other things being equal, the correlation between the working hours of one domain and those of another is negative.

At the bottom of the chain of subcontractors, daily laborers in such flop-house quarters as Sanya in Tokyo and Kamagasaki in Osaka sustain mainly the construction industry. They find a job on a daily basis through recruiters, many of whom have gangster connections. These laborers work on construction sites and engage in demanding physical tasks. They inevitably compete in the labor market with foreign workers.

(c) Maverick and Venture Businesses

Type C companies are characterized by their relatively large firm size and their management's capacity to make decisions without much interference from big businesses. Many of these companies have made independent innovations in product development, production technology, and marketing, thereby establishing significant shares in markets which large corporations failed to develop. As mid-sized enterprises, these innovation-orientated firms maintain superiority over rival companies not only in capital procurement, plant, and other hardware areas, but in technical know-how, human resource development, and other software spheres.[14] Increasingly, enterprises in this category include venture businesses that depend upon knowledge-intensive technology and new service businesses that rely upon the diversification of consumer interests.

These small enterprises can adapt to changes in market demands more flexibly than large bureaucratic corporations. Some expand by developing "crevice businesses," business opportunities which big companies have left open but which have much potential. Others commit themselves to speedy, entrepreneurial styles of decision-making and to flexible responses to clients' requests.

The entrepreneurs in this sector may lack social prestige and the status which large-company businessmen relish, but possess confidence and find satisfaction in their work. Independent and highly motivated, the leaders of this group seek self-actualization rather than organization dependency, thereby developing a life-style and value orientation different from that of people working primarily within the keiretsu system. These small-business elites generally possess higher levels of assets than career employees of large firms, and tend to be the chūsan type middle class rather than the chūryū type into which big-business white-collar elites tend to fall.[15] Panasonic, Honda, Sony, and Nintendo, which have become household names around the world, emerged from this sector.

(d) Independent Small Proprietors

Type D businesses are mainly those of independent small proprietors such as small neighborhood retail shop owners, snack-bar managers, barbers, hairdressers, rice dealers, public-bathhouse operators, liquor merchants, stationers, dry cleaners, and the like. This sphere also includes some professionals who manage small offices, including general medical practitioners, lawyers, and tax accountants.

The subculture of small-business proprietors differs considerably from that of "organization men" in large firms. On the whole, non-professional self-employed people do not place a high priority on university education and find vocational training more relevant to achievement of their occupational goals. Many have gone through high schools specializing in vocationally oriented teaching for industry or commerce. In recent years, special vocational schools for high-school graduates have offered further education for those who aim at managing small businesses of their own. Many who seek to manage such small-scale establishments as barber shops, beauty parlors, and restaurants often go to these special vocational schools with a view to succeeding to the management of their parents' independent businesses.

A further difference between small proprietors and company employees is that the former tend to pass on their businesses from one generation to another. Approximately two-thirds of self-employed business people inherit the business of their parents or parents-in-law.[16] This rate is highest in the non-agricultural sector and suggests that this group has its own process of class reproduction. The overwhelming majority of this group live in city areas, and a high proportion appear to live with their parents upon marriage, another reflection of intergenerational continuity in this sphere.

Self-employment is institutionalized as a desirable occupational career path.[17] Typically, those who choose this track initially work for a company to acquire skills for the future, then establish independent businesses either on their own or with their family members. In other words, many small proprietors themselves used to be workers employed by small independent businesses.[18] During their time as employees, they acquire special knowledge, skills, and personal connections while working in inferior conditions as trainees or apprentices. Upon completing high school, a person from this group might first work as an attendant at a gasoline station, then as an auto mechanic at another station, and thereafter learn how to manage such a business. Having amassed considerable savings and successfully negotiated a bank loan, he may later establish a gasoline station of his own and become an independent proprietor. In traditional urban Japan, it was an established practice for such an apprentice to serve under an independent merchant for a long period from his teens, become his head clerk, and finally set up his own shop with the blessing of his master. This practice, known as *noren wake* (splitting a shop sign curtain), is less common today in its original form but persists in transformed shape as an arrangement for establishing a solid career route for those who start without educational credentials or material resources.

Small business owners who are not necessarily connected with *keiretsu* networks work longer hours than their employees. Some are willing workaholics who enjoy their company life above all things and have very limited communication with family members.[19] Others work long to economize on labor costs. On average, owners of petty enterprises in the service and entertainment business with thirty or fewer employees take only sixty-six days off per annum, with total annual working hours amounting to sixty-five hours per week.[20]

Independent small-business people are prominent in community organizations and events. In particular, those who manage small shops have a stake in maintaining good relations with their communities and are frequently involved in community festivals, district events, and local fund-raising. This group produces many leaders and active members of the neighborhood associations which make political and social decisions about community affairs. Unlike salary-employees who normally work in firms distant from their homes, these community-based independent shop owners, who live and work on the same premises, combine business with pleasure in promoting the social cohesion of their localities.

3 The Situation in the Manufacturing Industry

The subcontract relationships of small businesses with large firms diversify with the decline in the proportion of subcontract transactions of each small firm. Diversification also increases as a consequence of small businesses increasing the number of large parent companies with which they interact. As Table 4.5 indicates, a government survey shows that small businesses in the manufacturing sector are almost equally divided into two groups: those who have maintained exclusive or quasi-exclusive relationships with large companies (Types A and B), and those who have diversified their connections either considerably or greatly (Types C and D). With less dependence on parental companies, the latter types enjoy more autonomy in managing their operations.[21]

The variety that exists in the small-business community suggests that the value orientations and life-styles of its workers differ greatly depending on firm size and the degree to which firms are free of the control of large companies. Some are submissive, passive, and evidently exploited.

Table 4.5 Small businesses in manufacturing (1990)

Percentage of subcontract transactions	Number of parental companies		
	1	*2–5*	*> 6*
> 90	(A) Exclusive type (15.8%)	(B) Quasi-exclusive type	
70–90	(B) Quasi-exclusive type (36.8%)	(C) Quasi-diversifying type (38.0%)	
< 70			(D) Diversifying type (9.4%)

Source: Small and Medium Enterprises Agency, *Chūshō Kigyō Hakusho* (Small Business White Paper) 1991.

Others are innovative, participatory, and openly entrepreneurial. These facets manifest themselves in different circumstances in different ways. One must be cautious about stereotyping Japanese small business employees, especially as they constitute an overwhelming majority of the labor force.

4 Blue-collar Workers and Their Life-styles

Blue-collar workers make up about a third of Japan's workforce.[22] In both small and large enterprises, the culture of blue-collar workers differs significantly from that of office employees. Generally, blue-collar workers view their work as a means of livelihood and not as a source of gratification and fulfillment. They see themselves as holding ignominious and inglorious positions on low rungs of the social ladder. On the whole, blue-collar workers begin each working day early and prefer to leave their working environment as early as possible.[23] They find more satisfaction at home and in community life than do white-collar employees. Generally, they value family life and take an active part in community affairs. In community baseball teams, after-hours children's soccer teams and other sports clubs, blue-collar workers are prominent. They pursue these leisure activities to compensate for their *honne* sense of cynicism, alienation, and dissatisfaction with their workplace.[24]

II   The Dominant Framework of Large Corporations

White-collar employees in large companies, although a tiny minority in the workforce, have attracted disproportionate attention in labor studies in Japan because of the enormous power they wield in the business world both at home and abroad. In this sector firm-based internal labor markets function in conjunction with the so-called permanent employment system. Typically, a company will recruit a batch of new graduates every year, conduct intensive in-house on-the-job training, and rotate employees laterally from one department to another to make them multiskilled and versatile. For instance, a fresh employee may be assigned first to the accounting department, then to the sales division, and switched after a few years to the advertising section. The employment arrangements are based not so much on formal contracts as on informal agreements; a new recruit may be given a statement that he or she has been hired, but not an explicit covenant which spells out job specifications. Salaries are generally determined by length of service in the firm and structured in such a way that intercompany movement would not pay off in the long run. Employees have a strong incentive to work hard and improve enterprise performance since the bonus system is built into salary structure to distribute corporate gains among them.

Large corporations take initiatives to provide their employees with corporate welfare facilities ranging from company housing to recreation facilities. By establishing themselves as acceptable workers within the corporate framework, employees qualify for long-term low-interest company loans so that they may purchase houses or fund their children's education. To gain access to these schemes, however, employees must demonstrate resolute commitment to their corporate lives, and thus strong corporate allegiance. Once established, such an arrangement ties them more firmly to their company and increases their dependence upon it. Japan's white-collar employees are often sarcastic about their controlled life, likening it to *miyazukae*, the unenviable life of officials in the service of the court in ancient Japan, who had to put up with various kinds of humiliation to survive in highly bureaucratic government organizations. To a considerable extent, the life-styles of today's salarymen resemble those of samurai warriors who devoted themselves to their feudal lord and to the expansion of the privilege and prestige of his house and fief.

The top management of large companies is composed of long-serving successful ex-employees who have risen through the ranks; stockholders have little influence in the decision-making processes of their company, giving rise to a sharp distinction between corporate ownership and management. Furthermore, because large companies have chains of subsidiary and subcontract firms based upon *keiretsu* and other arrangements, they can function with relatively small bodies of employees in relation to their scale.

These features of large corporations have prompted many observers to argue that Japan's capitalism differs from its Western counterpart.[25] Some analysts maintain that Japanese firms have developed "corporationism" (*kaishashugi* or *kigyōshugi*) in which employees are completely tied to the company.[26] Others propose a distinction between "stockholder capitalism" (*kojin shihonshugi*) and "corporate capitalism" (*hōjin shihonshugi*), and maintain that the latter type now predominates in Japan.[27] In stockholder capitalism, as it is found in Western societies, companies function as incorporated bodies formed to maximize stockholders' returns. In corporate capitalism, each corporation becomes a substantive and personal entity as though it had a personality of its own, with its interests overriding those of individuals connected with it.[28]

Since companies are thus anthropomorphized and deified, they become omnipotent and omnipresent in the lives of their members, executives, managers, and regular employees alike, compelling them to dedicate themselves to the companies' "needs" and "commands." Thus, these "corporate warriors" are expected, in an almost military fashion, to devote themselves to the requirements of the enterprise at the expense of individual rights and choices. In return, virtually all Japanese companies pay bonuses to their regular employees in summer and winter, the amount depending upon company performance in the preceding term. Many firms also arrange and pay for company excursions and conduct company funerals when managers and directors die. Some firms even maintain company cemeteries.

To maintain these semi-totalistic characteristics, Japan's large companies use diffuse and nebulous rhetoric in evaluating employees' ability in terms of their personal devotion to the company, and likening the firm to the family.

1 Manipulative Definition of Employee Ability

Large Japanese companies evaluate their employees, both white-collar and blue-collar, annually or biannually throughout their occupational career. These appraisals, which determine employees' wage levels and promotion prospects, take a range of abilities into account. In this regard, the Japanese vocabulary distinguishes three types of ability: *jitsuryoku*, manifest ability which one demonstrates in a particular project or undertaking; *soshitsu*, latent ability that one possesses in relation to a particular domain of activity; and *nōryoku*, latent, undifferentiated, general, and overall ability that one has as a person. The third element is imprecise and comprises vague ingredients of "human character," "personality traits," and "psychological makeup," but it plays a crucial role in personnel evaluation in the firm-based internal labor market.[29] This market presupposes the production of generalist employees who can cope with multiple job situations, and therefore each employee is expected not only to display a job-specific manifest ability but to possess a wide range of attributes that are not necessarily connected with his or her job but are consistent with the broad goals of the firm. This means that the expected attributes encompass such nebulous components as *hitogara* (human quality) and *jinkaku* (personhood) that go beyond the specific requirements of one's occupational duties. Workers are aware that they are assessed in terms of the extent to which they are cooperative, obliging, and harmonious in their interpersonal relations.

Once personnel evaluation places a significant emphasis upon these ambiguous areas of *nōryoku*, employees have to compete with each other to demonstrate that they have general, latent qualities compatible with corporate goals. This is why some employees arrive at the office every morning earlier than the stipulated starting time to clean their desks and office furniture. For the same reason, many office workers stay after normal working hours until their boss leaves the office. Somewhat similarly, subordinates often assist with the preparation of the funeral of a relative of their superior. Employees engage in these tasks because they know that their human quality and personhood outside their job specifications are constantly subject to corporate appraisal. In this sense, their behavior springs not from altruism but from calculations regarding the presentation of personality traits that might affect their chances of promotion and salary increases. Their *tatemae* has to be unqualified loyalty to corporate norms but their *honne* lies in the maximization of their interests in the system. This is why some employees slack off during the day and come back to their desks after five o'clock to get the real work of the day done, in the name of devotion to the firm (although in reality they actually want paid overtime).

Meanwhile, their superiors are far from being free of similar compulsion. They cannot expect to lead their subordinates smoothly without exhibiting their own human quality and personhood beyond the call of job-specific duties. Thus, at their own expense Japanese managers take their subordinates to pubs and restaurants after work, visit their subordinates' relatives in hospital, and act as go-betweens for their subordinates' marriage. In so doing, managers can expect to count on the support and dedication of the employees of their department in tasks beyond its designated responsibilities.[30] Managers who can command their subordinates in this extra-duty realm are regarded as competent and as having the above-mentioned third element of ability, *nōryoku*.

Employees' levels in large companies rise in accordance with the length of their service to the company, moving up sharply towards the end of their career (in their fifties). The seniority-based wage structure makes employees reluctant to move from one company to another in the middle of their career; they can maximize their salary benefits by staying in the same firm.

In the face of the prolonged recession, increasing off-shore corporate operations and gradually rising unemployment in the 1990s, some large companies started to examine their salary and promotion structure and began to introduce a system which places more emphasis upon employees' manifest abilities and concrete achievements. Head-hunting is not unusual, and some middle managers now receive annual salaries on the basis of their performance in the previous year. There are signs that the life-time employment system and seniority-based salary scheme are collapsing in some sectors of big business, though these are a tiny minority in the mid 1990s.

2 The Family Metaphor as a Socialization Device

Japanese corporate leaders have used the family metaphor to inculcate the norm of total commitment in their employees. The key formula of this strategy is to liken a company to a family. An enterprise expects its employees to cultivate close internal relationships, develop family-like warmth and order, and regard the company as a center of their lives more important than their own families. Intriguingly, when speaking of their company to outsiders, many employees call it *uchi* (our house or home) and when speaking of competitor firms use a suffix, *san*, normally attached to a family name. Toshiba, for example, is referred to as Toshiba-san, and Nissan as Nissan-san. This approach is based upon the clear sense of *uchi–soto* distinction and immerses individual employees in their work without an overt sense of alienation, though it does not work fully for blue-collar workers. Whether one calls such immersion complete commitment or total exploitation, this Japanese management technique focusses on moralistic indoctrination and introduces expressive symbols to accomplish instrumental processes.

It goes without saying that a business is a complex organization engaged in profit-making and capital accumulation. The firm has to compete, expand, and exploit to achieve these goals. It is far from being altruistic, compassionate, and empathetic. In contrast, the presumed principles of the family are based upon self-sacrifice, mutual assistance, and harmonious affection. It is supposed to be the prototype of communal organization. The *tatemae* of the firm being the family manipulatively conceals the *honne* of corporate operations. The Japanese management method has shown that it is effective to use communal symbolism to attain the goals of business organization; it may well be more effective than the legalistic, impersonal, and bureaucratic vocabulary which some Western companies appear to prefer.

Within this framework, corporations invest heavily in socialization programs for their employees. They normally have morning sessions not only to prepare for the day but in many cases to cite company mottos and sing company songs. At a formal level, major companies hold intensive training sessions for several weeks for new employees, in an endeavor to infuse company policies and practices into their minds. Some of these sessions even attempt to rid the corporate rookies of their sense of self and ego. Some companies require them to sing songs in a busy street without feeling shy. Others compel them to perform physical exercise to the point of near exhaustion. These training programs have no bearing on the substance of the trainees' future work. Instead, the drills are designed chiefly to mold the newcomers into selfless and egoless employees who are willing to subject themselves to company orders no matter how unreasonable they may be. Many firms organize resocialization sessions of these and other kinds for low and middle managers.[31] In German sociological language, Japanese companies put up a facade of being *Gemeinschaft* (community) though they are *Gesellschaft* (association) in reality.

At a more informal level, middle managers are expected to take their subordinates out after work not only to listen to their complaints and troubles but to moralize upon the importance of devotion to company work. The managers play the role of corporate socializer in this way because their chances of promotion partly hinge upon their success in this area.

Thus, application of the family metaphor to a corporation has played havoc with the family itself, which has increasingly become subject to the imperatives of the corporate world. In this twisted sense, the corporation is a family and the family is a corporation, in contemporary Japan.[32]

III Social Costs of Japanese Workstyle

The ideological framework of these work practices in Japan has had both positive and negative consequences. No doubt it has greatly contributed to the *omote* dynamism and achievements of Japanese economic institutions. However, it has also produced a number of social costs on its *ura* side, impinging not only upon individual rights but also upon the health of many workers.

1 Long Working Hours

The Labor Standards Act, amended in 1993, stipulates that the statutory norm for working hours in Japan is forty hours per week. Any work performed over this limit is supposed to be treated as overtime with an additional payment of 25–30 percent. In reality, however, small businesses, particularly petty ones, are allowed, as a transitional measure, to maintain the old norms of forty-four to forty-six hours per week.

Total working hours per annum, which is the crucial index of the work ethic, is much higher in Japan than in most Western societies. The Japanese level hovers at around two thousand hours, estimated to be nearly three to four hundred hours longer than in Germany and France.[33] Although Japanese workers are entitled to paid annual leave of twenty days, they take only about nine days off on average, using less than half of their entitlement.[34] Overtime per worker remains about 150 hours annually.[35] Workers now tend to build overtime payments into their household budgets to cover housing loan repayments and education costs, and thereby compel themselves to work beyond normal working hours.

Furthermore, Japanese companies maintain the practice of "service overtime" where employees work after hours without receiving overtime allowances. On average, at least 10 percent of their actual working hours are estimated to fall into this category.[36] Although the practice contravenes the Labor Standards Act it prevails among many firms, which take advantage of the weak status of employees who are conscious of being assessed constantly regarding their level of devotion to corporate requirements.[37] Employees also normally use part of their annual paid recreation leave as sick leave, as most Japanese companies do not have clearly defined provisions for paid sick leave. Therefore, employees have little choice but to use their paid recreation leave when they are sick. When employees suffer from long-term ailments, it is generally at the company's discretion whether and how long they are paid during their illness.

Article 36 of the Labor Standards Act stipulates that a company's management can require employees to work overtime or on holidays as long as it has a written agreement with a labor union representing more than half of its employees and submitted it to the head of the labor standards supervision bureau concerned. The conclusion of such an agreement enables employers to avoid criminal prosecution even if they impose overtime on unwilling workers. However, legal scholars disagree over the extent to which employers may demand overtime of workers. At one end of the spectrum, it is argued that the signing of an agreement binds all unionists to corporate overtime requirements. At the other end, it is maintained that each worker has a right to refuse to work overtime even after an agreement has been reached between management and labor. The reality is that many Japanese employees find it difficult to leave the office before their bosses because they are under constant pressure to demonstrate their loyalty to the company by staying late.

In this context, the judiciary often side with the "corporation first" philosophy. On November 28 1991, for example, the Supreme Court dismissed the claim of a former employee of Hitachi that he was wrongfully fired because he refused the company order to work overtime. The ruling was that employees are required to comply with company regulations, including those concerning overtime, as long as they are "within reason."

2 Karōshi

With long working hours established as a norm of corporate life, an increasing number of employees have shown symptoms of chronic fatigue; some have worked themselves to death. The term *karōshi* (which literally means death caused by excessive work) has been coined to describe sudden deaths brought about by extreme exhaustion and stress resulting from overwork. Heart attacks, cardiac insufficiency, cerebral or subarachnoid (membrane) hemorrhage, and other heart and brain malfunctions top the list of causes of *karōshi*.

Legally, *karōshi* falls into the category of work-related casualty which industrial injury insurance is supposed to cover. In reality, however, it is difficult to prove *karōshi*. During 1988–90, 2,053 families lodged applications for worker compensation, but government labor authorities recognized only 92 as cases of *karōshi* – an approval rate of about 4 percent.[38] This extremely low percentage is attributable to the general reluctance of corporate management to release crucial data. The Industrial Injury Insurance Law requires that applications for worker compensation be accompanied by detailed reports on the work schedule of the relevant employee prior to his or her death. The bereaved family therefore must submit detailed documentation to the government Labor Standards Inspection Office, which assesses and authorizes their claims for industrial injury compensation, but companies tend to deny access to full information about the working hours of the deceased for fear of the corporate reality of inordinate hours of labor becoming public. Instead, the company management often provides the family with a gift of money in token of their sympathy and pays part of the funeral expenses in an attempt to cover up the circumstances leading to *karōshi*.

Initially, *karōshi* occurred among such front-line workers as truck drivers, migrant workers from rural areas, and local government employees, but it became increasingly frequent among middle managers of small enterprises and more recently at top management level. *Karōshi* takes place most often in tertiary industry, particularly in the service sector, where working hours remain inordinately long. Volunteer lawyers organized the National Council Against *Karōshi* and established *karōshi* hotlines across the nation to provide workers and their families with legal advice.

3 Tanshin Funin

The firm-based internal labor market system assumes that the firm constantly conducts on-the-job training to develop the skills of its employees. They are required to be rotated from one job to another, from one department to another, and from one office to another. Lateral and diagonal job rotation forms an essential component of the development of employees with diverse skills. This system, however, has not only economic benefits but social costs.

Nearly half a million Japanese married employees live away from their families because they have been transferred to a branch or factory distant from their family residence.[39] This practice, which is known as *tanshin funin* (single posting), is most prevalent among large corporations and national and local governments. These have about half the *tanshin funin* population, two-thirds of whom are between thirty-five and fifty-four years of age, and about half of whom are white-collar employees occupying managerial, professional, technical, and clerical positions.[40] A conservative estimate focussing upon corporations with a thousand or more employees[41] indicates that approximately one in five transfers of married workers falls into this category. The public utility industry, including electricity, gas, heat, and water supply, has the highest proportion, with one in three married transferees being a "company bachelor" of this kind. The Supreme Court and lower courts have ruled that *tanshin funin* is legal as long as it is arranged "because of corporate requirements."[42] The judiciary takes the position that employees should endure the disadvantages caused by *tanshin funin*, which is "not illegal even if it vitiates the stability of the family."[43]

In some cases, employees accept *tanshin funin* because it involves promotion. But difficulties regarding education, housing, and family health problems stand out as the major reasons for their acceptance of this practice.[44] The largest proportion of *tanshin funin* employees attribute their acceptance to problems concerning their children's education. High-school students in particular often face difficulty in transferring from one school to another, because admission to a high school is normally granted to those who have successfully passed an entrance examination in the final year of middle school. Transfer procedures and requirements are often cumbersome and complicated. Moreover, many pupils in elite institutions, even at elementary and middle school levels, are reluctant to move to a different prefecture for fear of having to study at a school of lower standard and possibly losing in the race to enter a prestigious university. These problems mean that when the father takes up his new position he leaves his family behind.

The second major reason for company bachelorship concerns housing problems. In many cases, house-owning employees would have to let their houses if their family moved with them, but the Tenancy Law gives much protection to tenants, to the extent that they can continue to claim occupancy unless landlords have "justifiable reason" to reoccupy their property. Because of frequent disputes between tenants and landlords, house owners who are ordered to transfer are often disinclined to let their houses, and choose to temporarily separate from their family.

The third reason for *tanshin funin* relates to the health problems of family members.[45] Many middle-aged salarymen live with their ageing parents, some of whom are seriously ill or even bed-ridden. When transferred to a distant office, these employees choose to leave their spouse to the task of nursing the ailing parents, and to move to the place of their new assignment alone.

These dark sides of Japan's economic development are partly attributable to the docility of Japan's labor unions, which often put corporate business imperatives ahead of workers' rights.

III Enterprise Unionism and Labor Movements

By and large, Japanese labor unions are enterprise unions which do not cut across company lines. Each enterprise union draws its membership from the non-managerial employees and some lower-level managers of a firm, regardless of their job classifications, and independently of whether they are blue-collar assembly-line workers, clerical office workers, engineers, or company accountants. About nine out of ten unionists in Japan belong to enterprise unions of this kind.

1 Skewing and Decline in Union Membership

A majority of workers in Japan, particularly those in small businesses, are not unionized and have no organized way of defending their rights against management. The unionization rate declines with the size of the firm; more than 60 percent of workers in corporations with one thousand or more employees are labor union members, but only 4 percent in small companies with fewer than thirty employees are unionized.[46] Labor movements in Japan are essentially a large-corporation phenomenon. They tend to defend the interests of large-corporation employees, often at the expense of their small-enterprise counterparts.

The proportion of the workforce that joins labor unions has declined to less than a quarter. As of 1994, the unionization rate was about 24 percent, less than half of its peak of 56 percent in 1948 (see Figure 4.1). Management groups at all levels have consistently attempted to weaken organized labor throughout the postwar years, but at least three additional factors have contributed to its downfall. The first of these is the change in the industrial structure of the Japanese economy. The manu-

Table 4.6 Unionization rate by firm size (1991)

Firm size (employees)	Unionization rate (%)
< 30	4
30–99	5
100–999	23
> 1000	61

Source: Labor Union Basic Survey of the Ministry of Labor.

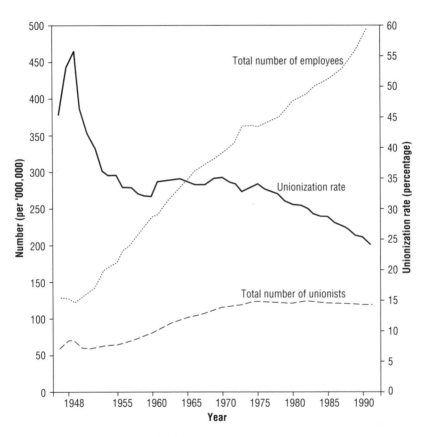

Figure 4.1 Changes in unionization rate

facturing sector, particularly the textile and shipbuilding industries, where the unionization level was high, went through intensive rationalization programs and lost a considerable number of workers. Concomitantly, the service sector where unions had traditionally been weak expanded rapidly, and the number of part-time and casual workers increased dramatically in this sector. These changes in the industrial structure of the Japanese economy stood in the way of unions' attempts to maintain their membership. The second negative factor was the implementation of privatization and deregulation programs which the government brought into effect in the 1980s. These programs attenuated, fragmented, or abolished public-sector unions which had formed the bastion of postwar Japanese labor movements. In this process, the Japan Railways Union and the Japan Telecommunications Union, which had engaged in numerous nationwide militant labor disputes in the past, vanished from the forefront of the labor movements. The third catalyst for the decline in union membership was the increasing apathy of the younger generation toward political causes, reformist activities, and organized protests.[47] Once a potent political force pertinent to the interests of a large proportion of the working population, most labor unions in Japan have become almost irrelevant to a majority of their former constituency.

2 Capital–Labor Cooperation

The union militancy which swept the nation immediately after World War II and before the high-growth period is now a thing of the past. At the firm level, the enterprise union structure makes it difficult for workers of the same job classification to form an intercompany alliance. At the national level, labor has often acquiesced in management's call for controlled wage increases and long working hours in the name of defending the international competitiveness of the Japanese economy. Behind these conciliatory styles of Japan's labor lies a union structure in which only a tiny fraction of union leaders remain labor advocates throughout their career. A significant proportion of union officials at the enterprise level assume their posts as a stepping-stone to managerial positions. Within the framework of enterprise unionism, union leaders who know that their term of office is limited often cultivate connections with high-level executives when dealing with management. This experience gives an advantage to ex-union officials who seek promotion within the company. Thus, over two-thirds of management personnel in large firms have served as union officials in the earlier stages of their career.[48] In many companies, the head of the personnel department or the labor division is an ex-union leader. This makes it difficult for union members to lodge serious complaints against managers with union leaders, who might secretly communicate with the management. In most cases, company management provide union offices and pay union officials' wages. Thus, in many large corporations, enterprise unions often act as the "second management" to pacify the labor force.

Enterprise unionism provides a major obstacle to the reduction of working hours. Each enterprise union engages in decentralized, firm-based negotiations with company management, but no firm can find it easy to shorten working hours without knowing what competing firms might decide about the issue. Since a one-sided reduction may weaken the company's competitive edge, employers would press for a trade-off between a reduction in working hours and an increase in productivity, which enterprise unions would not necessarily accept. In contrast, Germany, Sweden, Norway, Denmark and the Netherlands have been able to shorten working hours because these countries have institutionalized centralized collective bargaining systems.[49] Within this structure, agreements that unions and employers' organizations make at the center bind all firms in the relevant industry, and ensure that uniform practice prevails. With regard to working conditions, and specifically working hours, then, the centralized system of bargaining frees both employers and unionists from the anxiety of intercompany competition that is embedded in Japan's enterprise unionism makeup.[50]

In the world of blue-collar workers, Japan's large corporations successfully reorganized the system of management and supervision throughout the 1960s and 1970s. As the core of the rearrangement, they attempted to open an avenue for promotion for blue-collar workers beyond the level of foremen and thereby lower the wall between them and white-collar workers.[51] In the steel industry, for instance, management instituted the rank of *sagyōchō*, operation managers responsible for the overall administration of production lines. Placed between the plant manager and foremen, these blue-collar middle managers were placed in charge of production control and personnel surveillance. As the proxies at factory-floor level of high-level managers in corporate headquarters, they were fully authorized to make performance evaluations, attitude assessments, and bonus appraisals of the rank and file in their unit. The operation-manager system paved the way for a new career structure in which blue-collar workers could expect to be able to move up not only to middle-management level but eventually to the rank of plant manager. The system drove blue-collar workers to compete fiercely. The scheme gave a fresh sense of direction to the newly appointed operation managers, who had lost respect and influence as foremen because technological innovations had made their production skills outmoded. They emerged as workplace figures of authority embodying the directives of the company. Furthermore, with enterprise unionism in place, operation managers were union members, and often union officials. This virtually closed off the possibility of unions taking up blue-collar grievances and frustrations as the central issue of labor–management negotiations.

In fact, the posture of most labor unions has been compatible with the ideology of competition. Invoking the principle of equality, they have pressed for implementation of a structure in which blue-collar workers have the opportunity of promotion beyond the demarcation line between blue- and white-collar workers. When the barrier was removed or at least obscured, unions approved and even encouraged competition among blue-collar workers seeking those opportunities; in that sense, labor and capital have been in accord.

On the whole, unions of large companies have accepted the management's reasoning that an increase in productivity would lead to the enlargement of the "size of the pie," that would eventually lift wage levels and improve the living standard of workers. This argument gained credibility among union officials at the time of the high-growth economy, and since the 1960s unions have generally cooperated with management in productivity increases, technological innovation, and organizational restructuring.

3 Decline in Labor Disputes

The internal structure of organized labor is not uniform. To be sure, the "all-member-entry" type enterprise unions where company employees of all classifications are supposed to be union members form the core of Japan's unionism. However, there are two other types of unions.[52] One type consists of "plural-type" unions, which co-exist separately within an enterprise and compete with each other as majority and minority unions. In many cases, one tends to be anti-management and the other pro-management. These plural-type unions account for a substantial portion of labor dispute cases in the private sector, handled by the Central Labor Relations Committee (*Chūrōi*). The other type of unions, "new-type" unions, operate mainly in the margin of the workforce and tend to be craft unions based on occupational similarities and transcending enterprise lines. Cases in point include unions of temporary and part-time workers, of the mentally ill and physically handicapped, and of female workers. These unions attract membership mainly from workers in medium, small, and petty firms, and represent interests vastly different from those of workers in the core sector.

These union activities, however, remain peripheral as mainstream organized labor tries to find its way into the Japanese establishment and to acquire influence in national decision-making. Increasingly conciliatory and yielding, unions resort less and less to strikes and other forms of industrial dispute. In addition to the corporationism making inroads into workers' lives, the strategy of the national leadership of organized labor has contributed to the decline in union militancy.

An overwhelming majority of enterprise unions are organized under the umbrella of their industrial national centers, such as the All Japan Prefectural and Municipal Workers' Union, the Confederation of Japan Automobile Workers' Unions, the All Japan Federation of Electric

Machine Workers' Unions, and the Japanese Federation of Textile, Garment, Chemical, Mercantile, and Allied Industry Workers' Union. These industrial unions are further centralized into the Japan Trade Union Confederation, popularly called *Rengō*. It came into existence in 1987 with the amalgamation of separate national federations of unions in the private sector, such as *Sōhyō* (the General Council of Trade Unions), *Dōmei* (the Japanese Confederation of Labor), *Chūritsu Rōren* (the Federation of Independent Unions of Japan), and *Shinsanbetsu* (the National Federation of Industrial Organizations). With the incorporation of public-sector unions mainly under *Sōhyō* in 1989, *Rengō* has a total membership of eight million. A competing national union federation, *Zenrōren* (the National Confederation of Trade Unions), which is more politically oriented and closely associated with the Japan Communist party, has a much smaller membership amounting to about a tenth that of *Rengō*.

Notwithstanding their general partnership with management, Japanese unions try to represent labor interests and combat managerial interests with regard to wage and bonus increases. *Rengō* and other industrial federations orchestrate labor demands in this area every March and April in their "Spring Offensive" in a bid to win national benchmarks of annual wage and bonus increases for each industry. During this season, the national industrial unions, with varying success, negotiate with their national counterparts in industrial management in an attempt to gain as high an increase as possible.

The Spring Offensive has established the system in which all participating enterprise unions in the same industry come to agreements with their management in such a way that the annual salary increase is set to virtually the same figure. While this used to help unions form a united front against management groups during the high-growth period, the across-the-board figures tended to be settled at the level of low-performance firms in the stagnating or recessionary economy in the 1990s. Also, this style of bargaining became counterproductive in the context of growing diversity in the labor composition, salary structure, and working hour requirements of firms in the same industry. The Spring Offensive used to be accompanied by acute industrial action but this is no longer the case. The overall level of serious strikes has declined so much that strikes have virtually been contained. Japan has become practically a strike-free society.

V Distribution of Corporationism

In response to the oil crises of the 1970s, Japan's large firms implemented a scheme of lean management, a strategy which minimized the number of employees who had well-paid and well-protected jobs with numerous fringe benefits. This program involved shifting some of these workers to small businesses under the control of the large corporations, the expansion of the external labor market of part-timers and casual workers, and an intensification of the work of the employees who retained the privilege of remaining in the internal labor market.

The lengthy recession during the early 1990s further eroded the treasured lifetime-employment system in large firms and allowed them to justify corporate restructuring. With the strong yen and the concomitant increase in off-shore operations, many firms began to suffer from the oversupply of career-line white-collar employees who had expected to occupy managerial positions. Economic imperatives overshadowed the cultural rhetoric of companies as families, resulting in redundant employees being dislodged from their positions or simply fired. The alleged Japanese culture of group harmony has little substance in this context.

The restructuring of Japan's large firms also entails the partial collapse of the seniority-based wage structure and the introduction of a wage system which uses the achievement of tasks as the prime criterion of assessment. Some employees are now given a set annual salary depending more upon their performance in the previous year and less upon length of service to the company.

The changing values among youngsters coincided with the degeneration of the life-time employment ideology. Nowadays, one in three male university graduates moves from one company to another within ten years of graduation.[53] Some attribute their job change to long working hours in the firm they left. Others claim that they have made a choice because other enterprises offered a more attractive deal. In either case, the younger generation is less willing to identify itself with the doctrine of achieving one's position in an organization through long-term patience and perseverance.

Thus, the workforce that exemplifies the business practice which is allegedly distinctive of Japan, the life-time employment arrangement, has declined in size. The fact that th`s elite group of employees was a small minority to begin with corroborates the hypothesis that Japan's work culture is much more diverse than that of workaholism, job dedication, company loyalty, and group orientation.

Though corporations wield relentless power over the everyday life of many Japanese, there is considerable difference in the way in which individuals are linked to the corporate world. In pondering such variation, it may be useful to consider two analytical dimensions. One is the situational dimension, which gauges the extent to which an individual occupies a career-line position in an established enterprise. The other is the ideational dimension, which measures the degree to which an individual is socialized into the values of the corporate

Table 4.7   Distribution of corporatism

Socialization into corporatism	Career prospects in corporation structure	
	High	*Low*
High	(A) Corporate soldiers	(C) External aspirants
Low	(B) Internal skeptics	(D) Latent escapees

community. Correlation of these two dimensions yields four profiles corresponding to four possible types of Japanese workforce, as Table 4.7 indicates.

Cell A represents the corporate soldier type who holds a promising position in a major company and believes in corporate reasoning. Elite salarymen who are committed to the expansion of their company belong to this group. They are the stereotype of Japanese businessmen. Industrious workaholic owner-managers of small enterprises have similar corporate commitments.

Cell B exhibits the internal skeptic type who is employed in an internal labor market and occupies a post with good income and security but does not accept the ideology of corporationism at the *honne* level. An example would be a career-track employee who gives higher priority to activities outside his company and has little interest in devoting himself to corporate work. Another illustration might be an upwardly mobile department head who works slowly during business hours, stays late only to maximize overtime payments, and does not really care whether the company performs well.

Into Cell C falls the external aspirant type, who embraces the dominant values of large corporations but does not have a position within their structure. Cases include backstreet factory workers who want to let their children have a good education in order to acquire a job in a top company, and a non-career clerical worker with limited education who shows an extremely high level of company loyalty and devotion in the hope of being recognized and promoted in the corporate hierarchy.

Cell D is composed of the latent escapee type, who has little to do with the elite course of the corporate world and has no sympathy with the dominant corporate values. Examples are blue-collar workers who are mainly interested in after-hour leisure activities. Many young female office workers also fall into this category.

While the description of Cell A type workers is given undue emphasis in images of Japanese workers, they actually represent only a small portion of Japan's labor force. Greater balance is required in studies of work in Japan.

Notes

1 Granovetter 1984, p. 334.
2 This pattern is not unique to the Japanese situation but universal across advanced capitalist economies. The observed reality contradicts the long-held view that the development of capitalism would annihilate small-scale enterprises to pave the way for monopolistic domination by large companies, although oligopolies do dominate and control small businesses.
3 Some areas in tertiary industry are exceptions to this general definition. For the wholesale sector, the employee and capital ceilings decrease to one hundred persons and thirty million yen respectively. For the retail and service sectors, the cut-off figures are much smaller, fifty employees and ten million yen each.
4 These patterns do not change even if one eliminates agriculture, forestry, and fisheries from the calculations.
5 Based upon the Establishment Census conducted in 1991 by the Management and Coordination Agency.
6 Ishida 1989.
7 There is a debate over whether the life-time employment system has been a unique Japanese structure. Koike 1988, for example, contends that long service workers are so numerous both in Europe and the United States that Japan is not unique.
8 For instance, Yoshitani 1992.
9 Nakamura 1992 stresses this line.
10 Ōsono 1991, pp. 8–53.
11 One of the best descriptions of the lives of workers in small contract firms is in L'Hénoret 1993.
12 A survey carried out by the Small and Medium Enterprise Agency (Chūshō Kigyōchō) of the Ministry of International Trade and Industry in 1991.
13 It is no coincidence that Yamagata prefecture in northern Japan, which has the highest proportion of subcontracting companies, records the longest working hours in the nation.
14 Nakamura 1990 and 1992.
15 Kiyonari 1985, pp. 68–9.
16 SSM III, pp. 123–4.
17 Imada 1982.
18 SSM I, pp. 124–5.
19 Nippon no Shachō Kenkyū-kai 1994.
20 A fact-finding survey of labor conditions of small-scale establishments, conducted in September 1993 by the Central Federation of Societies of Commerce and Industry.
21 Types A and B correspond to the "high" column in Table 4.2, and C and D to its "low" column.
22 1990 census data.
23 NHK 1992, pp. 82–3.
24 Hamashima 1991, p. 362.
25 For instance, Johnson 1990.
26 Sataka 1992a, 1993a and 1993b; Matsumoto 1991.
27 Okumura 1991.

28 The Japanese legal system selectively adopts these assumptions in favor of anthropomorphizing corporations as juridical persons. Like individual persons, they are allowed to make political donations and to engage in political activities. However, Japan's criminal law does not subject enterprises to criminal charges, on the grounds that they are fictitious, impersonal entities.

29 The discussion here follows Iwata 1981, pp. 117–45.

30 Befu 1990b.

31 According to Sataka (1992b), a major electronics company requires workers to participate in "soul purification sessions" in the remote countryside in which they wear only loincloths and collectively dip themselves in a river to the shoulder. He also cites a case of a training session for company executives of car sales companies, in which a participant who had high blood pressure fell sick and was hospitalized after yelling loudly a few times in public at the instruction of a session leader.

32 The situation generated many popular expressions referring to the inability of company-first men to fit into the family environment. In the 1980s, they were sarcastically called "huge garbage" of no use to family life. Around the same time a popular saying was in circulation in the mass media: "it is best for the husband to be healthy and not at home."

33 The 1992 figure of the Monthly Labor Survey of the Ministry of Labor. It is difficult to make a systematic comparison with the figures of other countries because Japanese data do not include workers in firms with fewer than thirty employees, nor do they cover part-timers.

34 The Leisure Development Center's survey, as reported in AM March 18 1993, p. 11.

35 The 1992 figure based on the Monthly Labor Survey of the Ministry of Labor.

36 There is a difference of about 10 percent between the working hours reported by companies and recorded in the Monthly Labor Survey of the Ministry of Labor, and those reported by individual workers and recorded in the Labor Force Survey of the Management and Coordination Agency. This difference is attributed to the practice of "service overtime."

37 A survey conducted by *Sōhyō* in 1988 showed that two out of five workers replied that they were subjected to this practice in one form or another.

38 A legal practitioner estimates that the actual number of *karōshi* incidents amounts to tens of thousands and potential *karōshi* victims may reach hundreds of thousands (Okamura 1990, p.16).

39 According to the 1991 estimate of the Management and Coordination Agency, the number is about 455,000 (AM January 8 1993, p. 1).

40 Rōdōshō Kanbō 1991b.

41 Rōdōshō Kanbō 1991b, p. 13.

42 The Supreme Court's reasoning in July 1986.

43 The Tokyo District Court ruling in September 1993.

44 Rōdōshō Kanbō 1991b, pp. 27–36; AM December 31 1995, p. 26.

45 The survey result of the Research Center for Industry and Labor in 1995.

46 The Labor Union Basic Survey conducted by the Ministry of Labor in 1991.

47 Despite the overall decline in unionization since the mid 1970s, the construction industry has had a sharp increase in union membership. *Zenkensōren*, the National Federation of Construction Workers, enlarged its membership from 274,000 in 1980 to 385,000 in 1987. The Federation is composed mainly of construction workmen.

48 A survey result in 1978. See Eccleston 1989, p. 83.
49 Deutschmann 1991.
50 The collaboration of labor with capital in this fashion puts overseas labor unions at a disadvantage. The metal workers' union in Germany, for instance, finds it difficult to argue against management's claim that the reduction of working hours in Germany will erode the capacity of the German metal industry to compete effectively against its Japanese counterpart which operates on much longer working-hour arrangements. This hampers the German workers' struggle to win a thirty-five hour working week (*Japan Times*, March 20 1992, p. 22).
51 Watanabe 1990, pp. 87 and 189–90.
52 Kawanishi 1986 and 1992.
53 A survey of twenty thousand graduates, conducted by the Japan Labor Research Institute in 1992.

5

Diversity and Unity in Education

I Demography and Stratification

The postwar Japanese education system is patterned on the American model. At the age of six children enter primary school, which has six grades. They then proceed to middle school, which comprises three years; completing it is mandatory. Some 97 percent of those who complete compulsory education then progress to three-year high school.[1] Thus more than nine out of ten students complete twelve years of schooling, making high-school education virtually semi-mandatory. All government schools are coeducational, but some private schools are single-sex.

Beyond this level, four-year universities and two-year junior colleges operate as institutions of higher education. Nationally, only two in five students proceed to this level, and those who graduate from four-year universities comprise only about one-quarter of the relevant age group. While the proportion of students enrolling in tertiary institutions has steadily increased, those who possess university degrees amount to some 12 percent of the entire population. Japanese who are university-educated are a tiny minority; the vast majority of Japanese have had little to do with university life.

Outside the sphere of universities and colleges, an increasing number of unregulated, private commercial schools called *senmon gakkō* (special vocational schools) run vocation-oriented courses for those who have completed high-school but who are unable or unwilling to gain admission to universities and colleges.

The average formal educational level of the Japanese is among the highest in the world. Parents and students in Japan are conscious both of the prestige associated with higher educational credentials and of the

107

long-term pecuniary rewards that they bring. As Figure 5.1 indicates, the average level of life-time salaries and wages of university graduates is twice that of those who completed only middle-school education. Interestingly, some studies have cast doubt on the popular view that one's educational qualifications influence one's long-term monetary rewards more decisively in Japan than in Western societies.[2] With the general rise of living standards, however, parents are increasingly prepared to invest in education in the hope of their children acquiring a comparative material advantage in future life.

The most visible class cleavages emerge at the level of entrance to high school. There are various types of high schools. Some are government

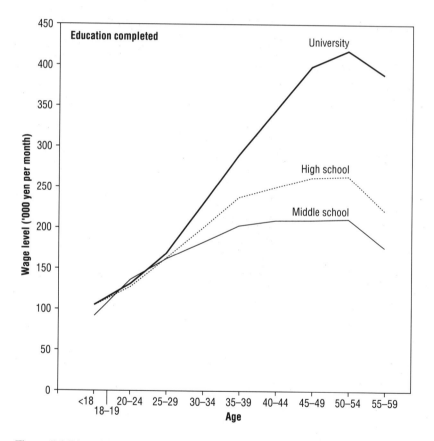

Figure 5.1 Disparities of age-based wages among male employees with different educational backgrounds
Source: Shimono 1991, p. 127, based on the Basic Statistical Survey of Wage Structures of the Ministry of Labor (1981).

funded and others are privately funded, the respective student numbers being in the ratio of seven to three. With regard to curricula, high schools are divided into two main groups: those providing general education with the expectation that a significant proportion of their students will advance to universities and colleges, and those specializing in vocational education (such as for agriculture, industry, and commerce) on the assumption that their students will enter the job market of their specialization upon completion of their studies. The distinction between the two types is somewhat blurred; some general school students start working immediately after finishing high school, while some vocational students proceed to universities and colleges. A further significant proportion enters private vocational schools (*senmon gakkō*). The demography of the high-school student population is given in Table 5.1.

1 Two Paths of Schooling: Academic and Vocational

Three major options are open to those who complete high school education.

The first is taken by about a third of all high-school graduates who progress straight to universities and colleges. Though nearly half of all high-school students aspire to a tertiary education in some form, the number of places available is limited.

A majority of institutions of higher education provide four-year degree courses. Such institutions are of three types. The first comprises national

Table 5.1: Demographic distribution of the high-school student population

School type	Academic path (universities and colleges)	Vocational path 1 (jobs)	Vocational path 2 (private vocational schools)	Approximate percentage
Government	A	C	E	70%
Private	B	D	F	30%
Approximate percentage	30%[a] (plus 10% as *rōnin*)	30%	30%	100%

Notes

Percentage figures are rough estimates based on 1994 data extracted from the School Basic Survey of the Ministry of Education.

[a] In 1994, this figure was made up of 22% for four-year university tracks and 14% for two-year junior college routes.

universities supported financially by the central government, including many of the most prestigious, for example Tokyo and Kyoto Universities. The second type comprises a small number of public universities funded chiefly by prefectural or municipal governments. The third group consists of private universities and colleges, including such well-known institutions as Waseda and Keiō Universities. Out of a total of over five hundred four-year universities and colleges, approximately three-quarters are private institutions. Institutions of higher education differ greatly not only in repute but in the nature and quality of the education they provide and the quality of their students. Though called universities and colleges, most cases in the bottom half of this group of institutions do not really deserve the label.

In addition, there are junior colleges which provide two-year degrees. Some 90 percent of students at this level are female, contrasting with four-year univrsity courses, where only 30 percent of students are female. With little academic motivation, many of them regard their time in these institutions as a phase between high school and marriage. Though junior colleges are classified as academic institutions, most of them are private and similar to vocational schools in their educational substance, with much emphasis placed upon training for home-making and domestic science.

It is widely believed that the Japanese educational structure is of a "tournament" type in which losers who have failed in their teens are virtually unable to take up the same challenge in life. This propels students, particularly in elite schools, to make fervent preparations for university entrance examinations. Upon close inquiry, however, the Japanese system is closer to the "league" type where one defeat is not the end of the road because a "return match" is built into the system.[3] It induces many unsuccessful candidates to devote another year or even two or three years to prepare for the entrance examination of their desired faculty. These students, who are between high school and university levels, are popularly labelled *rōnin* (lordless samurai), as they are attached to no formal educational institution and are therefore regarded as "masterless." Many *rōnin* attend private cramming schools which train students specifically for entrance examinations. This group constitutes about 10 percent of the total number of high-school graduates.

The second available route is the employment track, which approximately 30 percent of high-school graduates opt for. Most vocational or commercial high schools prepare their students for this path, and some students who have graduated from general high schools also choose it. One should bear in mind that more than half of Japan's youth do not advance beyond high-school level, and most make no preparation for university entrance examinations. With clear vocational orientations, the second-sector students are less achievement-driven and more practical. The well-publicized "examination hell" belongs to less than half of Japanese youth.

The 30 percent or so of high-school leavers who do not succeed in entering the tertiary education path or the employment route take a third option: that of attending privately managed vocational schools. These include schools for secretarial assistance, English conversation, cooking, sewing, bookkeeping, nursing, computer programming, flower arrangement, and so forth. Such vocational schools, which have thrived outside the formal education system, absorb potentially unemployed youth into a vocational training environment. To a considerable extent they mask the extent of latent unemployment.[4] Enrollments in these vocational schools have expanded since the mid 1970s concomitantly with the decline in job vacancies open to high-school graduates. These private institutions accommodate many of those who have completed studies at low-ranking general high schools but who cannot pass a university entrance examination or get a job; in this sense they provide a rescue mechanism for mediocre and low performers at high school. Privatized, commercial, and profit-orientated, these institutions remain outside government regulations and subsidies, drawing their earnings almost wholly from students' tuition fees on the basis of a full-fee user-pays principle.

Students entering universities and colleges and *rōnin* students may be grouped together as being in the academic route. One can also lump together the second and third paths as the vocational route. Those on the academic route are fewer than those on the vocational route. Because of the increasing commercialization of Japanese education, the route students take increasingly hinges upon their parents' financial resources.

2 The Ideology of Educational Credentialism

The ideology of educational credentialism pervades Japanese society and spreads an examination culture across considerable sections of Japan's schools. In the distribution of occupational positions in Japan, it is believed that educational background plays an exceptionally important role. At the level of higher education, universities are rank-ordered in terms of prestige and reputation in such a way that degrees from top-ranking universities are regarded as essential qualifications for high positions in the occupational hierarchy. Large corporations and the public bureaucracy in particular are believed to promote employees on the basis of the university they graduated from. Such a belief induces many candidates for university examinations to choose prestigious universities rather than disciplines in which they are interested or departments which have good reputations. Thus, those who aspire to tertiary education are intensely competitive in preparing for the entrance examinations of prestigious universities.

The increasing severity of the competition at this level has filtered down through high school in such a way that middle-school pupils struggle to get into high schools which produce large numbers of successful entrants to highly ranked universities.[5] Pupils who begin this process early commence their preparations in elementary school, so that they may gain admission to established private secondary schools which have systematic middle- and high-school education geared to university entrance examinations and high pass rates for entry into prestigious universities.[6]

Extensive mass media coverage of these tendencies influences the normative framework of Japanese education, making its top layer the model to be emulated. In fact, Japanese children spend more time in school than their Western counterparts, being required to attend school on Saturdays for half a day fortnightly, and having shorter vacation periods. Students are expected to digest a considerable amount of material to reach the levels demanded by the examinations of high schools and universities.[7]

The examination-orientated culture of Japanese education necessitates an elaborate system of criteria for assessing students' knowledge. On the pretext of avoiding subjective evaluation, these criteria give priority to the supposedly objective appraisal of pupils' capacities to memorize facts, numbers, and events and solve mathematical and scientific equations. This framework attaches little importance to the development of creative thinking, original problem formulation, and critical analysis in the area of social issues and political debates. Thus, rote learning and repeated drilling are the predominant feature of Japan's education, particularly at secondary-school level, where examination culture permeates deep into the classroom. Consequently, Japanese students rank high in international comparisons of mathematical and scientific test results. The nation's school system produces an army of youngsters who have had excellent training in basic factual knowledge but limited education in critical social thinking.

3 The Commercialization of Education

Education in Japan is an expensive business. The system imposes a considerable financial burden on families because, except in public primary and middle schools, all students must pay tuition fees. Education is especially costly for those studying in private schools and universities.

University education in Japan is regarded as a private privilege rather

than a public commodity. Public universities funded by national, prefectural, or municipal governments constitute only a quarter of institutions of higher education. They charge their students tuition fees which
amount to about 10 percent of the national average income of salary
earners. Though partially subsidized by national government, private
universities and colleges have much higher tuition fees plus considerable
entrance fees, which exceed the national average annual income at some
institutions. Scholarships are few in number and low in value. Furthermore, since most tertiary institutions are clustered in major metropolitan
centers, students from rural and provincial areas must pay considerable
accommodation costs. Accordingly, students depend heavily on their
parents' financial support during their university years. Thus, parents'
capacity to support their children affects their advancement to the tertiary level.

Parents' willingness to invest in their children's education has paved
the way for "shadow education"[8] outside formal schooling. There is an
examination industry which controls and makes profits from extra-
school education. Most important in this industry are *juku* schools, after-
school coaching establishments that thrive because of the intense
competition over school and university entrance examinations. These
schools range from large-scale, private training institutions to small,
home-based, private tutorial arrangements. At the primary- and middle-
school levels alone, over forty-five thousand were operating in 1993,
attended by about five million pupils – more than one-third of the
relevant population. At the middle-school level, nearly two-thirds of
students go to *juku* after school.[9] Some attend to catch up with school
work. Others prepare for entrance examinations. Still others regard
these schools as places for spending time with their friends. Whatever
their reasoning, the mushrooming of *juku* means a decline in youngsters'
leisure time after school. The *juku* phenomenon also implies that schools
have failed to satisfy students' educational needs.

The extent to which parents can invest in the education of their
children depends very much upon their resources, and those youngsters
who finish their education in government high schools and start working
at the age of eighteen (Cell C in Table 5.1) mostly come from families
lacking economic resources. Some well-placed and well-resourced parents put their children into expensive, elite private schools (Cell B)
which have single-stream middle-school and high-school curricula. Some
of these schools have links with private universities or track records of
producing students successful in obtaining admission into prestigious
universities.

In the overheated climate of examination fervor, commercial education firms developed a statistical formula to measure the test result of

each student in a large sample with a view to predicting the probability of his or her passing the entrance examination of a particular school or university. This measure, called *hensachi* (deviation score), is designed in such a way that the mean of scores for a group of students taking a test is always fifty and the standard deviation ten. From time to time, commercial test companies organize prefecture-wide or nationwide trial examinations taken by a large number of students from various schools. Locating each applicant's *hensachi* score on the distribution curve, the companies measure the likelihood of success with high accuracy on the basis of past data on the minimum entry score for the school or university department in question. These scores have provided valuable information for applicants wishing to decide which institution they should apply to enter.

This system of measurement is so widely used that until 1992 most middle schools allowed commercial test companies to conduct *hensachi*-producing tests in their classrooms. The Ministry of Education banned this practice in 1993 in a bid to stem increasing commercialism in school precincts. However, students remain interested in obtaining pre-examination numerical data on their scholastic attainments compared with those of students from other schools. Consequently, firms in the examination industry have continued to conduct examinations outside schools. In the absence of interschool comparative data prior to high-school entrance examinations held in January and February, teachers and parents too choose to rely on commercial tests that produce students' *hensachi*.

At the top end of the high-school hierarchy in major metropolitan areas, reputable private high schools (Cell B in Table 5.1), which have a stake in the business of recruiting high-scoring middle-school students, give them "acceptance commitments" mid-year, well in advance of formal entrance examinations, on the basis of their early third-year marks. While officially prohibited, this underhand practice continues unrestrained, appearing to emulate the corporate practice of firms which offer advance contracts of employment to promising university students who are to graduate the following year.

Hensachi arrangements are routine among high-school students vying for university places. They sit for commercially organized trial examinations which provide candidates, both third-year high-school students and *rōnin*, with fairly accurate ideas of their chances of getting into their preferred university. These scores not only rank students, but do so in relation to a numerical ranking of universities.

Education culture within the elite school setting has gradually come to reflect corporate culture within the enterprise environment. Just as ability-based salaries increasingly represent the human worth of each employee, so too are the numerically calculated *hensachi* marks treated as though they were the sole indicator of the total value of each student. Educational sociologists regard the situation in academic-track schools as a "convergence of various human abilities into an index of *hensachi*,"[10] a "*hensachi*-based linear hierarchical definition of essentially multi-dimensional abilities,"[11] and a "one-dimensional system of the rank ordering of abilities measured solely by *hensachi* scores."[12]

4 School–Business Interactions

Companies in Japan make a practice of recruiting fresh graduates through schools' guidance-counselling units. Therefore, Japanese schools interact intensely with the business community in providing job placements for students. In this nexus, many dedicated high-school teachers devote themselves to finding jobs for their students. The teachers in relatively disadvantaged schools where most students go into the job market immediately after high-school education play a vital role in helping them secure jobs.[13]

Through the assistance of these school officers, high-school students who wish to find work would normally start looking for a job and sit employment examinations for various companies in the summer or fall of their final year. New recruits complete high school in March and commence work *en masse* on April 1, the first day of Japan's financial, school, and academic year. On this day throughout the nation, companies conduct formal ceremonies where new employees assemble in large halls to listen to pep talks given by their executive bosses. An overwhelming majority of job-seeking high-school students – over 80 percent – found work this way in the 1990s.[14]

The school-based recruitment system, which is legally supported by the 1949 revised Employment Stabilization Law, became a widespread practice in the 1960s and 1970s, allowing employers to choose the schools to which they would send job-application forms and related employment information. Students attending schools which companies do not approach have virtually no way of gaining an interview. If prospective employers are dissatisfied with the quality of students they hire from a given school, they can switch their preference to other schools. This situation causes guidance-counselling teachers to maintain and expand recruitment channels with companies, in rivalry with their counterparts at other schools. In turn, corporate personnel officers compete with each other to secure a constant supply of quality students from quality schools. Locked into reciprocal transactions, schools and enterprises thus form a central nexus in the recruitment market. These school–firm interactions also shape the hierarchical ranking of schools in each area, a school's ranking reflecting its standing with companies as a supplier of quality job applicants, and the standings of the companies it deals with. Within this context, counselling teachers go to great lengths to find a job for every student.[15] Their dedication and commitment in this regard make the scheme work.

A similar system prevails at university level. Prospective graduates commence job hunting early in their final year, but large corporations (prestigious ones in particular) consider applications only from students of the universities that they have designated in advance. Students from mediocre universities have no opportunity to be evaluated by these firms. This practice, which is known as the university designation system and which operates either openly or covertly, is the major reason for the stratification of tertiary institutions in the job market. Corporations justify the system on the grounds that, in the absence of dependable detailed information about the quality of each student, the most reliable indicator is the level of the university which he or she has succeeded in entering: the more difficult it is to get in, the more ability the prospective employee must have.

From a corporate manager's point of view, the level of difficulty of entry to each department of each university can be measured most credibly by its entrance examination score as reflected by the *hensachi*. With the *hensachi*-based university designation system firmly established, high-school students who wish to advance to higher education must pass an entrance examination of a university with a high *hensachi* standing in order to have the prospect of obtaining a good job after graduation. Given that employment opportunities with the best material rewards exist in the internal labor market, particularly in the large-corporation sector, students' *hensachi* scores not only represent their chance of gaining admission to a reputable university but are constant reminders of their position in the race for good employment.

Superimposed upon the three regular paths for high-school graduates is the external labor market, composed of part-timers, casual workers, temporary agents, and other non-regular employees. This has grown as a consequence of the shrinkage of the internal labor market. While on-the-job training of an enterprise's regular employees is a concomitant of the internal labor market, the continual expansion of the external market raises the question of who should be responsible for training its workers and bearing the cost involved. Given the fact that vocationally oriented *senmon gakkō* produce many who enter the external market, the numerical expansion of these institutions provides a partial solution to this problem.[16] Further, more middle-level life-time employees are switching companies, thereby creating a new external job market.

5   Articulation of Class Lines

Educational institutions are in principle meant to provide avenues for upward social mobility and to perform equalization functions among different social classes. Provided sufficient educational opportunities are available, the bright son of a laborer in a rural area should be able to pursue higher education and to climb to higher positions in the social hierarchy. Most Japanese perceive that this is not really the case. They regard the education system as more unfair[17] than the areas of wealth, occupation, and gender.[18] Educational-class lines are discernible in at least three areas: differences in family socialization processes, stratification in high-school culture, and macroscopic patterns of social mobility.

(a)   Differentiation of Family Socialization

The ideology of achievement-based meritocratic competition in schools often veils who defines what is meritorious and who gains an advantage over whom on the basis of defined criteria. An example is the way in which class background affects the process of acquiring language skills. A study of compositions written by upper-level primary-school children[19] shows that city pupils tend to use a wider variety of conjunctions, adverbs, and adjectives than rural pupils. City children also appear to identify the subject of a sentence more frequently than their countryside counterparts. With regard to patterns of conversational communication, urban, middle-class children are distinctly superior to urban, working-class children and to rural children in both descriptive and abstract sentence construction. These observations give credibility to the proposition that pupils with disadvantaged backgrounds are generally deprived of chances to develop formal language skills and gain overall linguistic ability.

The educational ambition of girls is conditioned by the occupational position of their fathers. A study of high-school girls in Tokyo[20] found that most daughters of professionals and managers aspire to advance to four-year universities, while the daughters of small-business owners and blue-collar workers expect to go to junior colleges, or to end their education after completing high school. At an early age, girls are immersed either in a cultural environment that takes it for granted that girls should obtain university degrees, or one that assumes girls do not need academic qualifications. The value orientations of mothers also greatly influence their daughters' aspirations. In families where the mother does not hold the conventional view of gender-based role differentiation, her daughter is likely to aim to achieve higher educational goals. The extra-school milieu thus determines the educational selection process in a fundamental way.

(b) Stratification of High School Culture

High-school students' interests differ significantly between high- and low-ranked schools. "Examination hell" in high-ranking schools provides merely a partial picture. A study of high-school students in the Tokyo metropolitan area[21] reveals that students at the bottom rungs of the school ladder find more significant meaning in their part-time jobs outside school, regarding them as enjoyable, useful, fulfilling, and relaxing. Many of them hardly study at home, distance themselves from class work and extra-curricular activities at school, and self-actualize in outside work where they willingly acquire a sense of responsibility, and the qualities of perseverance and courtesy. These job-orientated students expect to live independently of their parents, to become self-supporting in their future full-time job, and to marry earlier than school-orientated students. In this sense, part-time jobs facilitate students' self-reliance, self-support, and independence. In comparison with students in schools at the top of the school hierarchy, those near the bottom acquire real-life experiences outside school and mature relatively quickly.[22]

At the lowest end of the scale, students who do not measure up to the standards gauged by the *hensachi*-based yardstick – many of them being in cells C, D, E and F of Table 5.1 – find it more realistic to drop out of the school system entirely. In fact, the consolidation of the *hensachi* system has been accompanied by a rise in the number of dropouts. Furthermore, because the emphasis on *hensachi* marks generates a culture in which scholastic ability is viewed as the only measure of individual competence, low *hensachi* performers also tend to have low self-esteem. This leads these students into the so-called *tsuppari* subculture – a tendency to defy school and community authorities and to obstinately have their own way.

A study of the Osaka area identifies four subcultural types of high-school students.[23] The first type shows a strong orientation to academic achievement. The second cluster places an emphasis upon fun and friendship in school life, cultivating social skills and having a good time among classmates. The third group is orientated to social activism, with involvement in student council activities, participation in social movements, and interest in philosophical issues. The fourth orientation displays a non-conformist tendency, unwillingness to study hard, or get involved in school events and activities. Positive academic orientations are strong only in elite schools; other orientations are distributed variously among all types of schools. The same study also observes that, while a large proportion of elite-school students aspire to occupational success, a majority of students in vocationally orientated schools are primarily interested in having an ordinary but stable family. Students' *honne* appears to differ depending upon the school type.

At the bottom of the high-school hierarchy are more than one thousand evening schools which operate throughout the nation. These schools cater to a wide range of students numbering more than one hundred thousand. Though little attention is given to this segment of the student population, these evening high schools accommodate a broad variety of disadvantaged students:[24] underachievers at middle-school level, so-called "problem children," ex-sufferers of "school phobia," drop-outs from daytime high schools, and the physically handicapped. Other students include middle-aged and elderly adults who could not go to high school in their youth, and foreigners who work during the daytime.

The current profile of evening high-school students differs significantly from that of earlier decades. In the 1950s and 1960s an overwhelming majority were, for economic reasons, blue-collar workers by day and self-supporting students by night. In this period the number of students who studied in evening classes exceeded half a million and constituted more than 20 percent of the high-school student population. Since the 1970s, the number of evening school students has declined with improvement in the standard of living. These schools began to enroll a more diverse range of students who suffer problems of a non-economic nature. Though small in number, they too are part of Japan's high-school culture.

(c) Macro Patterns

At the macroscopic level, the SSM project presents three major findings in this area. First, the impact of class background upon the probability of advancing from middle school to high school has diminished. Family occupational and educational background has a declining influence on whether students proceed to high school. At this level, therefore, educational opportunities have been equalized. Second, the class background of high-school graduates continues to influence their likelihood of proceeding to university or college, and the amount of influence has not significantly changed. Accordingly, educational stratification remains relatively constant. Third, students from families of high educational and occupational background have much better chances of entering prestigious universities, and this pattern has intensified over time. In this area, a restratification of educational opportunities has transpired.

The social backgrounds of students at Tokyo University are concentrated in the elite sector.[25] The average income of their parents exceeds 150 percent of the national average income of male wage-earners in their late forties and fifties. About half the students at this university come from the top twenty high schools, eighteen of which are private high schools connected with their own middle schools; students in these schools are trained in a six-year continuous course.[26] With regard to parental occupation, income and school background, there is little doubt that the children of those who occupy the higher echelons of the social hierarchy and possess greater economic and cultural resources comprise an overwhelming majority of the student population of Japan's most prestigious university. Class plays a major role in determining high-school students' access to top institutions of higher education.

III State Control of Education

The Japanese education system is characterized by a high degree of centralization and domination by the national government. This pattern derives from the fact that Japan's modern school system was developed in the last quarter of the nineteenth century at the initiative and through the intervention of the powerful Ministry of Education. Japan had an extensive community base in education towards the end of its feudal years, in the form of many grassroots temple schools run by priests and local intellectuals, as well as schools for youngsters of the samurai class managed by feudal lords. But the strong leadership of the central government determined not only the tempo of the spread of schools as modern institutions, but also the shape and content of their curricula. And although the education system was decentralized and democratized immediately after World War II, the postwar liberalization process never overturned the dominance of the state in the management of schools. Even today, the Ministry of Education controls the content and tone of all school textbooks, supervises curricula throughout the nation, and has considerable power over the administration of universities. The vestiges and legacy of prewar centralized education remain a potent force, which maintains a wide range of practices common to most schools in the country. Because of the concentration of power in the Ministry of Education, its political and ideological stance has provoked heated controversy throughout the second half of the twentieth century. This structure counteracts the diversification of school culture and propels the unification of education in a number of ways.

1 Textbook Censorship

The Ministry of Education has the power to censor the contents of all textbooks used in primary, middle and high schools. In prewar years, it compiled its own textbooks and enforced their use at primary and secondary levels throughout the nation. After World War II, the system of state textbooks was abolished, and numerous commercial publishers began producing their own textbooks for various subjects. However, the Ministry retained the authority to modify the matter and wording of any textbook and made it a legal requirement that no textbooks could be distributed without its authorization. Because of its power of censorship, the Ministry's policy on the contents of textbooks on social studies and Japanese history has often galvanized the public. By and large, the Ministry's textbook inspectors have sought to censor descriptions of Japanese atrocities during World War II, depictions of political dissent and social movements against the government, and discussions of individual rights and choices. They have tried to sway the writers towards emphasizing nationalism and patriotism, submission and obedience to social order, and duties and obligations to society.

The Ministry attracted international criticism in the 1980s for its directives that the textbook description of Japan's military activity in Asia in the 1930s and 1940s be changed from "aggression" to "advancement." Similar emphatic disapproval was voiced when it was revealed that textbook examiners insisted that Korea's independence movements during the Japanese colonial period be portrayed as violent rebellions, and attempted to dilute the depiction of Japanese wartime activities.

The constitutionality of the government textbook authorization system surfaced as a controversial issue with a series of lawsuits brought by Professor Saburō Ienaga, an eminent historian, against the Ministry of Education. The Supreme Court ruled in 1993 that the system was constitutional and maintained that the state had the right to control the substance of education.

The present system enables examiners to reserve judgment and to provide "opinions for revision." The writers cannot expect to pass further screening without complying with these "opinions." Authors of social studies textbooks cite instances where the Ministry advised them to change their wording from "the rights of senior citizens" to "the welfare of senior citizens" and from "the rights of consumers" to "the life of consumers," and also suggested they should include a sentence about the legality of the Self Defense Forces.

Furthermore, approved textbooks are chosen for use in the classroom not by individual teachers or by schools but by the education committee at prefectural, county, or municipal level, and are bought and distributed en bloc. Because of the size and profitability of the textbook market thus organized, publishers cannot avoid making pecuniary calculations in dealing with Ministry textbook examiners. Thus, market-driven conformity prevails because of monetary considerations on the part of publishing houses.

2 Curriculum Guidelines

The Ministry exercises further control over the substance of education through its requirement that schools follow *gakushū shidō yōryō*, the detailed guidelines on what is to be taught and how it is to be taught at each grade from primary school to high school. It has been debated among educators as to whether these guidelines legally bind individual teachers, but in reality the Ministry uses them as a directive to force teachers' compliance with the educational framework established by the government. For example, the 1989 guidelines (the sixth revised version since the first provisional guidelines of 1947) abolished social studies and introduced life studies at junior grades of primary school, and split social studies into two separate subjects, geography and history as one subject and civics as the other. The new guidelines also required all schools to hoist the Rising Sun flag as the national flag on ceremonial occasions and to sing the Kimigayo song as the national anthem. The public is still divided over these requirements because the flag and song were used as symbols of nationalistic moral education during the war years, but the Ministry remains adamant.[27]

3 Conformist Patterns of Socialization

The fact that Japan's education structure has developed under the guidance and domination of the central government has left its mark in the way in which routines, conventions, and practices cut across regional lines. Several common patterns of socialization at school deserve attention.

(a) Militaristic Ethics

Japanese schools invoke militaristic ethics for the "personality formation" of students. These ethics have multiple layers but all embrace the notion that some physical training is needed to produce a socially acceptable person.

At the mildest level, Japanese children are expected to follow various forms of military discipline in classroom. It is part of Japanese classroom routine for a classroom leader to shout at the beginning of a session, "*Kiritsu!*" (stand up), "*Rei!*" (bow), and "*Chakuseki!*" (sit down) – calls that the entire class are expected to follow as their greeting to the teacher.

It is also customary for teachers to arrange their pupils by height order in classrooms and assemblies. While this gives the external appearance of sequence and regularity, the underlying presumption is that the taller the better; students are always conscious of their physical location in the height order of their classmates.

The most standard school uniform for boys is still a semi-military style of black jacket with a stand-up collar, and black trousers. Some schools, and many school sports clubs, require male students to have their hair cropped close, a practice similar to that applied to soldiers in the Japanese military before and during World War II. This convention prevails in more than a quarter of government middle schools throughout Japan and remains most entrenched in Kyūshū and Shikoku districts, with a majority of schools at this level making it compulsory.[28] The idea is that Spartan simplicity in school life will cultivate a strong, manly, and austere personality.

The system of quasi-military age-based hierarchy is ingrained at the interpersonal level. Commencing at secondary school, pupils are introduced to a pervasive student subculture in which junior students (*kōhai*) are expected to show respect, obedience, and subservience to senior students (*senpai*). Even outside school, *kōhai* students are expected to bow in greeting when they encounter *senpai* on the street. Inside school, the *senpai–kōhai* relationship is perhaps most intense and articulated in sports club activities; the new members, who are usually first-year pupils, are normally required to engage in menial tasks for the initial phase of their membership. At the instruction of older members, they must serve as ballboys or girls, clean the playing field and equipment, and even wash team members' clothes, without being allowed to practice or train themselves for the probationary period. This convention stems from the rationale that one can become a good player only after one has formed a submissive personality, willing to follow orders from a coach or captain. The belief is that one can develop a proclivity for subservience by being chastened by a series of humiliating tasks.

Every day after school, children must clean their own classrooms, school hallways, stairways, toilets, playground, and so forth. Behind this practice is the notion that pupils learn to be both humble and hardworking through sweeping with a broom, wiping the floor with a damp cloth, and getting their hands dirty. This routine is supposed to train pupils to be compliant, cooperative, and responsible citizens.

(b) Psychological Integration

Schools in Japan have developed techniques to promote psychological uniformity and cohesion among pupils. It is standard routine in many subjects for a teacher to instruct an entire class to read a textbook aloud, in unison. This gives the class a sense of working together and makes it difficult for any child to deviate from the set pattern. Not only high and middle schools but all primary schools in Japan have their own school song, which pupils sing together at morning assemblies, sporting events, and other ceremonial occasions to promote emotional integration.

Every school has a few annual events for which pupils collectively prepare and which are designed to generate a sense of group cohesion and achievement. A sporting day (*undō-kai*) which all schools have in fall is among those key events. On that day every pupil competes in running, hurdle races, relays, and so on. By convention, pupils are divided into red and white groups which vie with each other for a higher total score. Teachers and parents participate in some races, and *undō-kai* is usually an exciting community affair. A day for dramatic and musical performances is another important occasion on the school calendar. Before an audience of the entire school, each grade performs a drama, some classes sing several songs, and some clubs play music, traditional and Western. Every pupil is expected to take part in this occasion, for which a full day is reserved.

All children in Japan also learn standard gymnastic exercises in groups; these are practiced to the accompaniment of certain tunes broadcast by the Japan Broadcasting Corporation (NHK). The so-called radio gymnastics program has been broadcast every morning since prewar days, and schools across the nation adopted it as part of their physical education curriculum. As a result, most people in Japan know how to perform the exercises. Not only are these exercises expected to be performed in physical education classes, but also at athletic meets and many other sporting events. On such occasions every participant is expected to perform the exercises to a standard tune, generating an atmosphere of unity and solidarity.

(c) Check-ups and Self-policing

Japanese schools generally have excellent physical examination programs. Each school has a school doctor or doctors who conduct physical check-ups of all pupils on a regular basis. All schools in Japan keep good records of the height, weight, and vision of every pupil, measured at least once a year. No doubt this meticulous concern with pupils' physical condition contributes to early detection and treatment of their health problems.

A similar interest in the well-being of pupils extends to their attitudinal and behavioral "correctness." Slogans with such designations as "goal for this week" and "aim for this month" usually fill the walls of Japanese classrooms. These class aims are normally of a moralistic nature: "Let us not run in the corridors," "Let us try to answer teachers clearly," "Let us keep our school toilets clean," and so on. In some cases teachers set the objectives; in other cases pupils are instructed to collectively formulate them in class discussions. These exercises, designed to keep pupils in line, are followed by "soul-searching sessions" in which the entire class is expected to discuss whether the set objectives have been attained and, if not, what should be done in the future. In many schools, each class has pupils in charge of school discipline (*fuuki iin*) or "students on weekly duty" (*shūban*), who are expected to maintain class morals. These students assist teachers in ensuring that all pupils comply with school norms.

IV Regimentation and its Costs

1 Excessive Teacher Control

Rigidity, stringency, and regimentation have increasingly dominated Japanese education since schools increased teacher control of pupils in the 1970s and 1980s. This trend reflected the response of educators to the rise of political protests in secondary schools in the late 1960s and to the growth of school violence in the late 1970s and early 1980s. To suppress potential deviance from school norms, school administrators and teachers tried to tighten their grip on students by shaping their outward behavioral patterns into a uniform mode. This tendency gave rise to what many commentators call *kanri kyōiku*, the regulatory style of education that underscores control of students' bodily expressions and tries to standardize their appearances and personal effects.

School teachers are not a uniform body which supports this trend unreservedly. Many resisted the moves and attempted to maintain the relatively decentralized, liberal structure of education established immediately after the end of World War II. This was most visible in a series of confrontations which the Japan Teachers Union mounted against the Ministry of Education. The union took a firm stance in the name of democratic education against almost every move to reverse postwar educational reform and tighten state control. Though the union gradually lost ground to the Ministry, and lost membership as part of the overall decline in unionization, some teachers still maintain a genuinely progressive spirit. More importantly, many teachers are sincerely concerned about the well-being of their pupils, anxious to see them develop their potential fully, and eager to introduce innovative methods of teaching. Accordingly, one must look at the cost aspects of Japanese education in some perspective. Nonetheless, the price of regulatory education is increasingly visible in many aspects of school life.

(a) Corporal Punishment

It is illegal in Japan for teachers to use force on pupils. However, in reality some teachers resort to physical violence to control them, occasionally inflicting serious injuries.

Some cases which have attracted national attention show the tip of the iceberg. For instance, seven teachers buried two middle-school children up to their necks on a beach in Fukuoka in the summer of 1990, as a punishment for the students' acts of intimidation. In 1992, in a Chiba District Court ruling in favor of the plaintiff, it was confirmed that a student required medical treatment for five months in 1986 because his teacher had forced him to sit on the floor, and had twice kicked him hard in the face because he was late for a school lunch. The student received lacerations to his lower lip, two of his front teeth were knocked out, and his tooth nerve became paralyzed.

These are of course extreme cases, not incidents that occur in Japanese schools every day. Nonetheless, teachers' violence against students is not a rare occurrence, and many cases remain unreported for obvious reasons.[29] Some Japanese educators, particularly many teachers of physical education, believe that the military style of training is necessary to make pupils face the world. They see education as a way of fostering in pupils what they call *konjō*, the fighting spirit, tenacity, and doggedness. These teachers rationalize the use of violence as necessary to achieve this goal.

To make the matter worse, a considerable number of parents encouraged or connived at the imposition of illegal corporal punishment on pupils at primary and secondary levels. A national survey on human rights conducted by the Prime Minister's Office in 1988 reveals that one-third of respondents regard it as an acceptable practice.[30] Some discipline-oriented parents praise violent teachers as educators full of zeal, enthusiasm, and motivation to teach children. These teachers presume on this sort of community attitude.

(b) School Regulations

Another area of national controversy is the extensive application of detailed school regulations. These rules include a range of trivial restrictions on the length and color of hair, mode of dress, size and type of school bags, type of shoes, and so forth. In many schools, teachers stand near the school gate every morning to ensure that pupils wear the correct items in the correct way, in accordance with school regulations.

The strict application of rigid school rules has led to tragic occurrences. In Kobe in 1990, a high-school girl died when she attempted to run into the school grounds to avoid being late for school. The school made it a rule to close the machine-operated school gate at exactly 8:30 a.m., locking out tardy pupils. The girl tried to force her way in but the teacher on duty, knowing of the girl's attempt, nevertheless closed the gate. As a consequence, her head got caught between the gate and the wall and was crushed. She was killed instantly, and the teacher in question was found guilty on a charge of professional negligence resulting in death. While he was tried in a court of law, the real issue was the rigidity of school rules which make students fearful of the costs of deviating even minimally from the expected standards.[31] In this sense, this was not an isolated case.

The Japanese education system displays patterns contrary to trends in other industrialized societies where a style of learning shaped by permissive choice-orientated guidance is favored over authoritarian training. Ironically, since commercialism and consumerism dominate the world outside school, the very discrepancy between these two spheres of life induces some students to indulge in deviant behavior.

2 Costs of Regulatory Education

The regimented style of education leads to student frustrations, which are often translated into the gloomy situation which some observers call the "desolation of school culture." Its two aspects have formed the focus of national debate.

(a) Ijime

Ijime (bullying) has become rampant in schools since the mid 1980s, the very time when Japan's economic performance became the envy of other industrialized nations. *Ijime* is a collective act by a group of pupils to humiliate, disgrace, or torment a targetted pupil psychologically, verbally, or physically. In most cases of *ijime*, a considerable portion of pupils in a class take part as supporting actors. In this sense, it differs from other types of juvenile delinquency whose actors are restricted to a few individuals. In *ijime*, a majority brings ignominy upon a minority of one; a strong group gains satisfaction from the anguish of a pupil in a weak and disadvantaged position; and a large number of spectator pupils acquiesce in such harassment for fear of being chosen as targets themselves. In the peak year of 1985, some 155,000 cases of *ijime* were officially reported across the nation.[32] Although the number has declined in the 1990s, school bullying remains a constant feature of Japan's school life.[33]

Some children victimized by acts of *ijime* have committed suicide. An example is a widely discussed incident in Tokyo in which pupils and teachers played "funeral" with a pupil who had been subjected to bullying. During this student's absence from school (because of injuries he had received when skateboarding) a group of pupils who had bullied him for some time pulled his desk near the blackboard, positioned his photo on it and next to it placed a milk bottle in which they put some flowers, to set up his mock funeral. The group also prepared a square sheet of paper on which they wrote "A farewell to you" and circulated it around his and other classes. A considerable number of his classmates and pupils in other classes wrote in such mourning phrases as "Rest in peace" and "You should die as quickly as possible," with their signatures. A few teachers, including his classroom teacher, also signed the sheet and it was placed on the desk altar. For the "repose of his spirit," participants in the game put some candles on the desk and a Chinese citron into which they stuck a stick of incense. When the targetted pupil stepped into this scene, he smiled and did not show much emotion. He was later found in a toilet where he had hanged himself, at a station near his grandmother's house in Morioka in northern Japan, with a note saying that he had lived his life in a "hell on earth."

This case epitomizes *ijime* problems in contemporary Japan in at least three ways. First, bullying often takes a "soft" form in damaging victims psychologically rather than physically, and even presents the appearance of being playful rather than manifestly violent. Second, teachers frequently side with the bullies rather than the bullied. Third, even the judiciary tends to acquiesce in school authorities' positions regarding teacher and student bullying of this sort. In the ruling in the "funeral game" trial, the court declared that it is extremely difficult to eradicate bullying practices completely and "children must be exposed to *ijime* in the process of growing up." To the extent that the world of children reflects that of adults, the *ijime* phenomenon appears to mirror the way in which the pressures of conformity and ostracism operate in work environments and the community at large.

(b) School Phobia, Dropouts and "Rehabilitation"

The regulatory education system that emphasizes corporal control produces students who suffer from "school phobia." Refusing to attend school, they stay at home in their own rooms and often take on autistic tendencies, not even communicating with their parents. Some of these children become violent, inflicting injuries on family members. The number of middle-school students who failed to attend school more than tripled in the decade from 1975 to 1985. In 1992, the number of primary- and middle-school children who attended school for no more than thirty days a year exceeded seventy thousand.[34]

The sudden increase in school-refusal cases since the mid 1970s appears to coincide with the rise of the authoritarian style of education and to show the growth of "corporal resistance" among some students against corporal control in schools. Cases of school refusal are in a sense children's body language or body messages in response to school attempts to control their bodies.[35]

Against this backdrop, unofficial and unlicensed "rehabilitation schools" have thrived. These are organized by individuals with no formal teaching qualifications, who claim that they have special techniques to retrain problem children. Some parents turn to these as a last resort. In reality, many of these rehabilitation schools confine children in accommodation in a remote area and subject them to violence, which their trainers regard as an essential component of the rehabilitation program. These trainers contend that they can change the children by putting them through a series of severe physical tests. As a consequence, many cases of serious injury and death have resulted.[36] These self-appointed educators vigorously attempt to mold pupils and students into a narrowly defined confine of acceptable behavior, either manipulatively or by force. Such teacher action meets only a limited challenge and finds considerable acceptance in the community.

Violence, dropouts, and other "problems" in schools are not unique to Japan. Casual observations suggest that their frequency and intensity may be less in Japan than in other developed countries, though no firm comparative data in this area are available. The cost aspects of Japanese education must therefore be examined against what it has attained. In fact, Japan can take pride in its achievement in high literacy and numeracy. Despite a complicated system of writing, virtually everyone who has gone through Japanese compulsory education can read and write, making Japan almost free of illiteracy. Japanese shop assistants rarely make calculation errors, an indication that Japanese schools teach pupils numeracy skills with meticulous precision. The regulatory-style education system has made youngsters responsible and cooperative; stations, trains, and other public areas in Japanese cities are generally clean and free from graffiti, unlike some cities in Western countries. At the same time, the world of education has met the demand for the production of the conformist and submissive individuals that Japan's corporationism requires. This has led some observers to argue that many Japanese schools have become education factories reflecting the ideology and practices of the corporate world.[37] It is difficult to dismiss this claim as totally groundless.

V University Life as Moratorium

One irony of Japan's education scene lies in the sharp contrast between stringent schools and slack universities. While primary and secondary education in Japan produces highly trained pupils, Japan's universities remain a resting space or "leisure land" for many youngsters. Exhausted both mentally and physically by examination hell, they seek relaxation, enjoyment, and diversion in their university life.[38] Japanese students can afford to be lazy because Japanese firms hire university graduates not so much on the basis of what and how much they have studied, as by the *hensachi* ranking of their university. The employment race is more or less over after the university entrance examinations, and grades achieved in university subjects do not significantly alter the situation. University students are aware that employers are not interested in what students have learned in university, and rely on on-the-job training and other intracompany teaching techniques to train their new university graduates.

It is true that ambitious students who intend to pass competitive state examinations for the legal profession or for elite public service jobs study hard. The same is true of medical, engineering, and some other science students. But on the whole, Japanese students do not see their university life as a value-adding process for enhancing their qualifications but as a moratorium period to be enjoyed, prior to their entry into the job market. Higher education means not so much productive pursuit of knowledge as a consumption phase of relatively uncontrolled leisure time.

Because of the high expenditure that university life requires, most students engage in so-called *arubaito* (casual or part-time jobs), ranging from private tutoring of primary and secondary pupils to various kinds of manual work: working in restaurants, serving as shop assistants, delivering goods by truck, cleaning offices after working hours, and so on. While university students work as part-timers and casuals all around the world, such work is almost built into Japanese student life, and the Japanese economy depends heavily on the external labor market filled by university students' *arubaito*.

By and large, university staff are lax in their duties and are prepared to pass most students without a thorough evaluation of their academic performance. They are allowed to cancel their classes a few times a year without arranging substitute sessions. Students take this for granted and are often delighted to see class cancellation announcements on campus notice boards. Above all, faculty members in non-science, arts-based departments are derelict in their duty to seriously assess their students, and it is more or less assumed that, once one is admitted to a university, one rarely fails to graduate from it. This is why a maverick professor at Meiji University attracted national attention in 1991 when he failed a significant proportion of students in his subject who had already received job offers from major corporations.

The hierarchical structure of Japanese academia resembles that of Japan's business community in several respects. A system of *keiretsu* akin to the corporate world is widespread among institutions of higher education, with low-ranking universities being affiliated with established high-status universities. Professors of major prestigious universities have informal power to transfer their postgraduate students and junior staff for appointment to minor universities under their control, just as large companies relocate their employees from time to time to smaller enterprises under their command. In universities of repute, "inbreeding" remains the governing norm, with alumni occupying the high tiers of faculties. Upon retirement of a full professor holding a chair, his or her associate professor is normally promoted to the chair. In top-ranking universities, very few outsiders who have graduated from other institutions are appointed to high-status posts, though this pattern has been relaxed in recent years. Just as large corporations maintain a system of life-time employment, so do universities of high standing fill their positions with their own graduates. In both cases, long-term insiders occupy the executive or professorial posts, and outsiders even of high merit find it difficult to make inroads. Universities normally do not publicly advertise vacant positions; these are, in most cases, filled by internal deliberations on candidates recommended through personal networks of high-ranking academics.

VI Some Unresolved Issues

Japanese education appears to be both first-class and uncreative. It looks premodern in some areas and postmodern in others. The somewhat contradictory picture of Japanese education has given rise to a variety of scholarly and policy-orientated debates. Three areas require particular attention.

First of all, scholarly views of the overall quality of Japanese education differ greatly. At one end, many praise its high standards, egalitarianism, and meritocratic orientation.[39] Some take a very positive view of what they regard as the harmonious, group-cohesive, and collectivist emphasis of Japanese education. Others are explicit in suggesting that American schools must learn from Japanese schools.[40] At the other end, a number of observers point out that Japanese education is geared to producing students who are good at answering multiple-choice questions but who lack creativity and originality in thinking.[41] These analysts maintain that Japanese schools suppress spontaneous behavior and enforce discipline so harshly that bullying and other forms of deviant behavior darken school life. For these analysts, Japan's education represents a case not to be emulated. The two competing perspectives reflect some fundamental ideological differences among researchers regarding the extent to which educational institutions should perform functions that legitimize the existing order and transmit social values and basic skills from one generation to another, or should liberate youngsters from past conventions and traditions.

The second issue concerns the degree to which educational credentialism actually prevails in Japanese society. There are studies which suggest that, in the private sector, promotion rates of graduates from prestigious national universities are in fact lower than those of graduates from some less well-known private and local institutions. This finding has been debated at length, and points to the possibility that the promotion structure of Japanese companies may be based more on competition among individuals and on merit than on a rigid ranking according to educational background, particularly their *alma mater*.

Practical attempts have been made to weaken the influence of university ranking on status attainment in the occupational sphere. In recruiting fresh graduates, some companies have instituted a practice of refraining from asking the name of the university from which an applicant is graduating. The government instructed the national bureaucracy in 1993 to reduce the proportion of graduates of Tokyo University in its career-track positions to below 50 percent by the end of the century. Whether these attempts erode the elitist bastion against egalitarianism or have little bearing upon the overall trend, the fact remains that the upper echelon of the Japanese hierarchy is embroiled in debate over the definition, extent, and consequences of educational credentialism in Japan.

Finally, there are signs that the business community and the public bureaucracy are increasingly at odds with each other over the degree to which the state should regulate the education system. In the governmental Extraordinary Education Advisory Council in the late 1980s, a strong group of businessmen and academics successfully pressed for what they called the liberalization of education, in line with the philosophy of privatization and deregulation that advocates reduction of government control and the operation of the free market; overly obedient workers without much initiative are counterproductive to the increasingly internationalized Japanese economy.

The Ministry of Education warns against the expansion of education outside formal institutions, such as the spread of *juku* and the examination industry. In 1993, for example, it attempted to stop government middle schools sending pupils' *hensachi* to private high schools. The Ministry has long refused to hold informal talks with the representatives of *juku* groups for fear of giving the public the impression of recognizing them officially. With this tug-of-war developing, it is inevitable that the rift between the state bureaucracy and commercial interests will affect Japan's education at all levels.

Notes

1 The percentage is the 1994 figure based upon the School Basic Survey of the Ministry of Education.
2 For example, Ishida 1993 shows that the relationship between the two variables is stronger in the United States and the United Kingdom than in Japan.
3 Takeuchi 1991a. He argues that the US system is closer than the Japanese system to the "tournament" type arrangement.
4 Inui 1990, p. 230.
5 In response to the increasing trend for a five-day working week in industry, Japan's education hierarchy is studying the possibility of introducing a five-day week into the school system. Hopefully, this would provide pupils with more time outside school to play and enjoy individual freedom. Ironically, however, the proposed system would provide the commercial education industry with the opportunity to compete intensely for the expanded Saturday market. With more and more students studying at *juku* and other after-school establishments, the planned arrangement might simply transfer a large section of the student population on Saturdays from the formal school system to the commercial sector.
6 Though in comparative terms they are few, pupils who go through the so-called examination hell are overrepresented in media stories and scholarly writings partly because most journalists and academics themselves trod this elite path, and tend to identify with those who follow it. Newspapers and magazines play up how hard these students work to pass a series of examinations – curtailing sleep, abandoning summer and winter vacations, and studying unceasingly during weekends. The public is accustomed to annual media hype over which high schools produced how many students successful in gaining admission to which universities. Each year, public commentators routinely lament the negative impact of examination hell on the psychological well-being of students.
7 In total, they attend school 240 days a year, two months more than Americans, and three months more than the French. In addition, Japanese high-school students spend nineteen hours a week studying outside their school classes, middle-school students spend sixteen, and primary-school pupils spend eight hours. See Koyasu 1992, p. 26. A Japan–United States comparative study suggests that, including extra-school studying hours in calculations, Japanese pupils spend twice as much time studying as American pupils. *Yomiuri Shimbun*, morning edition, November 5 1991, p. 7.
8 Stevenson and Baker 1992.
9 Ministry of Education survey conducted in October 1993.
10 Horio 1979.
11 Tōyama 1976.
12 Inui 1990.
13 See Okano 1993 and 1994 for detailed ethnographic studies in this area.
14 Inui 1990, pp. 155–6.
15 See Okano 1993.
16 The third report of the Extraordinary Education Advisory Council in 1987 recommended the establishment of a life-time education system and a national certification system. This endorsement is consistent with the

expansion of the third track made up of *senmon gakkō*, which would benefit from the introduction of such systems.

17   Kosaka 1994, p. 200, Table 10.1.

18   Kosaka 1994.

19   Nakano 1974.

20   Miyajima and Tanaka 1984.

21   Fukutake Shoten 1992. The study was conducted in 1991, with a sample of 3,346 students in sixteen high schools.

22   Takeuchi 1993, pp. 120–1.

23   Yonekawa 1978.

24   AM April 5 1993, p. 10.

25   Tokyo Daigaku 1991.

26   NHK TV, *"Daigaku o tou"* ("Questioning universities"), special program televised on April 1 and 2 1992.

27   The response to the Ministry of Education on this issue has been regionally diversified. Most prefectures followed its instructions, but two prefectures (Kyoto and Okinawa) staunchly resisted the government position on the national flag and the national anthem. Kyoto was the only stronghold of the Japan Communist party, and Okinawa had a postwar history very different from that of the rest of Japan.

28   MM September 16 1993, p. 1. In Kagoshima prefecture in the southern part of Kyūshū, 99 percent of government middle schools retain this practice.

29   According to the Ministry of Education inquiry, a total of 698 cases of illegal corporal punishment were reported, with 1,271 pupils being the victims of teacher violence.

30   AM December 4 1988, p. 1.

31   The statement by the principal of that school, before some fifteen hundred students at assembly the following morning, indicates the degree to which school regulations are modelled on corporate norms. He stated: "If you can save one minute each, one thousand and five hundred minutes are produced. If you save five minutes each, more time will be manufactured. Corporation managers say these things frequently, but I think that I am entitled to make a similar statement to you. If you get up only ten minutes earlier, teachers do not have to give you instructions in a loud voice not to be late for school" (*Shūkan Asahi* October 27 1990).

32   Ministry of Education statistics show that, even in 1992, reported cases still exceeded twenty-three thousand.

33   A survey of 13,444 middle-school children conducted by the Ministry of Justice in 1994 indicates that 58 percent have observed instances of *ijime*, 43 percent have conducted and 36 percent have been subjected to it (AM April 17 1995, p. 31).

34   AM December 28 1993, p. 1.

35   Imazu 1991, pp. 80–8.

36   The best-known case with such an outcome is that of the Totsuka Yacht School which operated in Aichi prefecture. This school received many dropouts from around the country for reeducation, as it claimed that yacht training could effectively treat those "emotionally disturbed children" who were chronically violent at home or who refused to attend school. At the request of their parents, the yachting coaches picked up these children from their homes; if the children resisted they were often beaten, handcuffed, and then taken away. At the institution they were virtual prisoners, subjected to violent discipline, including beatings, kicking, and other forms of physical

punishment. A few deaths during the program in 1982 led to criminal prosecutions, but the court ruling of 1992 was ambivalent. The mass media also had divided attitudes to this case, reflecting the strength of community support for the use of physical violence against children who deviate from the general expectations of the public.

Another incident involved a small private facility, Kazenoko School, on Kosaki Island, Hiroshima prefecture, where parents sent children who had tendencies towards emotional disturbance or juvenile delinquency. Two children died of heatstroke in the summer of 1991 after being locked in a freight container for two consecutive days as a punishment for having smoked cigarettes.

37 Kamata 1984.
38 The total study time per week of Japanese university students amounts to only thirteen hours and compares quite unfavorably with the fifty-three hours of their American counterparts (Katō 1992, p. 85).
39 Cummings 1980; White 1987a.
40 Stevenson 1992; Stevenson and Stingler 1992; Vogel 1979.
41 Wolferen 1990; Schoolland 1990.

6

Gender Stratification and the Family System

The life conditions of Japanese women have been less visible and less subject to systematic examination than men's in the literature of Japanese studies until recently, though slightly over half of the Japanese population are women. The rise of feminism outside and inside Japan, however, has sensitized observers to gender stratification in Japanese society and directed their attention to a wide range of questions. In what ways are Japanese women subjected to a Japan-specific system of gender control? What kinds of gender barriers exist in Japan's labor market? How is female sexuality regulated in Japan? How are women disadvantaged in the Japanese family structure? This chapter examines these issues as the most fundamental problems of stratification, arguably more pivotal than other forms of inequality in contemporary Japan. Specifically, we will examine the patriarchal family registration system which is embedded in gender relations and the family system in Japan, the women's employment situation in the labor market, the issues of sexuality and reproduction, marriage and divorce, and various types of family life.

I The Family Registration System and *Ie* Ideology

Beneath Japan's gender relations and family system lies an elaborate system of registration which penetrates into the life of every Japanese and controls it in a fundamental way. The *koseki* (family registration) system is the cornerstone of the scheme, representing the usually veiled *ura* aspect of Japanese family structure. The basic unit of *koseki* is not an individual but a household. The records of each individual's gender, birthplace, date of birth, parents' names, position among siblings, marriage, and divorce are kept in detail in each household *koseki* and filed in the local municipal office.

The concept of family lineage is built into the *koseki* system. Technically, one can remove one's name from the current register and establish an independent *koseki* at any time, but most people do this at the time of marriage. Up to two generations, typically a couple and their children, can be included in a *koseki*. A three-generation register is legally unacceptable; for example, if grandparents, a married couple and their children live under the same roof, the grandparents must keep their own *koseki* and the two younger generations keep a separate one. How each individual branched off from a previous *koseki* register is an important piece of information in the current register.

In the hands of organizations the *koseki* has become a powerful instrument, providing full personal information about their members, as it has become widespread practice for organizations to require potential members to submit a copy of their *koseki* when they seek membership. *Koseki* data are required for many other crucial occasions. In the past, companies required job applicants to submit their *koseki* papers. Minority groups, particularly the buraku activists, vehemently opposed this practice, because the companies were able to discriminate against burakumin whose minority backgrounds were indirectly identified by the papers showing their birthplace and permanent address. While this convention was gradually abolished in the 1970s in response to the protests of buraku movements, the system works as a powerful deterrent to deviant behavior, as "stains" in *koseki* negatively affect the life-chances of all family members; since each *koseki* is organized on a household basis, those who acquire a copy can examine the attributes not only of an individual but also of his or her family members.

Supporting the family registration system, a resident card (*jūmin-hyō*) system requires each household to register its address and membership with the municipal office of its current place of residence. Accordingly, when a family moves from area A to area B, it must remove its old residence status from the municipal office of area A then report its new address and other family information to the municipal office of area B. In this way, the Japanese government secures detailed information about each household and its history through local governments. The resident card used to contain information identifying the gender, sibling order, and legitimacy status of each child, but the scheme was revised in 1995 in such a way that he or she is now listed simply as "child," a change which feminist groups had long demanded.

Behind the twin institutions of the family registration system and the residence card system lies the ideology of *ie*, which literally means house, home, or family but signifies something much more than these English words imply. *Ie* represents a quasi-kinship unit with a patriarchal head and members tied to him through real or symbolic blood relationship.

In the prewar civil code, the head was equipped with almost absolute power over household matters, including the choice of marriage partners for his family members. The headship of *ie* was transferred from one generation to another through primogeniture, whereby the first son normally inherited most of the property, wealth, and privilege of the household as well as *ie* headship. As a general rule, the second and younger sons established their own branch families, which remained subordinate to the head family. For the continuation of *ie* arrangements, it was not unusual for a family without a son to adopt a boy from a different family. Each *ie* unit was expected to provide fundamental support for the imperial system. The postwar civil code considerably dismantled the patriarchal system through introducing the general principle of gender equality. However, the ideology associated with the *ie* system still persists as an undercurrent of family life in Japan, and some of the key ingredients of the *ie* practice survive in the second half of the twentieth century in the maintenance of the *koseki* system, which disadvantages women in a number of ways.

1 The Notion of Household Head

The system makes the household the source of information and requires each household to nominate its head.[1] In reality, nearly all heads are male: some 98 percent of couples who married in 1990 nominated the husband as head of the household.[2] The head is listed at the beginning of the register separately from his individual entry as a member of the household. His permanent address (*honseki*) becomes that of his household, requiring its members to assume the same *honseki* as long as they remain listed in the same register. When the household head changes his surname for some reason, the members of the household must change their surname in the *koseki* to match his. Even when the household head dies, his headship continues in his household register as long as other members of the household remain listed in it. Accordingly, in many cases, a widow remains in her husband's *koseki* even after his death.[3] Furthermore, a baby born within three hundred days of a formal divorce is entered into the *koseki* of the household head, who is the ex-husband in nearly all cases. This requirement applies even if he is not the baby's biological father. Thus, the *koseki* scheme deters women from divorcing, preserves the male advantages of the patriarchal order, and protects the *ie* system in a fundamental way.

2 Children Born out of Wedlock

The *koseki* system makes a status distinction between children born in lawful marriage and those born out of wedlock. For a child of legitimate birth, gender identity and sibling order are designated, for example, by the description "first daughter" or "second son." However, a child born outside marriage is recorded simply as "child" until the father acknowledges paternity and marriage occurs. Thus, the family registration scheme categorizes children born in *de facto* relationships and children not acknowledged by their father as second-class citizens although, as mentioned earlier, the resident card system has removed these distinctions.

With respect to inheritance, Japan's civil code stipulates that the spouse of the deceased is entitled to half the estate, with the remaining half to be distributed equally among the children of the deceased. This is a big change from the prewar code, in which the first son inherited the property and wealth of the household almost exclusively. However, children born out of wedlock are entitled to only half the entitlement of legitimate children. The Tokyo High Court ruled in June 1993 and in November 1994 that this provision of the civil code violates Article 14 of Japan's constitution, which guarantees equality under the law. Though the government administrative council recommended in 1996 that the stipulation be amended in the next the revision of the civil code, conservative politicians remain cautious about the proposed change on the grounds that it would fundamentally alter the Japanese traditional family system.[4]

The *koseki* system requires births to be recorded on the mother's family documents even if the child is given up for adoption. Since the system records illegitimate births as a matter of public registration, women often opt for abortion to avoid the social stigma which would result from having an illegitimate child recorded on their official papers. In the late 1980s, a doctor was prosecuted for encouraging women who became pregnant out of wedlock to give birth rather than to have an abortion, and for making arrangements for childless couples to adopt and register as their own children the babies thus born. The case stirred a nationwide debate because, although the doctor's action was illegal under the family registration law, it was argued that it could be morally justified given the large number of unwed pregnant women who wanted neither to have an abortion nor to keep a baby born outside marriage. There were also numerous childless families desperate to adopt a baby. The family registration system thus socially penalizes single mothers and their children, thereby serving as a powerful apparatus to preserve the traditional family structure and values.

3 Deterrence to Divorce

The family registration system has been an important deterrent to divorce. The divorce rate in Japan has progressively increased since the 1960s, reaching a postwar peak in the early 1980s. However, it has never matched the level recorded in the last quarter of the nineteenth century when couples freely chose to marry or divorce in conformity with their local customs. The highest recorded divorce rate (divorces per one thousand persons) was 3.39 in 1883, while the postwar peak was 1.51 in 1983, exactly one century later.[5] With the enactment of the nationally uniform civil code at the turn of the century and the national consolidation of the *koseki* system, marriages and divorces became a matter of government regulation and official registration, and the divorce rate in the first half of the twentieth century declined sharply. Though the annual total of divorces has increased in postwar Japan, the divorce rate remains close to the level immediately after World War II, and is among the lowest recorded in industrially advanced nations.

Economic considerations are, of course, the predominant reason why many women stay in a marriage; those who depend upon their husband financially have little choice but to continue to live with him. In addition to this major constraint, the *koseki* system puts another restraint upon the possibility of divorce. Divorce requires two separate family registers to be established, and if the couple have had children each child must be shifted into one of the new registers, in most instances the mother's. Because copies of these papers are often required on such crucial occasions as employment and marriage, people can be stigmatized as the children of divorced parents through this public documentation. Fearful of a "tarnish" being placed on their children's registers, many married couples, particularly women who are deeply involved emotionally in their children's well-being, vacillate over divorce even when that option is a sensible one. Despite this, some women calculate that the social costs of divorce are less than its positive consequences. On the whole the system serves as as a deterrent to divorce, thus buttressing the patriarchal marriage structure.

4 Surname After Marriage

The *koseki* system requires that upon marriage wife and husband take the same surname, which must be one of their former surnames. Thus a married couple may not legally assume different surnames. When Ms Toyota and Mr Suzuki marry, they must both become either Toyota or Suzuki, and one of them must abandon her or his pre-marriage surname. In virtually all cases the woman abandons her surname and is entered into the register of her husband, who is usually listed as the household head.

Some women, mainly professionals, choose to use their maiden name as a *tsūshō* (popular name), promote the practice of *fūfu bessei* (different surnames despite formal marriage), and thereby challenge the rigid requirements of the family register system. In the early 1990s, a married female professor attracted national attention because the national university where she taught under her *tsūshō* refused to pay her salary unless she placed a name stamp of her registered surname, or her thumbprint, on salary receipts, and she took the matter to court, but lost her case. The Ministry of Education uses *koseki* names on appointments, promotions, and other official documents, regardless of whether women use their maiden names in practice. In many workplaces, *koseki* names rather than *tsūshō* are listed in internal telephone directories even if female employees use their maiden names in daily interactions with colleagues and clients.

In response to calls by women's groups for a more liberal approach to the surname issue, the governmental administrative council which considered the revision of the civil code recommended in 1996 that a couple should be able to choose an identical surname or different surnames at the time of marriage, when they should also decide whether their children would use their father's or mother's surname. According to the recommendation, all children's surnames must be identical, and those who are already married can assume different surnames upon the agreement of both parties if they report the change within one year of the enactment of the amended code.[6]

5 The Family Tomb

The practice of burial is closely linked with the *ie* system which functions in tandem with the family registration system. Following the convention of ancestral lineage, most families have family tombs where their ancestors are believed to be entombed. By convention, "descendants" include females who have married male offspring of the family genealogy. Because the *koseki* system is predicated upon the patriarchal logic that the wife belongs to her husband's family line as his subordinate, she is usually buried in his family tomb with his ancestors. But increasing interregional mobility, diversified family structure, and land price inflation have induced a substantial number of people, particularly women in urban areas, to reconsider the traditional methods. They object to the custom of family-tomb burial with its close links with *ie* ideology. Though the family registration system does not dictate where one should be buried, it provides a framework in which the patriarchal system governs women even after death.

6 Seki *and* Ie

In a broader context, the Japanese social system is supported by the notion of *seki*, the view that, unless one is formally registered as belonging to an organization or institution, one has no proper station in society. As *seki* pervades Japanese life fundamentally, most Japanese are greatly concerned about which *koseki* they are registered in and the form their entry takes. *Nyūseki* (entry into a register) and *joseki* (exit from a register) are cause for anxiety. The notion of *seki* also manifests itself in *gakuseki* (school registry), which is a national student dossier system. After death, one is supposed to be registered in *kiseki* (the registry of those in the posthumous world).

The *ie* system survives in community life in a visible way. Almost every Japanese household has a nameplate (*hyōsatsu*) on or near its gate or front door. The plate displays the surname of the household, often with the given name of its head. In some cases, the names of all household members are exhibited, with that of the household head first and in slightly larger characters. While aiding postal workers, newspaper deliverers and visitors, these plates serve as a constant reminder that the *koseki*-style ideology permeates the psyche of most Japanese.

Though every society has some system of registration – such as electoral rolls, social security numbers, birth and marriage certificates – Japan's family registration system differs from others in using the household as the unit, packaging a range of information into each *koseki*, and socially ostracizing those who do not fit into the male-dominated conventional family structure promoted by the *koseki* system. This is why *de facto* relationships are usually kept under the carpet, although *de facto* couples as well as sexually alternative groups have become more vocal in recent years (see chapter 9). The small number of *de facto* relationships occur mainly among professional women who relish economic independence and good career prospects, and among lower-class women who have little to lose from negative public perceptions. Thus, the understanding of gender relations in Japan requires an in-depth knowledge of the working of the family registration system, which affects all Japanese at every turn of their lives, functioning as an often invisible, but highly effective, way of maintaining patriarchal order.

II The Labor Market and Women's Employment Profiles

1 The M-shaped Curve of Women's Employment

The Japanese economy would not function without the female workers who, in 1991, constituted 40.6 percent of the total paid workforce. The workforce participation rate of Japanese women has shown a steady upward trend and in 1991 reached 50.7 percent; more than half of all women between fifteen and sixty-five years of age are engaged in waged labor. A significant majority of them (58.2 percent as of 1990) are married, and single women constitute only 32.7 percent of the entire female workforce. With regard to industrial classification, women are concentrated in tertiary industry, in particular in the service, finance and insurance, and sales sectors. In the manufacturing industry, women are conspicuous in light industries such as textile and food production, rather than in heavy industries. On the surface, these statistics suggest that women do not regard domestic labor as their only option and play a highly significant role in the labor market.

Unlike most men, however, the majority of women who explore the possibility of entering the job market solve complex equations involving many variables. From a life-cycle perspective, women must generally make decisions at three different times: at marriage, following childbirth, and when their last child commences schooling. Figure 6.1, which is based upon a study of a sample of married women at the age of fifty in 1989, shows that only about one-quarter of them remain in the workforce following childbirth.[7] When the initial child-rearing phase is over, about three-quarters of those who left work to have children return to the labor market. While most women aspire to work, their options are restricted by constraints to which few men are subject.

The strength of these pressures manifests itself in the so-called M-shaped curve of female labor-force participation (see Figure 6.2). The

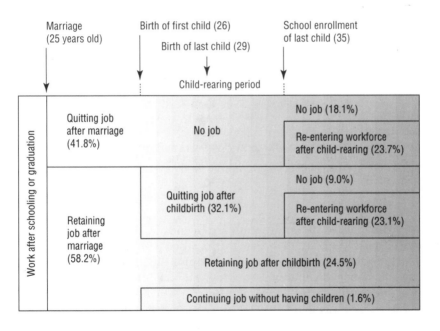

Figure 6.1 Relationship between work and child-rearing for women
Source: Rōdōshō 1991c, p. 77. The figure shows the result of the ninth Fertility Survey conducted by the Institute of Population Problems of the Ministry of Health and Welfare in 1987. The sample consisted of married women below the age of fifty.

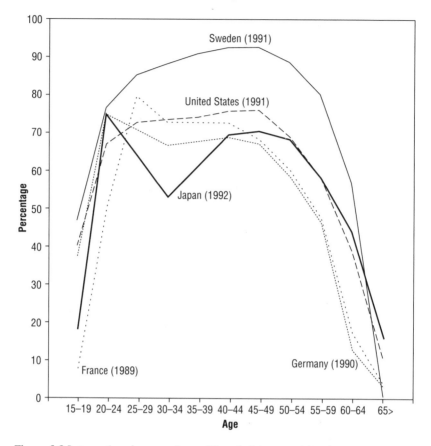

Figure 6.2 International comparison of female labor participation rates
Source: Adapted from Forum 1994, p. 33, based on ILO's *Year Book of Labour Statistics*. The German data are taken from West German statistics before unification.

curve ascends to the mid twenties, descends in the early thirties, and swings steadily upward to the late forties, when it finally begins to decline. The valley between the two peaks represents the phase in which women leave the labor force for child-rearing. The valley has become less steep over time, though the Japanese women's situation lags behind other industrialized societies where the M-shaped curve for women's participation in the workforce has almost disappeared, replaced by a reverse U-shaped curve with no visible drop in the arch.

The M-shaped curve began to emerge in Japan with the consolidation of fast economic growth in the 1960s, and part-time work has dominated as an option for women who wish to return to work after child-rearing. In the early 1990s, four out of ten women in the workforce were part-timers, and housewives constituted an overwhelming majority of this category, thereby creating a large "housewife part-time labor market."

In Japan the label of part-timer covers not only those employees with limited working hours but also those who work as long as regular full-time workers but who are hired on a fixed-term basis and paid hourly rates without fringe benefits. Of the part-timers belonging to the latter category, a majority are women.

In other words, to cope with the chronic labor shortage of the last three decades, Japanese capitalism has sought to recruit women, chiefly as supplementary labor, at low wages, and under unstable employment conditions. Feminist sociologists regard this as the second compromise between capitalism and patriarchy.[8] The first was the so-called Victorian compromise which assigned men to production roles and women to the reproductive function. The second compromise differs in generating a new gender-based division of labor which makes many women part-time wives and part-time workers. These women work not to secure economic independence, but to supplement their household income. On average, the contribution a woman makes to the family income remains less than a quarter of the total, an amount too small to achieve economic equality with her husband in their household. To the extent that the second compromise keeps women in deprived positions in wage labor as well as in domestic labor, it subjects women to the imperatives of both capitalism and patriarchy.

The proportion of married women who were housewives with part-time work surpassed that of full-time housewives in 1983. Part-time housewives can be divided into two groups.[9] In the first group, domestic work precedes outside waged work. The housewives of this category tend to suspend full-time work, dedicate themselves to child-rearing, and resume outside work later in life as part-time employees. The second group gives priority to waged work at the expense of domestic work. Those in this group do not generally interrupt their careers and end up with higher positions and better salaries in their middle age. In contrast with Euro-American and other Asian societies, where the second group of housewives dominates, the Japanese pattern indicates a predominance of the first group in the part-time housewife population. To the extent that this tendency persists, the interdependence between capitalism and patriarchy is entrenched rather than eroded.

2 The Two-tier Structure of the Internal Market

To consolidate this process, Japanese business leaders have split female labor into several tiers. At the level of regular full-time employees, they have implemented programs which attempt to classify female workers into two categories. One category is that of *sōgō shoku* (all-round employees), for whom companies arrange career paths much as for male career employees. These female employees are expected to accept the same conditions as male corporate soldiers. *Sōgō shoku* women must be willing to work overtime on a regular basis, to be dispatched to an office distant from their home for a few years (a practice known as *tanshin funin*), and to continue work without interruption during the child-rearing phase of their life-cycle.

Outside this small group of elite female employees is a larger category called *ippan shoku* (ordinary employees), who play less important roles in their workplace. They remain peripheral and subordinate workers with low wages, and management does not expect them to perform demanding functions or to follow a career path. Most women who prefer to give priority to family life opt for this category.

The Japanese business establishment justifies this two-tier system from a human-capital point of view. This perspective focusses upon the way in which management invests in the formation of company-specific skills in internal labor market structures. Japanese corporations place emphasis upon intensive on-the-job training and socialization, which commence immediately employees enter an organization. This practice disadvantages female employees who leave the labor force in the middle of their careers.[10] To optimize the returns of company spending in this area, employers target their investment at male employees, who are statistically more likely to provide continuous service than female employees. When women return to the workforce after a long break, they are far behind men of the same age bracket with regard to acquired skill. Employers therefore vindicate their position on the grounds of economic investment in human capital and find it economically rational to implement a system of statistical discrimination against women.[11] While advocating the *tatemae* of gender equality, the *honne* of many employers appear to be that the bulk of women should remain in subordinate positions in the workforce.

Japanese women have serious difficulty in securing managerial posts in companies.[12] Only a quarter of Japanese firms have female managers at or above the *kachō* (section head) level, and 73 percent of those who have attained managerial positions have not borne children. Nearly 70 percent of female managers who have borne children have relied upon the support of their parents or parents-in-law in caring for them.

Women in the *sōgō shoku* career path tend to come from a particular background. They must hold a degree from a four-year university, preferably a reputable one, and this means that their parents must have both the financial and cultural resources to support their education. Most of these elite women not only marry men within the elite course and thus gain double income, but also receive financial and other support from their parents who, in many cases, own substantial personal and real assets. This means that the cream of working women enjoy a triple income – their own and their spouse's salaries, plus their parents' contributions.[13]

Because of the diversification of women in the labor force, wage differentials between female workers are generally greater than those between male workers.[14] For women of the same age and length of service, the difference between wages in small firms and in big companies is greater than for men in the same categories. Likewise, wage differences between section heads and above on one hand, and the rank-and-file on the other, are greater for women than for men, as are the differences for those with university degrees and those without. In their forties and fifties, female university graduates earn nearly twice as much as those with middle-school education.

The increasing demand for female labor and the declining birthrate have caused law-makers and business leaders to institutionalize two provisions to enable women to stay in the workforce. One is the Equal Opportunity Law enacted in 1985, and the other is the Child-care Leave Law put into effect in April 1992. Neither has a penalty clause.

The Equal Opportunity Law held up an ideal of equality between men and women in the workplace, but it has no sanction clause and lacks the teeth to force employers to comply with its terms. Further, the principle of equality of opportunity operates among those with equal educational qualifications and therefore legitimizes discrimination between different educational backgrounds. Upon completion of high-school education, only 21 percent of girls advance to universities with four-year courses while 25 percent go on to two-year junior colleges. In contrast, 39 percent of boys proceed to four-year universities and only 2 percent to junior colleges.[15] In this context, the law has consolidated rather than broken down the practice of relegating women to the peripheral labor market. Female university graduates who get into the *sōgō shoku* career track comprise less than 1 percent of job-seekers who have just completed tertiary education.

Table 6.1 shows the harsh realities of gender inequality at the apexes of occupational pyramids. The boards of directors of major companies are the least open to females, who comprise only forty-eight of the 39,897 directors of the 2,128 corporations listed on Japan's eight stock exchanges. Of 5,573 public servants in the top four levels of the national bureaucracy, only fifty-eight are women. The world of mass media also has a dismal record in this respect.

The Child-care Leave Law requires all companies to allow female or

Table 6.1 Proportion of women in positions of power

Positions	%
Female members of the House of Representatives (1994)[a]	2.3
Female business managers	
at *jūyaku* (director and above) level (1993)[b]	0.1
at *buchō* (department head) level (1991)[c]	1.2
at *kachō* (section head) level (1991)[c]	2.3
Female union leaders in *Rengō* (Japan Trade Union Confederation) (1994)[d]	5.5
Female high-ranking officials at grade nine or above in the national bureaucracy (1989)[4]	0.7
Female judges (1990)[f]	5.0
Female prosecutors (1990)[f]	2.1
Female principals (1992)[g]	
at primary-school level	6.0
at middle-school level	1.1
Female full professors in universities (1991)[h]	5.1
Female journalists in newspapers (1992)[i]	5.6

Sources
[a] AM February 28 1995, p. 19. This percentage ranks 149th among 176 countries surveyed.
[b] *Jōjō gaisha yakuin dōkō chōsa* (Trend survey of directors of major companies) of Tōyō Keizai Shimpōsha. The figure covers only those 2,128 major companies listed on Japan's eight stock exchanges.
[c] The Basic Survey on Wage Structure of the Ministry of Labor. The survey covered only enterprises with 100 or more employees.
[d] The figure covers members of the executive committee of national industrial unions (*tansan*). AM August 24 1994, p. 26.
[e] Inoue and Ehara 1991, p. 151. The figures include the top four grades, the so-called designated posts (*shiteishoku*) and grades nine, ten and eleven.
[f] Bandō 1992, p. 99.
[g] The Statistical Survey on School Teachers of the Ministry of Education.
[h] The School Basic Survey of the Ministry of Education.
[i] The Japan Newspaper Association's survey of reporters in ninety-three newspapers and newsagencies. AE March 3 1993, p. 29.

male employees to take parental leave without pay for up to one year to enable them to care for a newborn child. After the leave period, companies must allow the employee to resume work in the same job, or a position of equivalent standing. This law, like the Equal Opportunity Law, has no penalty clause, as companies that fail to comply with it do not face legal prosecution.

An overwhelming majority of companies do not allow their employees to take leave to nurse aged relatives. However, it remains the norm that the family, rather than institutions, must care for the infirm elderly. Once an old person falls seriously ill or becomes completely bedridden, family members or relatives are expected to attend to them personally. This occurs in an overwhelming majority of cases, and only a small minority of families are willing and able to use nursing homes, hospitals, and other medical institutions. This places a heavy burden on women, because in almost all cases (more than 90 percent according to a national survey) bed-ridden senior citizens are cared for by women. While some sons do look after their ailing parents, the task is more frequently forced upon a daughter-in-law (see Figure 6.3). A married working woman, typically in her mid forties, who lives near or with her parents-in-law, faces the dilemma of choosing between her job and family obligations.

4 Four Types of Married Women

Women outside the primary labor markets are partially connected with the corporate world, but certainly are not socialized into its values as fully as male full-time employees. For example, women opt for more flexible work arrangements than men, and in comparison with male workers female workers give conspicuous priority to activities outside work. In this sense, women's life-styles appear to foreshadow the future work patterns of the Japanese labor force.

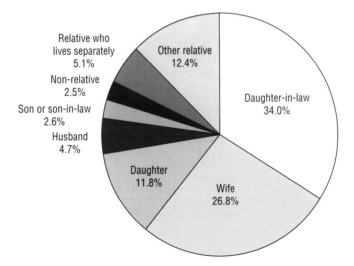

Figure 6.3 Who nurses bed-ridden old persons?
Source: The Welfare Administration Basic Survey of the Ministry of Health and Welfare (1984).

These observations suggest that the degree of structural penetration of corporate norms into individual life orientations differs between men and women: women are less indoctrinated with corporate logic than men. On the whole, women are at the periphery of capitalist production, and from this vantage point they can more critically examine and remodel the existing system. Some Japanese feminists argue that women should make men more "feminine" in every sphere of life instead of attempting to emulate men.[16]

The life of women can be seen in terms of the extent to which it is integrated into two types of social order. One of these is the capitalist order, which concerns the way in which the system of economic production and distribution is organized. Whether one engages in paid employment or not is the most conspicuous indicator of the extent to which one is involved in this order. The strongest factors influencing married women's decisions in this matter are their husband's incomes and their access to inheritable assets.[17]

The other dimension is the patriarchal order, in which male power controls women in family and community life. The more gender equality women achieve in this sphere the more free they are from this control, and the less enmeshed are their lives in the patriarchal order. Married women in Japan could perhaps be classified according to the degree of their incorporation into these two dimensions (see Table 6.2).

(a) Part-time Workers and Part-time Housewives

Cell A includes part-timers who are content with a family situation where the husband is the breadwinner and the wife plays a supporting role both financially and with regard to household chores. Women who choose to work as part-timers and casual workers see their work mainly as

Table 6.2 Permeation into the lives of married women by the capitalist and patriarchal orders

Patriarchal order	Capitalist order	
	Strong	*Weak*
Strong	(A) Family-supporting part-time workers and part-time housewives	(C) Full-time housewives accepting the status quo
Weak	(B) Career women, many in *sōgō shoku*	(D) Community activists and networkers not in workforce

supplementing the household budget. In daily life, one encounters these women working at cash registers, as hostesses at snack bars, and as sales assistants in shops and stores. Some women take up comparatively novel options.

One alternative is to register with a "temp" (*haken*) company which sends specialist workers on a fixed-term basis to firms that request them. These workers, who number only fifty thousand according to the 1987 Ministry of Labor survey, work in a range of areas from computer programming, interpreting, secretarial work, bookkeeping, and drafting to cleaning buildings. Women in their late twenties with some occupational experience make up most of the *haken* workers. Work in this area is attractive to them chiefly because they are assessed on their ability and performance rather than seniority, and partly because they are not bound to a single company. However, the prime reason for women choosing this type of work arrangement is its flexibility, which allows them to adjust their working hours and select their work environment to suit their personal situations and preferences.

Another option open to women in the external labor market is to start small businesses of their own. Some run *juku*, after-school private tutorial classes, in their homes. Others form groups that own small shops selling a wide variety of goods, ranging from women's clothing or accessories to crockery. Some groups manage various food-related operations, ranging from coffee shops to confectioneries. These businesses sometimes operate as part of a franchise network. Most women who take this alternative appear to be motivated by its compatibility with child-rearing and other home duties, and in particular by its allowing them to arrange their working hours flexibly and independently. Many in this category are in their mid thirties or older, whose children have reached school age.

Some women choose to work as hostesses in the evening in the bar and restaurant business. Called *mizushōbai*, this type of work is widely available in pubs, night clubs, saloons, taverns, high-class restaurants, and other entertainment places. Women in this business are expected to amuse male customers who eat and drink in these quarters before going home. While bordering on the sex industry, the *mizushōbai* world provides high wages for women who are prepared to work irregular hours. Though many of them are unmarried young women, married women and divorcees who want quick cash also work in this sector. A small minority of them even aspire to own places of their own and make their career in this world.

Generally, women's work styles are constrained by differences in the ways in which men and women structure their non-working hours. On average, a married working man with a working wife spends only eight minutes per day on such household tasks as cooking and child-rearing, while a married working woman with a husband who works has to devote four hours and twenty-one minutes to household tasks.[18]

Feminist studies suggest that the reference group for women in the part-time labor market is not career women (in group B) but full-time housewives (in group C). They want to be women of leisure but cannot because of their family's financial situation. Because they go out to work in order to be a "good mother," they feel some role strain but do not really find fundamental role conflict in their dual existence; they are satisfied to give priority to their family life rather than their work, and in that sense they are the women who "unfortunately failed to become full-time housewives."[19]

(b) Career Women

Cell B comprises career women who compete with men at work and who have a largely free hand in the management of their family lives. Most of the above-mentioned *sōgō shoku* types fall into this category. The political push for gender equality in recruitment and promotion in the workplace comes from this group.

(c) Full-time Housewives

Cell C comprises full-time housewives whose lives are subordinated to the requirements of their husband. This type accepts the trade-off between freedom from paid work and toleration of male-dominated family life.

At best, the power of full-time housewives remains equivocal. Banks in Japan do not allow married couples to establish joint accounts. To purchase daily necessities, it is not uncommon for a housewife to carry her husband's cashcard to use an automatic teller machine to withdraw money from his bank account (into which his company pays his salary). This pattern is routine for couples where the husband is the full-time breadwinner and the wife is the full-time housewife. Furthermore, ordinary families do not have checkbooks, but pay their monthly bills in cash through banks, a task usually performed by the wife. Accordingly, when it comes to living expenses, the wife generally controls the household purse. Despite this, the husband takes the leadership in making major family decisions. A national government survey shows that in only a small proportion of households the wife makes decisions on the purchase of such large items as land, houses, cars, and furniture; these decisions are usually made either collectively by the couple or mainly by the husband, as Table 6.3 indicates. Most people feel that the overall household decision-making power rests with the husband, not the wife. This suggests that the power of the wife in household matters in Japan may be

Table 6.3 Decision-makers in the household

Items for decision-making	Husband (%)	Wife (%)	Both (%)	Other (%)
Purchase of land or house	53.2	1.9	31.5	13.3
Purchase of furniture or large domestic electric appliances	23.2	20.1	43.7	13.1
Control of daily household budget	9.7	70.5	15.0	4.8
Overall decision-making power	61.7	11.6	20.5	6.3

Source: A survey on gender equality conducted by the Management and Coordination Agency in 1992. The sample was composed of 2,845 married men and women at the age of twenty or above. See Yuzawa 1995, p. 105.

exaggerated, although the trend is towards more equality between spouses.

(d) Networkers

Cell D consists of those who choose not to work in the business world but who at the same time pursue gender equality in the household. Many female community activists and networkers fall into this category.[20]

Some women choose to work in community-based organizations. These include, for example, workers' collectives which aim to establish alternative work structures, where employees can participate in decision-making processes on the basis of democratic principles. These collectives do not regard profit-making as their prime goal and attempt to provide communal networks among members. Some collectives organize community colleges or culture centers for adult education. Others establish recycling shops, and still others operate as links of a larger cooperative chain. In a variety of family service clubs, members help each other in such household chores as cleaning, shopping, washing, and infant nursing, for a nominal fee. Participants in these organizations receive remuneration for their work, but their interest in these activities centers on the establishment and expansion of autonomous women's networks in the neighborhood and beyond. These organizations tend to form a kind of horizontally structured society based upon linkages cutting across community lines.[21] Women in their late forties and fifties who have been liberated from the time and expenditure required for child-rearing and child education play a major role in these activities. With their husbands still working, they have plenty of time and sufficient financial resources to become heavily involved in these ventures. With little access to the established labor market at their age, these women have become a new type of proprietor in pursuit of self-realization through work.

Some networkers play major roles in reformist political groups at the community level. Some of these activists are involved in protest activities against development projects which would negatively affect residents' interests. Others object to the construction of high-rise condominium buildings in densely populated urban centers. Still others take part in movements against the extension of highways and roads, which cause noise and air pollution. Networkers orientated to environmental issues organize distribution networks of organically grown vegetables and fruit, selling them directly to consumers from farmers without intermediary dealers. The demands of these women are connected with community issues and family needs directly enough to affect local politics. With time available and good networking skills, these activists represent significant political voices in grassroots Japan.

III Sexuality and Control of the Female Body

1 Contraception and Abortion

Japanese health authorities are stringent in regulating available means of contraception and lenient in allowing abortion as a method of birth control. This diverges from the patterns in most other industrialized societies where a wide range of contraceptives, including the pill, are openly available but abortion issues have stirred bitter controversy. While Christianity played a significant role in shaping the abortion debate in the West, the *ie* ideology of the government and the stance of the medical profession mean that the pill has been generally unavailable for a long time in Japan.

Japan's Ministry of Health and Welfare has never legalized the pill as a contraceptive. As a consequence, the condom remains the most widely used method of contraception. About three-quarters of couples who practice birth control use condoms to prevent pregnancy.[22] To rationalize the prohibition of the pill, the Ministry presents both medical and moral justifications.

On the medical side, both the medical profession and the Ministry reason that its side effects have not been fully studied. This contention is built upon the chemical poisoning argument which led to the official banning of the pill as a contraceptive in 1972. Before then, Japanese were able to purchase it freely in drugstores without a prescription, officially not as a contraceptive but as a medicine for hormone- and menstruation-related problems. However, a series of chemical poisoning scandals in the 1960s led the Ministry to be concerned about the pill. The scandals (none related to the pill) included deformed babies born to women who had taken thalidomide during early pregnancy, and babies poisoned by arsenic in milk powder. The Ministry of Health and Welfare became extremely cautious, and in 1967 it prohibited Japanese pharmaceutical companies from producing the pill. Since 1972, the Ministry has classified the pill as a medicine available solely by prescription, and not as a contraceptive.

To complicate matters, the threat of Acquired Immune Deficiency Syndrome has enabled critics of the pill to take a new stance and argue that its liberalization would discourage the use of the condom, which is the most effective preventive method against the spread of AIDS. In 1992 this argument swayed the Central Pharmaceutical Affairs Council, the advisory body of the Ministry of Health and Welfare, against recommending the legalization of the pill. The Council, composed of medical experts, met regularly to discuss the pill issue, and made a negative recommendation despite the demands of feminist and civic liberalization pressure groups.

More importantly, the Ministry takes a moral stance, contending that the liberalization of the pill as a contraceptive would foster promiscuity and corrupt women's morals. The implication is that it would free women from the fear of pregnancy, encourage them to engage in sexual activity more liberally, and contaminate the allegedly respectable Japanese family system.

In reality, however, the sexual revolution has occurred anyway. A majority of youngsters find premarital sex acceptable (see Figure 2.4). Many popular magazines and television shows are full of nude pictures and sexual descriptions. Adult books and videos are readily available. Still, parents and teachers remain reluctant to give children sex education and do not regard it as their task.[23] An increasing gap between the moral pretenses of the adult community and young people's behavioral realities is conducive to numerous unwanted pregnancies and abortions, both reported and unreported.

Abortion has been a legal means of birth control in postwar Japan. The reported number of abortions is close to half a million per year.[24] These are regarded as conservative figures; women normally pay abortion costs in cash because national health insurance does not cover them, and for taxation purposes many doctors do not report all cases of abortion. Japan's Eugenic Protection Law allows women to have abortions for economic reasons.[25]

The abortion industry has a peculiar concomitant on the religious front. Some temples have an area which accommodates hundreds of small, doll-like stone statues called *mizuko jizō*, some covered with baby bibs and caps, others with toys beside them. Feeling guilty and contrite, some women who have had abortions have dedicated these costly stone carvings which symbolize the souls of aborted fetuses. With the sizeable market in mind, some temples openly advertise the availability of this service in newspapers and magazines, specifying costs and fees.

2 Domestic Violence

Violence at home takes many forms. In prewar Japan, a husband's violence against his wife was accepted. The practice still persists though it is more concealed, but there are few empirical studies in this area and their findings differ vastly as to the extent of domestic violence. A national survey conducted in 1992 by a domestic-violence study group indicates that 78 percent of women experienced violence in some form from their husbands or partners.[26] A survey in 1989 done by Hakuhōdō suggests that 49 percent of married men have punched or slapped their wife.[27] In a prefectural survey carried out in 1995 by the Policy Office for Women of the Kanagawa Prefectural Government, 10 percent of women replied that they were subjected to violence from their spouse.[28] In most cases, the man had hit his spouse or girlfriend with a fist, slapped her face, kicked her body, or twisted her arm. A considerable number of women reported being partially strangled, or hit with a baseball bat, a golf club or a belt. A considerable proportion of victims of physical violence suffered injuries, the worst including bone fractures, burns, and burst eardrums. These surveys show that violent men are not restricted to any particular class lines; they include doctors, university professors, and public servants in significant numbers. The proportion does not differ depending upon income level. Despite this reality, only seven community shelters for women operate in Japan, primarily on the basis of volunteer support with very limited government subsidies.[29]

Court data also show the extent of domestic violence which women suffer. When wives file divorce requests, the husband's domestic violence is usually cited as a major reason for the action, second only to "personality incompatibility."[30] While the exact extent of violence of this kind remains unidentifiable, in all probability it is much more widespread than is commonly believed. The nature of the problem makes it less visible than other social issues.

In recent years, the phrase "domestic violence" in the Japanese context has referred primarily to violent acts of children against their parents. There are no solid data on the sociological background of these children. Those who are violent towards their parents are mostly in the middle-school age bracket, and most cases involve a boy kicking, beating, and punching his mother. The family that produces most domestic violence of this kind is typically that with a father who pays no attention to the children and a mother who tries to control and protect the children excessively. To a considerable extent, these incidents reflect the predicament of many Japanese families in which the father works long hours and spends little time at home, and the lonely mother finds emotional satisfaction in excessive expectations of the children's success. In this respect, children's domestic violence indirectly represents injuries that Japan's corporate system has inflicted on Japanese families.

3 Sexual Harassment

The notion of sexual harassment has recently been imported into Japan from Western countries, although the practice has a long history. The shortened and Japanese version of the concept, *sekuhara*, has gained wide circulation from court cases that women have brought against men's behavior in workplaces.[31] The Ministry of Labor, which oversees work practices in firms, explains the notion of sexual harassment to the business community in productivity terms rather than from the human rights perspective. It defines *sekuhara* as a sexual act, either verbal 'and behavioral, imposed upon female workers against their will, causing "disadvantage to business performance" and "deterioration of the work environment."[32] Because of power relations in workplaces and ambiguities in the legal framework, many cases remain unreported, though some cases have surfaced since the concept of *sekuhara* gained public currency. Some women have charged that they were transferred or fired when they rejected their male superior's sexual advances. Others have complained that they experienced *sekuhara* during business trips, company excursions, and drinking parties. In metropolitan areas, working women complain about sleazy sexual harassment in packed commuter trains.[33]

IV Marriage and Divorce

1 Marriage

Japan is perhaps the only advanced industrial society in which a large number of couples marry through family arrangements, with a go-between serving as intermediary. It is estimated that as of 1985 about half of all married couples in Japan had been united in this way.[34] Love marriages have increased, however, and more than 70 percent of couples married since 1970 have married for love. Nonetheless, arranged marriages remain a practical alternative for some sections of the community.

Preparation for an arranged marriage commences with the parents of a child of marriageable age circulating his or her photograph and personal history through their network of friends and acquaintances. When two parties in the arranged-marriage market become interested in exploring the possibility of a match, they have an intermediary organize a *miai* session, a meeting where prospective marriage partners are introduced, normally in the presence of their parents who leave shortly afterwards. While there is no standard procedure from this point, the prospective partners usually arrange another meeting if they are mutually interested. This may or may not progress to marriage.

Even in love marriages, procedures can take forms similar to those of arranged marriages. Marriage ceremonies are conducted in the presence of a go-between couple, and on the understanding that the marriage represents a union between family A and family B. *Ie* ideology surfaces on these ceremonial occasions, attaching importance to family pedigree, lineage, and consanguinity.

For love marriages no less than for arranged marriages, the process of choosing a marriage partner is class-dependent; people are apt to find partners from the same occupational and educational background.[35] For instance, there are occupation barriers between agricultural and non-agricultural sectors, between non-manual and manual groups, and between professional/managerial and clerical categories. Intraclass marriages within occupational and educational categories remain dominant, and in that sense intraclass homogamy persists as an entrenched pattern. In this respect, one can make two specific observations.

First, marriages based on the similarities of parents' occupational classifications are most prevalent in the professional and managerial class.[36] This implies that intergenerational class continuity endures most firmly in the upper echelon of Japanese society. Lavish marriage functions held in first-class hotels are the norm in this stratum, implicitly confirming and celebrating its durability.

Second, the class traits of the parents of marriage partners are more random for arranged marriages than for love marriages.[37] This reflects the fact that arranged marriages are the consequence of the match-making practice available to those who cannot find partners through their own social networks on their own initiative. The redressing function of *miai* opens arranged marriages to a more diverse range of class backgrounds than love marriages. Meanwhile, ostensibly spontaneous selections of partners in love marriages are patterned in such a way that the class attributes of parents creep into the decision-making process whether consciously or not. In this way, ironically, the increasingly dominant culture of love marriage has solidified, rather than loosened, intergenerational class perpetuity.

On the whole, however, class affinity is more pronounced between the marrying couple than between their parents.[38] Similarities between partners' educational backgrounds appears to be greater than between their occupational positions. About 80 percent of female graduates from Tokyo University are married to graduates of Tokyo University, most of whom occupy managerial, specialist, or professional positions. At a macroscopic level, marriage remains one of the most powerful devices of intergenerational class reproduction.

2 Divorce

The divorce rate in Japan, though rising since the 1980s, remains low compared with major Western countries.[39] The lack of economic independence of many women is the primary reason for remaining married, but a few additional related constraints conspire to suppress the divorce rate.

Generally, husband and wife in Japan tend to have separate spheres of life.[40] In comparison with couples in the United States, Japanese couples rarely attend social functions together, have few mutual friends, and rarely converse with each other about their respective activities.[41] Communication gaps between couples are accepted realities in Japan. In this context, those who regard conjugal love as the essence of married life are a minority in Japan. Marriages of convenience are widely condoned in order to maintain family stability. In comparison with Western societies, Japanese data[42] show that only a significantly small proportion of women favor the proposition that "if one is dissatisfied with one's marriage partner, one is free to divorce." Japanese women tend to refrain from divorce out of consideration for their children and parents, and at the expense of their own connubial satisfaction.[43] With the stigma that is attached to divorce and recorded in the family registration system, men and women who have divorced have much more difficulty in remarrying than people in Western countries.[44]

Divorced women in Japan are penalized in many spheres of life. To begin with, a housewife who does not have a regular income is not likely to have joint ownership of the house or flat where she lives with her husband. Because banks do not make housing loans to those without a steady income, a wife normally does not jointly hold the title to the property with her husband. This means that a housewife who wants a divorce or a separation has no place to go, and must look for new accommodation at her own expense. This is why some Japanese women put up with quasi-divorce, where the wife and husband live under the same roof despite the virtual collapse of their marriage.[45]

In addition, though the mother obtains custody of her children in about three-quarters of all divorce cases,[46] she cannot realistically expect her ex-husband to share the cost of child-rearing. Legal authorities have limited the enforcement of any judgments of the family court, and it is a statistical reality that an overwhelming majority of divorcees raise their children without the financial support of their former husband.

Most divorces in Japan occur by mutual consent of the couple without intervention by the family court. Only about one in ten divorces involve judicial arbitration, judgment or ruling. Divorces by consent prevail among the young, whose divorce rate is high. Those in the middle-aged and elderly bracket, where the divorce rate is relatively low, tend to rely more on the family court. For older couples, divorce involves a wider range of conflicts over asset ownership, inheritance, and access to children.

Most divorce cases in postwar years have involved couples married for less than two years. Though this pattern persists to some degree, the trend since the 1970s has been an increase in divorces among couples married for more than ten years. This means that the number of children affected by divorce has increased. It is not uncommon now for a couple with several children to divorce.

In cities, particularly among the educated middle class, the gradual spread of feminism has weakened the stigma of divorce. With an increasing number of women in the labor market, women are more financially capable of leading independent lives and looking after their children following divorce. Moreover, women see divorce in a more positive light than men; while women tend to regard it as an act of courage and autonomy, men generally find it an occasion of unhappiness, rashness, and failure.

V Types of Family

1 Competing Images of the Japanese Family

Japan's family system has two apparently contradictory tendencies. On the one hand, some family sociologists note the vitality[47] and increasing stability[48] of Japan's family system in comparison with its counterparts in other industrialized countries. The numbers of *de facto* marriages, open homosexual partnerships and single mothers have increased, but not as rapidly or obviously as in many Western societies.

On the other hand, some analysts point to the "disintegration of the family"[49] and the "age of family-less families,"[50] and suggest that Japan's family system is undergoing a fundamental change and facing a serious crisis, perhaps slightly belatedly. They point out that many ostensibly content middle-class urban families in Japan function as families, but without the substance expected of the conventional family unit. In extreme cases, the husband works overtime until late in the evening, the wife attends evening classes or meetings, their children go to private after-school classes, and consequently they have dinner together only once or twice a week. Some families are "weekend families" in the sense that there is interaction of family members only on Saturdays or Sundays. The phrase "to do a family" has been coined to describe the behavior of those families who attempt under such circumstances to maintain the supposed order of an orthodox family in an artificial and contrived way.[51]

Both features can be seen in nuclear families and in extended stem families.

2 Nuclear Family Patterns

The declining birthrate brought about a sudden drop in the size of families in postwar years. The average household size hovered around five until about 1955 but declined to less than three by the 1990s,[52] a change that took about a century in major Western countries. While the number of extended families has remained almost constant, nuclear families with few children have dramatically increased during this period. Most families with children have chosen to have only one or two, bringing the average under 1.8.[53] Nuclear families in Japan today exhibit problems different from those of extended families.

On the whole, nuclear families enjoy a high degree of autonomy and independence; the wife does not have to worry about the daily interventions of parents-in-law. These nuclear families typically settle down first in a small but well-equipped apartment or condominium. They then move to a detached house, if their financial and social conditions allow. Condominium buildings that sprawl across and around major cities reflect the spread of small families with one or two children. Their self-contained, partitioned, and rather comfortable life-styles became consolidated with the wide availability of reasonably priced household electric appliances like refrigerators, vacuum cleaners, and washing machines. Freed from manual family chores, housewives in these circumstances have been free to raise a small number of children the way they like without interference from the older generation.

On the negative side, however, women in nuclear families in cities lead solitary and alienated lives. This is not just because their husbands devote themselves to their companies, rarely attending to family matters, but also because the numbers of children are fewer, the woman's parents may live far away, and interaction with other families in the neighborhood is rare. Consequently, full-time housewives find themselves directing all their energy to child-rearing, and develop fervent expectations regarding the future of their children in an attempt to obtain the psychological gratification that they cannot get from their spouse. Some analysts[54] call this predicament "mother–child adhesion," a situation that sometimes has pathological consequences.

Such attachment drives some to become "education mothers" who are obsessed with their children's marks and strive for educational success at all costs. Others suffer from "child-rearing neurosis" which, in extreme cases, results in a joint suicide of mother and child. Drawing upon his clinical experience as a pediatrician, Hisatoku[55] reports the growth of cases of chronic stomach-ache, diarrhea, asthma, school phobia, autism, and other psychogenic symptoms among children. Coining the phrase "mother-pathogenic disease," he attributes these disorders to the mother's excessive protection or interference in the sufferer's early childhood. The problem exists only among some middle-class children whose mother has inordinate expectations of them. Such apparently pathological tendencies on the part of these alienated mothers doubtless stem from their husband's truancy from child-raising; in that sense, the illness can perhaps more properly be called "father-pathogenic disease."

A majority of child-rearing mothers have some support system and can avoid the extreme forms of isolation often associated with secluded nuclear families. On the basis of her studies in Hyōgo prefecture, Ochiai[56] suggests that, despite the expansion of the number of conjugal families, parents or parents-in-law continue to assist in caring for their grandchildren especially if they all live together or the grandparents live nearby. In the absence of such grandparental support, women in the infant-rearing phase develop neighborhood groups for mutual assistance. They organize play groups, get together at a member's home on a rotational basis, and enjoy conversation while their children play together. Some even organize a voluntary association of mothers in need of mutual support for baby care. Those who live in the atomized urban environment must look for some non-kin support system in their neighborhood. Thus, grandparental backing and neighborhood-group support are two practical alternatives for young mothers. In the countryside, where three-generation families are prevalent and kinship ties are well established, full-time housewives can rely on parents or parents-in-law and participate in social activities outside home during their infant-raising period.

More and more working mothers use baby-care centers and day nurseries, but because these institutions are largely unavailable outside big cities, in rural areas it is more usual for infants to go first to a nursery school and then to a kindergarten before enrolling in a primary school. Moreover, in cities, mothers in nuclear families appear to share a sub-culture of mother–infant adhesion in which they interact with their children in a rather closed and isolated way. In contrast, children in the countryside or living in extended families enjoy interactions with a wider range of people, such as grandparents and neighbors.[57]

3 Endurance of Extended Families

Japanese family structure differs from that in other industrialized countries in its large proportion of extended families with two adult generations living under the same roof. The 1985 census figures suggest that nearly seven out of ten persons at or above the age of sixty-five live with their relatives, mainly with the family of one of their children. Calculated from a different angle, there is about one extended family for every three nuclear families. Because the nuclear family has 3.3 members on average and the extended family 5.5, some 64 percent of Japanese today live in a nuclear family setting, 31 percent in an extended family environment, and 5 percent in single households.[58] The persistence of the extended family system in contemporary Japan thus deserves notice even though nuclear families form the largest group, accounting for about 60 percent of all households. This pattern is inconsistent with the prediction of the modernization theory, that industrialization entails the overwhelming dominance of the nuclear family system.

In extended families, the traditional norm requires that the family of the first son reside with his parents. This often leads to bitter and malicious tension between his wife and her mother-in-law. Because of rapid changes in values between generations, such tension frequently becomes open conflict. The old mother-in-law who remembers prewar years expects submission and subservience from the young wife, who prefers an autonomous and unconstrained life-style. Soap operas on Japanese television abound with tales of discord and friction of this kind, reflecting the magnitude of everyday problems in this area. These programs are popular because many in the audience can identify with the characters and their predicaments.

Extended families show signs that they are adapting to the changing environment while retaining some traditional features. A study in Osaka shows that a majority of extended families still share a family budget between older and younger generations, although this practice is less prevalent than previously.[59] Research on extended families in Shizuoka shows that older-generation couples tend to live in extended family arrangements throughout their marriage, whereas younger-generation couples are inclined to choose this option at a certain phase of their married life. Another study in Osaka suggests that the designation of an heir continues to be strong even in family groups where parents and their children manage completely separate nuclear families.[60]

In *omote* terms on the surface, the durability of extended households in contemporary Japan appears to indicate the survival of traditional family values. In *ura* reality, however, most two-generation families make this arrangement for pragmatic rather than altruistic reasons. Given the high cost of purchasing housing properties, young people are prepared to live with or close to their parents and provide them with home-based nursing care, in the expectation of acquiring their house after their death in exchange.[61] Even if the two generations do not live together or close, aged parents often expect to receive living allowances from their children, with the tacit understanding that they will repay the "debt" by allowing the contributing children to inherit their property after death.[62] This is why aged parents without inheritable assets find it more difficult to live with their children or receive an allowance from them.

Meanwhile, studies of village families show much clearer patterns revealing the continued, and even increasing, strength of the extended family, although there are signs of decline in *ie* consciousness among younger villagers. The proportion of extended families in Japan's agricultural community increased from 42.2 percent in 1920 to 56.2 percent in 1970. During the same period, nuclear families declined from 46.4 to 36.3 percent.[63]

On ceremonial occasions, the symbols of family lineage and genealogy surface as an indication of the survival of the *ie* system. Marriage ceremonies and functions, for example, take the form of the union of two family lines.[64] Outside the venue of the wedding reception, a sign is normally displayed to indicate that a marriage is to occur linking House A and House B. Prior to a wedding ceremony, the two houses exchange betrothal presents as a kind of engagement ritual. These presents (*yuinō*) symbolize an agreement that the houses have entered a special relationship. The centerpiece of the exchange is the betrothal money that the parents of the groom are expected to give to the bride or her parents to enable her to purchase household goods and make other preparations for their married life. Other presents, which include food and sake, elaborately wrapped, reflect the traditional village custom in which members of the two households eat and drink together to mark the beginning of the special relationship of mutual assistance between them during harvest and other busy seasons.

Japan's funerals also exhibit the endurance of extended-family principles. The common practice is for the body of the deceased to be brought back home even if he or she died in hospital. A wake is held nearly all night beside the body at the house where the person lived. Memorial services are also normally held at home, before the body is taken to a crematorium. The ashes are buried at the family tomb.

4 Increase in Single Households

Households outside the conventional family structure dramatically increased in the 1980s. Single households constituted nearly a quarter of households in Japan at the beginning of the 1990s, partly reflecting the surge of youngsters who choose alternative life-styles: life-time singles, cohabitation without formal marriage, single mothers, and acknowledging one's homosexuality.

However, this does not mean that the Japanese are becoming more single-orientated. A national survey[65] suggests that only 2 percent of men and 4 percent of women have "no intention to marry throughout their lives." These percentages roughly correspond to the proportions of unmarried persons in their forties, and indicate that no fundamental intergenerational value change has taken place with respect to intention to marry. White-collar employees are more eager to marry than blue-collar workers, self-employed or unemployed persons. Contrary to popular belief, career women with university education expect to have a married life and are more intent on marrying than those with high-school or middle-school education. On the whole, the institution of marriage remains the most prevalent form of male–female relationship, although community acceptance of other forms appears to be gradually spreading.

5 Schematic Summary

To summarize the discussion in graphic form, it may be helpful to consider two dimensions of classification: type of residential arrangement, which ranges from extended family to nuclear family; and family norm, ranging from lineage orientation to conjugal orientation. Combining these two dimensions, one can envisage four family types, as displayed in Table 6.4.

Category A represents the most traditional type, in which the *ie* principle predominates and the married couple lives with the husband's parents. Category D consists of autonomous, modern nuclear-family types where the conjugal ideology prevails. Between these two extremes are two intermediate mixed varieties.

Category B includes families where two adult generations live in the same house but value conjugal relations more than lineal ones and lead mutually independent lives. Because of high property prices, city families, particularly in the Tokyo metropolitan areas, choose this life-style by building a two- or three-story residence with self-contained floors for each conjugal unit.

Category C includes nuclear families who believe in lineage-based

Table 6.4   Four types of family

	Type of residential arrangement	
Family norm	Extended family	Nuclear family
Lineage orientation	A	C
Conjugal orientation	B	D

Source: Adapted from Mitsuyoshi 1991, p. 141.

relations between generations. These families may live apart for occupational and other reasons, but closely follow traditional conventions governing marriage ceremonies, funerals, festivals, ancestral worship, family tomb management, and gift-giving among kin, and interact intimately with each other.

Formal studies of social stratification in Japan have long treated the occupational and educational attributes of the male head of a household as the basis for analysis and have given little attention to women, whose social status in such studies has been assumed to be identical with the husband's. This bias calls for the re-examination of the basic premise and format of analysis,[66] given the increasing numbers of unmarried women and women in the labor force, and in view of changes in domestic labor and the widening influence of feminist thought on sociology and other social sciences. Studies in the latter vein have revealed not only differences in the worlds of men and women and the structure of power relations between men and women, but also internal differentiation within the world of women.

Notes

1 The Ministry of Home Affairs defines the concept of household head in some detail on the basis of patriarchal principles:

1 In the case of the father and his first son both earning a living for the household, the father should be deemed its head in accordance with commonly accepted ideas even if the father's income is less than that of the first son.

2 In the case of the father being his first son's dependant in terms of income tax law and his first and second sons both earning a living for the household, the first son should be deemed its head even if his income is less than that of the second son.

3 In the case of neither the father nor his first son having any income and the second son being chiefly responsible for earning a living for the household, the first son should be deemed its head in accordance with commonly accepted ideas so long as he is regarded as only temporarily unemployed.

4 The wife becomes the household head when the husband has no income and the wife earns a living.

"Questions and answers concerning the Law on Basic Registers of Residents," a notice dispatched by the head of the Administration Department of the Ministry, cited in Satō 1991, pp. 138–9.

2 A survey conducted by the Ministry of Health and Welfare (Kōseishō) in 1990.

3 Sakakibara 1992, pp. 88–90.

4 AM January 17 1996, p. 1.

5 Yuzawa 1987a, pp. 166–7.

6 AM January 17 1966, p. 29.

7 The combined outcome of the ninth Fertility Survey conducted by the Institute of Population Problems of the Ministry of Health and Welfare in 1987 and the Population Dynamics Survey conducted in 1989.

8 Ueno 1990, pp. 214–21.

9 Ueno 1990, pp. 263–5.

10 See Brinton 1988 and 1992.

11 Brinton 1992, ch. 3.

12 Josei Shokugyō Zaidan 1990.

13 Ueno 1991, p. 153.

14 Josei Shokugyō Zaidan 1991, pp. 57–63.

15 The 1994 School Basic Survey of the Ministry of Education.

16 Ueno 1988.

17 Ozawa 1989; Ueno 1991.

18 Josei Shokugyō Zaidan 1991, p. 69.

19 Ueno 1991, pp. 154–5.

20 See Noguchi 1992.

21 More broadly, citizens' movements of various kinds are based upon the principles of horizontal networks. See Ishida 1996.

22 The twentieth National Family Planning Opinion Survey conducted by the *Mainichi Shimbun* in 1990.

23 See, for example, Forum 1994, p. 159.

24 Japanese doctors reported 466,876 abortions in 1989 and 456,797 in 1990.

25 On the advice of the Public Hygiene Council, the Ministry of Health and Welfare changed the period within which abortion is allowed from the first twenty-four weeks of pregnancy to the first twenty-two weeks.

26 *Tokyo Shimbun*, April 3 1993, morning edition, p. 15. The sample size was about eight hundred.

27 Hakuhōdō 1989.

28 AM January 14 1996, p. 14. The survey was distributed to five thousand potential respondents with a successful return rate of 53 percent. In this survey, some 2 percent of men replied that they experienced violence from their wife.

29 Reports compiled by the Women's Association of Yokohama City on the basis of studies conducted in 1994 and 1995. They report that more than twelve hundred shelters exist in the United States (AM January 14 1996, p. 15).

30 Yuzawa 1987a, p. 175.
31 A Labor Ministry survey of one thousand female employees which was conducted in March and April 1992 found that about a quarter said they had had an unpleasant sexual experience in their workplace (*Japan Times* March 1 1994, p. 4).
32 AM October 19 1993, p. 30.
33 AM August 22 1993, p. 5.
34 SSM IV, p. 129.
35 SSM IV, pp. 131–43.
36 SSM IV, pp. 142–3.
37 SSM IV, p. 141.
38 SSM IV, pp. 140–2.
39 The divorce rate, measured as the proportion of the number of divorce cases per thousand people, was 1.37 in Japan in 1991; it was 4.83 in the United States (1988), 3.39 in the Soviet Union (1989), 2.86 in Britain (1989), 2.22 in Sweden (1990), 2.04 in West Germany (1989) and 1.90 in France (1988) (Forum 1994, p. 22).
40 Yuzawa 1987a, p. 74.
41 This pattern is evident in surveys by the Prime Minister's Office on "Youth and Home" in 1982 and on "Public Opinion on Family and Home" in 1986. See also Yuzawa 1987a, p. 75, and 1995, pp. 98–9.
42 Forum 1994, p. 22.
43 Shikata 1984.
44 See Inoue and Ehara 1991, pp. 26–7.
45 This practice is known as *katei-nai rikon* (divorce within marriage).
46 Yuzawa 1995, pp. 182–3.
47 Morioka and Mochizuki 1993.
48 Yuzawa 1987b.
49 Nakano 1992, especially ch. 8.
50 Okonogi 1992.
51 Nakano 1992; Asahi Shinbunsha 1992, pp. 164–5.
52 The Basic Survey of National Life conducted by Kōseishō estimates that the figure as of 1993 was 2.96.
53 Kōseishō's survey in 1993.
54 Kimura and Baba 1988.
55 Kyūtoku 1979.
56 Ochiai et al. 1989.
57 Ochiai et al. 1989, p. 30.
58 Yuzawa 1987a, p. 6.
59 Tokuoka 1976.
60 Mitsuyoshi 1986.
61 Ōtake and Horioka 1994, pp. 235–7.
62 Horioka 1995.
63 Mitsuyoshi 1991, pp. 136–7.
64 See, for example, Edwards 1989.
65 A survey carried out by the Institute of Population Problems of the Ministry of Health and Welfare in 1982.
66 SSM IV.

7

Minority Groups:
Ethnicity and Discrimination

I Japanese Ethnocentrism and Globalization

Japan has frequently been portrayed as a uniquely homogeneous society both racially and ethnically.[1] Before the end of World War II, the Japanese leadership had inculcated in the populace the myths of Japanese racial purity and of the ethnic superiority which was supposed to be guaranteed by the uninterrupted lineage of the imperial household over centuries. In postwar years, many observers have attributed Japan's economic success and political stability to its racial and ethnic homogeneity.[2] In everyday life, racism and ethnocentrism still remain strong in many sections of the community and the establishment. The *tatemae* of Japan's racial and ethnic homogeneity goes hand in hand with the *honne* of many Japanese, who believe that "Japaneseness" has superior qualities and should not be contaminated.

Analysts of the social psychology of the Japanese suggest that the inferiority complex towards the caucasian West and the superiority complex towards Asian neighbors have played a major role in Japanese perceptions of other nationalities. The leadership of modern Japan envisaged a "ladder of civilizations" in which Euro-American societies occupied the highest rungs, Japan was somewhere in the middle, and other Asian countries were at the bottom.[3] Also notable is the persistence of the doctrine of *wakon yōsai* (Japanese spirit and Western technology), the dichotomy which splits the world into two spheres, Japan and the West, and assumes that the spiritual, moral, and cultural life of the Japanese should not be corrupted by foreign influences no matter how much Japan's material way of life may be affected by them.[4] Borrowing some elements of imported Western imagery, the Japanese mass culture industry has

169

portrayed blacks in derogatory ways in comics, TV programs, and novels.[5] Popular among business elites, books which perpetuate anti-Semitic stereotypes based upon the old propaganda of the "international Jewish conspiracy" hit the bestseller chart from time to time.

At the top of the national hierarchy, politicians have often expressed their *honne* and referred to the superiority of the Japanese race, a race uncontaminated by other racial and ethnic groups. In 1986, the Prime Minister, Yasuhiro Nakasone, publicly claimed the Japanese had a higher level of intelligence than Americans and attributed this alleged difference to Japanese racial purity and American racial heterogeneity.[6] In defending the policy of regulating imports of agricultural goods, Tsutomu Hata, who later became Prime Minister, claimed in 1987 that Japanese beef is more suitable to the Japanese because they have longer intestines than Westerners.[7] Michio Watanabe, former Foreign Minister of the Liberal Democratic party government, inadvertently incurred the ire of the US black community in 1988 by alleging in derogatory language that blacks are lax in financial matters.[8] In 1990, Seiroku Kajiyama, then Minister of Justice, likened the influx of foreign prostitutes into a red-light district in Tokyo to the movement of blacks into white communities in the United States.[9] Though these national figures retracted their comments, they made the remarks knowing full well that this type of view appeals to the *honne* of their supporters. To that extent, the top politicians reflect the belief of the community at large.[10]

At the same time, Japanese society is exposed to the international community on an unprecedented scale. With the appreciation of the Japanese yen, many Japanese firms have no choice but to move their factories off-shore and interact directly with the local population. The Japanese travel abroad in numbers unparalleled in history. Satellite television technology brings images of the outside world into the living rooms of many Japanese. Both cities and rural areas witness an increasing flow of foreign students, overseas visitors, and long-term residents from abroad. The attraction of the yen and the Japanese demand for manual labor have brought phenomenal numbers of foreign workers into Japan. Grassroots Japan is undergoing a process of irreversible globalization. This has sensitized some sectors of the Japanese public to the real possibility of making Japanese society more tolerant and free from bigotry.

Thus, contemporary Japanese society is caught between the contradictory forces of narrow ethnocentrism and open internationalization. Intolerance and prejudice are rampant, but individuals and groups pursuing a more open and multicultural Japan are also active, challenging various modes of racism and discriminatory practices.

II Deconstructing the "Japanese"

Japan has a variety of minority issues, ethnic and otherwise, which the proponents of the homogeneous Japan thesis tend not to address. As discussed in chapter 1, some 4 percent of the Japanese population can be classified as members of minority groups. In the Kinki area, the center of western Japan, the proportion amounts to some 10 percent. The minority issues are the *ura* and *uchi* realities of contemporary Japanese society.

This chapter will survey the contemporary situations of four main minority groups in Japan: the Ainu, burakumin, Koreans, and foreign workers. Their minority status results from different historical circumstances as sketched in Chapter 1 and detailed in later sections: the Ainu situation derived from the Honshū race's attempt at internal colonization of the northern areas since the sixth century; the buraku problem stems from the caste system in the feudal period; the Korean issues originated from Japan's external aggression into the Korean peninsula in the first half of the twentieth century; and the foreign workers' influx began with Japan's economic performance in the 1980s and the 1990s.

These minority groups bring to the fore the fundamental question of who the Japanese (*Nihonjin*) really are. One may consider at least seven aspects of Japaneseness – nationality, ethnic lineage, language competence, place of birth, current residence, subjective identity, and level of cultural literacy – as Table 7.2 indicates. While each dimension is in some respect problematic,[11] the main objective of the table is to show that there can be a number of measures of Japaneseness and multiple kinds of Japanese. In combining the presence or absence of their attributes, one can analytically classify the Japanese into numerous types.

If we do not define who the Japanese are solely on the basis of citizenship, on which bureaucrats make decisions, a number of questions

Table 7.1 Characteristics of minority groups

Group	Population	Geographical concentration	Cause of minority presence
Burakumin	3,000,000	Kansai region	Caste system during the feudal period
Resident Koreans	700,000	Kansai region	Japan's colonization of Korea
Ainu	24,000	Hokkaidō	Honshū inhabitants' aggression in northern Japan
Foreign workers	700,000	Major cities	Shortage of unskilled labor

Table 7.2   Various types of "Japanese"

Specific examples	Nationality (citizenship)	"Pure Japanese genes"	Language competence	Place of birth	Current residence	Level of cultural literacy	Subjective identity
Most Japanese	+	+	+	+	+	?	?
Korean residents in Japan	–	–	+	+	+	?	?
Japanese businessmen posted overseas	+	+	+	+	–	?	?
Ainu and naturalized foreigners	+	–	+	+	+	?	?
First-generation overseas who forfeited Japanese citizenship	–	+	+	+	–	?	?
Children of Japanese overseas settlers	–/+	+	+/–	+/–	–	?	?
Immigrant workers in Japan	–	–	–/+	–	+	?	?
Third-generation Japanese Brazilians working in Japan	–	+	–/+	–	+	?	?
Some returnee children	+	+	–	+	+	?	?
Some children of overseas settlers	+	+	–	–	–	?	?
Children of mixed marriage who live in Japan	+	+/–	+	+/–	+	?	?
Third-generation overseas Japanese who cannot speak Japanese	–	+	–	–	–	?	?
Naturalized foreigners who were born in Japan but returned to their home country	–	–	+	+	–	?	?
Most overseas Japan specialists	–	–	+	–	–/+	?	?

Source: Expanded from Fukuoka 1993, p. 5; Mouer and Sugimoto 1995, p. 31.

occur.[12] The distinction between Korean Japanese who differ only in terms of citizenship seems in many cases to be rather artificial. Should naturalized sumo wrestlers like Takamiyama and Konishiki be considered Japanese? What about two Japanese who work in similar situations overseas and who consider themselves Japanese, but one retains his citizenship while the other takes up citizenship in the country in which he resides? What about Japanese-born children growing up abroad, for whom English or some other language might be considered their first language? What about Japanese Brazilians who have come to live in Japan? What about Mr Fujimori, the President of Peru, who is seen by many Peruvians as Japanese? Who has the right to decide who the Japanese are?

The notions of biological pedigree and pure Japanese genes are widespread but controversial and questionable. Especially important is the ill-defined criterion labelled simply as Japanese cultural literacy. Depending upon which culture of Japan one refers to, the amount of cultural literacy one has differs greatly. For instance, many foreign workers in Japan may lack polite Japanese and know nothing about the tea ceremony, but be more knowledgeable than middle-class housewives about the culture of subcontracting firms in the construction industry. Some returnee school-children from overseas may not be fluent in Japanese but be more perceptive than their teachers about the culture of Japanese education observed from a comparative perspective.

There may be different interpretations of the rules which delineate Japanese from other peoples. One can be exclusivist and define only those who satisfy all seven criteria in Table 7.2 as Japanese. One can be inclusivist and argue that those who satisfy at least one criterion can be regarded as Japanese. There are also many middle-ground positions between these two extremes. Minority and ethnicity problems in Japan are linked to the larger questions of who the Japanese are and who has the right to decide the issue.

III The Buraku Problem

The largest minority group is that of burakumin, an outcast group who share the racial and ethnic origin of the majority of Japanese. There are no biological differences between burakumin and majority Japanese, nor is there any means of distinguishing them at sight. The burakumin have fallen victim to the bigoted belief that, since their ancestors belonged to a social category below ordinary citizens during the feudal period, they constitute a fundamentally inferior class. A wide range of nasty discriminatory practices against burakumin reflect an invisible caste system in Japanese society.

The term *buraku* means a settlement, hamlet, or village community and *burakumin* denotes the residents of such units. Unfounded prejudice has forced buraku members to live in secluded communities under conditions of relative impoverishment. The exact size of the burakumin population remains unknown because they are Japanese citizens by race and nationality, and discrimination is based upon elusive labelling. An official survey conducted by the Prime Minister's Office gives the number of buraku communities as 4,603 and that of their residents as 2,010,230.[13] This survey focussed upon localities which the government has designated as entitled to benefit from public projects aimed at the elimination of discrimination. There are at least one thousand localities whose status is the subject of dispute between the government and community groups. Taking these factors into consideration, informed guesses put the number of communities at six thousand and that of burakumin at three million.[14]

Some buraku communities have existed for nearly four centuries. Segregated communities began to emerge around the sixteenth century and were institutionalized by the strengthening of the class system of the Tokugawa feudal regime. This system classified the population into four recognized ranks – samurai warriors at the top, farmers in the second rank, artisans in the third, and tradespeople at the bottom – but placed the ancestors of present-day burakumin outside these ranks, locating them in separate neighborhoods.

Two types of outcasts dwelt in these communities. The first, known as *eta* (which literally means the amply polluted or highly contaminated), comprised several groups: workers in the leather industry, including those who butchered and skinned cattle and those who produced leather goods; low-ranking craftsmen such as dyers and bambooware and metal-ware makers; transport workers, including watermen and seamen; shrine and temple laborers; and irrigation workers and guards of agricultural fields. The second major category was that of *hinin* (which literally means non-human people), comprising entertainers, beggars, executioners, and so forth. While regarded as lower than *eta* in rank, those in the *hinin* classification were allowed to climb to non-outcast status (under limited circumstances), whereas those in the *eta* category were not.[15]

Prejudice exists against burakumin in marriage, employment, education, and many other areas. The marriage patterns of burakumin give an indication of persistent discrimination against them. A government survey of buraku communities[16] shows that two out of three marriages in the sample are between those who were born in these communities. Intercommunity marriages between burakumin and non-burakumin are in the minority, and marriages between a buraku male and a non-buraku female are much more frequent than between a buraku female and a non-buraku male. There are numerous examples of non-buraku parents or relatives opposing marriages with burakumin, refusing to attend marriage ceremonies, or declining to associate with a couple after marriage.[17] Discriminatory practices in marriage sometimes involve private detective agencies called *kōshinjo*. At the request of conservative parents, these agencies investigate the family backgrounds, friends, political orientation, and other private and personal details of a prospective bride or groom.

At the same time, there are signs that youngsters are gradually freeing themselves from entrenched prejudice and taking a more open stance. Intercommunity marriages have increased among the younger generation, the survey showing that they constituted more than half the marriages where the husband was less than thirty years of age. This appears to suggest that the attitude of the majority community is changing.

Several features of the employment patterns of buraku inhabitants are conspicuous. A significant proportion work in the construction industry; the proportion employed in the wholesale, retail, restaurant, and service industries remains relatively low. Compared with the labor force in general, workers from buraku are more likely to be employed in small or petty businesses at low wages. Yet a considerable improvement in work opportunities for young people is discernible, indicating that discriminatory practices in workplaces have gradually declined.

Discrimination against burakumin has been sustained in covert ways. It was revealed (mainly in the early 1970s) that some companies secretly purchased copies of clandestinely published documents which listed the locations of and other data on buraku communities. The companies engaged in such activities in an attempt to identify job applicants with a buraku background and to eliminate them at the recruitment stage. The companies were able to accomplish this by checking the lists against the permanent address that each job applicant entered on their *koseki* papers, which they were normally required to submit at the time of application. At least ten blacklists of buraku communities surfaced in the 1970s and 1980s. The resolute condemnation of this practice by buraku liberation movements revealed the way in which the *koseki* system was used to discriminate against minority groups. The protest led to the establishment of a new procedure requiring applicants to write only the prefecture of their permanent address on the application form, so that address details remain unknown to prospective employers.

Members of buraku communities have been disadvantaged culturally and linguistically too. The rate of illiteracy in buraku communities remains high partly because a considerable number of the older generation could not complete compulsory education in their childhood. Though the situation has improved considerably in recent years, one in five buraku inhabitants has some difficulty in writing.[18] This reality prompted buraku-movement activists to mount a literacy campaign across their communities. Buraku children go to high school at a lower rate than the national average, and there are pronounced differences between buraku communities and the Japanese population generally in the ratio of students advancing to universities and colleges. In the Kansai area, the proportion of burakumin students who go beyond compulsory education is 10–20 percent less than the national average, a situation traceable to their low test results.[19] A study in Osaka, which focussed upon the language development of infants, sheds light upon a complex process which hinders the full growth of language skills in buraku children. While more or less equal to other children in their development of verbal language, they fall behind in comprehension and use of sentences. Researchers attribute this to the lack of role-playing opportunities at home, and especially to its being less common for burakumin parents to read stories to their children.[20] Because written language dominates in formal education, children from buraku communities are disadvantaged early and face difficulties in dealing with an educational curriculum which is organized on the assumption that children receive considerable exposure to written language before entering school.

The government has introduced special anti-discrimination legislation since 1969 in an attempt to counter discrimination against buraku communities. These laws ensure that the government provides financial support to projects that will improve the economic, housing, and educational conditions of burakumin. These legal steps enabled burakumin to apply for special funds and loans to improve their houses, community roads, and business infrastructures, and to allow their children to advance beyond compulsory education.

The social movements of buraku organizations have been militant in pressing their cause for the eradication of prejudice and the institutionalization of equality. Their history dates from the establishment in 1922 of *Suiheisha*, the first national burakumin organization committed to their liberation. Because of its socialist and communist orientation and radical principles, *Suiheisha* was disbanded during World War II, but was revived in postwar years and became *Buraku Kaihō Dōmei* (the Buraku Liberation League). The largest buraku organization, it claims a membership of some two hundred thousand and takes the most radical stance, maintaining that buraku discrimination is deep-rooted and widespread throughout Japanese society. *Kaihō Dōmei* adopted the strategy of publicly confronting and denouncing individuals and groups that promote discrimination either openly or covertly. This method, known as *kyūdan* (impeachment), has often been accompanied by the tactic of confining the accused in a room until they make satisfactory self-criticisms. As the most militant buraku organization, the League has also mounted a number of legal challenges. The best-known case is the so-called Sayama Struggle, in which the League has maintained that a buraku man who was sentenced to life imprisonment for having murdered a female high-school student in 1963 was framed by police and the prosecution, who were prejudiced against burakumin.

As a means of combatting prejudice against minority groups, activists have pressed hard for exclusion of biased words and phrases from print and electronic media. The Buraku Liberation League, in particular, has targetted newspapers, magazines, television and radio stations, and individual writers and journalists who have used expressions that it regarded as prejudicial. Under pressure of public accusation by the League, many have been compelled to offer public self-criticism and apologies. Other minority groups have followed suit and have effectively shaken the complacency of the Japanese majority. No doubt this tactic has contributed to the increasing community awareness of the deep-seated unconscious prejudice built into some expressions.[21] The physic-ally handicapped, who also see themselves as a minority, are sensitive to the use of particular expressions and often publicly join the fray.

While the anti-discrimination campaign waged by buraku movements resulted in visible material improvements of buraku communities, their educational and cultural disadvantages remain relatively unchanged. With a shifting of emphasis to the software rather than the hardware aspects of buraku liberation in the 1990s, activists started reviewing the impeachment measures which terrified some sections of the majority Japanese. They now place emphasis on institutional solutions, campaign-ing for the legislation of the Buraku Emancipation Basic Law, which would make it a national imperative to root out buraku discrimination and prejudice.

The buraku movement is not uniform. *Zenkoku Buraku Kaihō Undō Rengōkai* (the National Federation of Buraku Liberation Movements), which is affiliated with the Japan Communist party, takes the view that buraku discrimination is disappearing and that desegregation is pro-gressing well. With a membership of about eighty thousand, this group maintains that the excessive militancy of buraku movements will con-solidate rather than end prejudice, and slow the integration process. The third buraku organization, *Zenkoku Jiyū Dōwakai* (the National Federation of Freedom and Integration), is a small conservative group.

IV Korean Residents

Resident Koreans comprise the largest minority group with foreign origin. According to Ministry of Justice figures they number about seven hundred thousand, and an overwhelming majority of them are second- and third-generation residents who do not have Japanese citizenship but whose native language is Japanese. After the colonization of Korea in 1910, the Japanese establishment brought their parents and grand-parents to Japan as cheap labor in mining, construction, and ship-building. In 1945, some 2.3 million Koreans lived in Japan and about 1.7 million, nearly three-quarters, returned home during the six months after the end of World War II. The remaining six hundred thousand chose to settle in Japan, realizing that they had lost contact with their connections in Korea and would have difficulty in earning a livelihood there. As second-class residents, Koreans in Japan are subjected to dis-crimination in job recruitment, promotion, eligibility for pensions, and many other spheres of civil rights.

Because the Korean peninsula is divided into two nations, capitalist South and communist North, the Korean population in Japan is also split into two groups: the South-oriented organization *Mindan* (the Korean Residents Union in Japan) and the North-affiliated *Chongryun* (the General Association of Korean Residents in Japan). At a rough estimate, about two-thirds are oriented to South Korea and about one-third to North Korea,[22] though increasing numbers have become non-committal. The North-oriented groups, once highly influential among resident Koreans, have gradually lost their political clout due to the decline in North Korea's international status. But they remain active in ethnic education, managing a total of 144 full-time ethnic schools across the country, including one university and twelve high schools, in an attempt to maintain the Korean language and culture among young, now mainly third- and fourth-generation Koreans.

Political conflicts on the Korean peninsula are often translated into tensions in the Korean communities in Japan. During the Korean War in the early 1950s, the two Korean organizations engaged in bitter confront-ations at the community level. With the international strain over North Korea's suspected nuclear arms development intensifying in 1994, there were hundreds of incidents where Japanese right-wingers and bigots slashed the ethnic uniforms (*chima chogori*) of Korean female students on trains and at railway stations and made them frequent targets of physical and verbal abuse.

Japan's nationality law reflects the imagery of a racially homogeneous, patriarchal society. The law adopts the personal rather than territorial principle of nationality, determining one's nationality according to that of one's parents rather than according to the nation of one's birth. For-eign nationals' children born in Japan cannot obtain Japanese citizen-ship, while children whose father or mother is a Japanese national auto-matically become Japanese citizens at birth regardless of where they are born. Therefore, the second- and third-generation children of Koreans resident in Japan can become Japanese only after they take steps towards naturalization and the Ministry of Justice approves their application. The nationality law still requires that applicants should be persons of "good conduct," an ambiguous phrase which permits the authorities to use their discretion in rejecting applications.

From the Korean perspective, the Japanese government's position on the Korean nationality question has been inconsistent. During the colonial period, Koreans were made Japanese nationals though a separate law regulated their family registration system. Accordingly, male Koreans had the right to vote and to be elected to national and local legislatures; some were in fact elected as national parliamentarians and city legislators. However, with the independence of South and North Korea and the enactment of a fresh election law immediately after the end of World War II, Korean residents in Japan were deprived of voting rights. On May 2 1947, one day before the promulgation of the new postwar constitution, the Japanese government put into effect the Alien Registration Ordinance which virtually targetted Koreans in Japan, classified them as foreigners, and made them register as alien residents. Following the outbreak of the Korean War and the intensification of the Cold War in eastern Asia, the Japanese authorities hardened their attitude towards Koreans in Japan and enacted the Alien Registration Law upon the termination of the Allied occupation of Japan and the advent of independence in 1952.

Koreans are subject to discrimination on many grounds. First, they are barred from holding public office, though barriers have been gradually eroded. Non-Japanese cannot apply to sit examinations to become government officers at either the national or local level. In practice, since the 1970s, an increasing number of municipalities in the Kansai and Kantō areas have removed the nationality requirements for public office, but they remain a minority. The nationality requirement was removed for mail workers (although all postal workers are public servants) and nurses in public hospitals and health centers. But the Ministry of Home Affairs maintains the position that those who do not hold Japanese citizenship cannot be appointed to positions which involve the "execution of public power" or the "formation of the will of local municipalities." This means that non-Japanese nationals can hold only professional or clerical positions in local government which do not have executive or managerial responsibilities. Such governmental policies lend justification to private-sector discrimination against Koreans.

Housing discrimination against Koreans is widespread and often surreptitious. Some owners of flats and apartments openly require occupants to be Japanese nationals. Some real estate agents make it a condition for applicants to submit copies of their resident cards for identification purposes. This excludes non-Japanese because foreign residents have alien registration certificates but do not have resident cards, which are issued only to Japanese.[23]

The Alien Registration Law stipulates that foreign nationals who intend to reside in Japan for one year or more must be fingerprinted at the beginning of their stay; those who refuse to comply with this provision are liable for up to one year's imprisonment and/or a fine of two hundred thousand yen. The law was enacted in the context of the intense Cold War in East Asia. National security authorities regarded Koreans, especially those with links to North Korea, as potential security risks. In response to persistent protests by Korean organizations in Japan and by Korean governments, the Japanese authorities have made piecemeal revisions to the law, loosening its provisions relating to the legal status of Korean residents in Japan. In the 1991 amendment, they were given the status of "special permanent residents" who cannot be deported as easily as other long-term residents. This applies not only to first- and second-generation Koreans but also to the third generation and thereafter.

A 1993 amendment removed the fingerprinting requirements for permanent residents, who are mainly from the former Japanese colonies of Korea and Taiwan. However, these residents are still required to carry their alien registration cards at all times, and a failure to do so incurs a fine. Even when taking a walk or jogging, a Korean resident must carry his or her card to avoid the risk of being fined. The card lists the names and dates of birth of the Korean resident's family members as well as his or her photo and signature. Long-term residents without permanent residency status, such as business people and missionaries, are still fingerprinted. These permanent residents must report any change not only of their place of residence but also of their place of work to the local authorities.

Another contentious issue is the names that naturalized Koreans may assume. The Japanese government long took the position that foreigners must officially assume Japanese-sounding names as a condition of naturalization. Those Koreans who acquired Japanese citizenship had to give up such Korean names as Kim, Lee, and Park for more Japanese-sounding names such as Tanaka, Yamada, and Suzuki. Though this requirement has been removed, the name issue is a particularly sensitive point among Koreans in Japan because of the historical fact that the Japanese colonial regime in Korea forced all Koreans to assume Japanese surnames and to officially register them with government offices. The program known as *sōshi kaimei* (creation and revision of names), which reflected the Japanese method of total psychological control, humiliated Koreans.

The Ministry of Education takes a dual position on the appointment of foreign nationals to teaching positions. At the level of higher education, the 1982 legislation allowed non-Japanese nationals to occupy permanent teaching posts, for example as professors and lecturers, at national and public universities. However, the law includes a proviso that they cannot assume positions of authority, for example as chairpersons, deans, and presidents, on the grounds that these posts are offices through which "governmental power" is exercised. Many foreign academics regard this as academic apartheid. At secondary and primary levels, the Education Ministry has attempted to thwart the appointment of foreigners to permanent teaching posts. In 1982, the Ministry was quick to send an official notice to prefectural governments (which had the power to appoint school teachers), warning that it would not tolerate Koreans and other foreign nationals teaching in schools as permanent staff. Significantly, some prefectural governments have defied the Ministry's stance, and by the beginning of 1990 had appointed a total of thirty non-Japanese nationals, mainly resident Koreans, as primary and secondary teachers. In 1991, with the visit of the Korean President to Japan, the Japanese government softened its requirements and allowed public schools to hire Koreans and other foreign nationals as "full-time instructors," a move that some activists see as an attempt to consolidate the existing discrimination.

Graduates of Korean high schools in Japan are not entitled to enter Japanese universities. Because the Ministry of Education classifies these schools as vocational schools, not as high schools, their students do not automatically qualify to take entrance examinations for about three-quarters of all Japanese universities and colleges, including all national universities. The Ministry justifies its position with the claim that these schools aim at ethnic education, emphasize the teaching of the Korean language, history, and culture, and fail to follow the curricula specified by the Ministry. This gives rise to numerous anomalies. For example, if a boy graduates from a Korean high school in Seoul, he can apply for admission to Japanese universities as a foreign student from overseas. But if he moves to Japan and completes his schooling at a Korean high school in Tokyo, he is not entitled to lodge an application with most universities in Japan.[24]

Pension eligibility is another contentious issue. The National Pension system was altered in 1982 to enable Koreans and other permanent residents to join the scheme. For twenty-two years until then, they had had no access to the Japanese pension program. Under the new arrangement, those who were more than thirty-five years old at the time of the amendment are not entitled to old-age pensions, on the grounds that pensions are paid only to the individuals who have made contributions to the scheme for twenty-five years or more, until sixty years of age. This means that first-generation Koreans and many of the second generation are not eligible. With regard to pensions for the physically disabled, similar restrictions are imposed on foreign residents who were in and past their twenties in 1982.

Within the Korean community, a generation gap is discernible. The first generation, now a numerical minority that nevertheless retains considerable influence over Korean organizations in Japan, remains committed and loyal to their home country and government, some hoping to eventually return home. Second- and third-generation Koreans born and raised in Japan have little interest in living in Korea, but feel ambivalent towards both Korean and Japanese societies. Many had to struggle to learn Korean as a second language in the Japanese environment. An overwhelming majority have studied in Japanese educational institutions, have only limited knowledge of Korean society and history, and enjoy Japanese popular culture as much as the Japanese. Some have the traumatic experience of discovering their real Korean name only in their adolescence, because their parents used a Japanese name to hide their ethnic origin. Few have escaped anti-Korean prejudice and discrimination in employment, marriage, and housing. The second and third generations, committed permanent residents with interests in Japan, increasingly put priority on the expansion of their legal, political, and social rights.

Despite the changing climate, marriage between Koreans and Japanese remains a sensitive issue. Many first- and second-generation Koreans who retain memories of Japan's colonial past and its direct aftermath feel that marrying Japanese was a kind of betrayal of Korean compatriots. Over time, however, the proportion of intra-ethnic marriages between Koreans has declined. After the mid 1970s, Koreans who married Japanese outnumbered those who married Koreans. The youngest Koreans, many of whom are the fourth generation and in their twenties and younger, do not accept the older generations' argument that Koreans should marry Koreans to maintain their ethnic consciousness and identity.[25] Incapable of speaking Korean and acculturated into Japanese styles of life, young Koreans find it both realistic and desirable to find their partner without taking nationality into consideration: some 70 percent of Koreans now marry Japanese nationals. Likewise, the younger generation is more prepared to seek naturalization as Japanese citizens.[26]

Overall, the time since the end of Japan's colonization of Korea in 1945 has altered the shape of the Korean issue in Japanese society. An overwhelming majority of Korean residents now speak Japanese as their first language and intend to live in Japan permanently. With an increase in inter-ethnic marriages with Japanese and the rise of the South Korean economy, many Japanese Koreans are reluctant to take a confrontationist stance and are eager to establish an internationalist identity and outlook, taking advantage of their dual existence. Against this background, young Koreans have become divided about the extent to which Koreans should remember and attach importance to the history of Japan's colonization and exploitation, and the degree to which they are attached to Japanese society as the environment where they have grown up. Combining these two factors, Fukuoka constructs a model of four types of Koreans, as shown in Table 7.3.[27] At the practical level, young Koreans differ in terms of the language they use in everyday life, and whether they use a Korean or Japanese name.

The first type (Type A) of Koreans have a strong sense of loyalty to their home country and define themselves as victims of Japan's annexation of Korea, who reject any form of assimilation into Japanese society.[28] Many Koreans of this type were educated in ethnic schools and became bilingual. Generally, they take pride in being Korean, use Korean names, and hold membership in the North-orientated General Association of Korean Residents in Japan (*Chongryun*). Sharply critical of Japanese discrimination against Koreans and primarily reliant upon Korean business networks, they tend to form closed Korean communities, have close friends only among Koreans, and see themselves as foreigners in Japan.

In contrast, Koreans with individualistic orientation (Type B) neither take much notice of the past relationship between Korea and Japan nor have strong attachment to Japanese society. They seek to advance their

Table 7.3 Four identity types of Korean youth in Japan

| Attachment to Japanese society | *Importance attached to Japan's colonial history* | |
	Strong	*Weak*
Weak	(A) Fatherland orientation (we are Koreans who happen to be in Japan) Bilingual Korean name	(B) Individualistic orientation (we seek self-actualization privately) Mostly speak Japanese; eager to learn English Not concerned about the name issue
Strong	(C) Multicultural orientation (we want to find ways of cohabitating with Japanese) Primarily Japanese Korean name	(D) Assimilation orientation (we want to be Japanese) Japanese only Japanese name

Source: Adapted from Fukuoka 1993, p. 89.

career in an individualistic way without depending upon organizational support. Cosmopolitan, achievement-orientated, and confident of their ability, they are interested in acquiring upward social mobility by going to top Japanese universities or studying in the United States or Europe. Most of them are not concerned about the name issue, use Japanese in most situations, and are eager to learn English as the language of international communication.

The multicultural type (Type C) represents a new breed of Koreans who remain critical of the legacy of Japan's attitude to Korea, have a strong Korean identity, and use Korean names. However, unlike Type A, they regard Japanese society as their home base and establish a multicultural life-style in which they live with the Japanese without losing their sense of Korean autonomy and individuality. Many used Japanese names in the past to hide their Korean identities but became conscious and proud of their ethnic duality while taking part in anti-discrimination movements with Japanese citizens. Having studied in Japanese schools, most of them consider Japanese their first language but some study the Korean language on their own initiative. These Koreans are politically conscious and reform-orientated, while having a deep attachment to the Japanese local community in which they were brought up. The activists of this group work closely with Japanese groups to press for equal rights for Koreans and other foreign nationals in Japan.

Assimilationist Koreans (Type D) put the first priority on becoming Japanese in every way. Brought up in a predominantly Japanese environment, they are totally Japanese culturally and linguistically and believe that what's done cannot be undone with regard to Japan's past colonial policy. Many attempt to remove their "Korean characteristics," adapt themselves fully to Japanese society, and thereby seek to be accepted by the Japanese. Most of them become naturalized Japanese nationals.

Over time, the Japanese authorities have taken a conciliatory position, with local governments in particular assuming generally sympathetic stands towards Korean communities. In response to Korean residents' appeal, the Supreme Court ruled in 1995 that the constitution does not prohibit permanent residents from having voting rights in local elections. At the same time, reform-minded Japanese are vocal in their claim that Japan cannot be an internationalized society without cultivating genuine openness and tolerance towards the largest ethnic minority in Japan.

V Indigenous Ainu

The Ainu race, the indigenous population of northern Japan, now comprises some twenty-four thousand persons and seven thousand households living mainly in Hokkaidō.[29] For more than ten centuries, they have suffered a series of attempts by Japan's central government to invade and deprive them of their land, and to totally assimilate them culturally and linguistically.[30] In this sense, their history resembles that of American Indians and Australian Aborigines.

Immediately after the Meiji Restoration, the Tokyo government took steps to designate Hokkaidō as "ownerless land," confiscated the Ainu land, and established a governmental Land Development Bureau. The dispatch of government-supported militia paved the way for the assault of Japanese capital on virgin forests. Until recently, the national government regarded the Ainu as an underdeveloped and uncivilized race, took a high-handed assimilation policy, and demolished much of the Ainu traditional culture. Governmental and corporate development projects are still degrading the conditions of the Ainu community. The most contentious such project is the construction of a dam near Nibutani in the southwest of Hokkaidō, where the Ainu have traditionally captured salmon.

Occupationally, many Ainu work in primary industry or the construction industry, with a considerable number being employed as casual day laborers. Sharing a plight common to aboriginal people subjected to the commercial forces of the industrialized world, Ainu have often been portrayed as leading exotic lives and made showpieces for the tourism industry. The Ainu community is increasingly cautious about the exploitation of the curiosity value of their arts and crafts. Nonetheless, the fact remains that Ainu culture differs fundamentally from the culture of the majority of Japanese, bearing further testimony to the diversity of Japanese ways of life. Some ecologists and environmentalists find fresh inspiration in the customary Ainu mode of life, which emphasizes "living with nature". Ainu culture is based upon a world view which presumes that everything in nature, be it tree, plant, animal, bird, stone, wind, or mountain, has a life of its own and can interact with humanity. But only the very old remember the songs and folklore which have been orally transmitted through generations, because the Ainu language has no written form. With most Ainu being educated in Japanese schools and their everyday language being Japanese, the preservation of Ainu culture requires positive intervention, without which it might disappear entirely.

While Article 14 of Japan's constitution stipulates that, "All of the people are equal under the law and there shall be no discrimination in political, economic or social relations because of race, creed, sex, social status or family origin," no reference is made to discrimination based on ethnicity. This appears to reflect the fact that even postwar democratic reformers did not recognize the significance of ethnic minority issues in Japan.[31] The law governing the Ainu population, *Kyū-dojin hogohō* (Law for the Protection of Former Savage Natives), has not altered its name despite a series of amendments of its substance. The occupation-led land reform, which equalized land ownership for the agrarian population in general, had the reverse effect for the Ainu community, because Ainu land that non-Ainu peasants had cultivated was confiscated on the grounds of absentee land ownership. As a result, Ainu lost approximately one-third of their agricultural land in Hokkaidō.

The continuance of discrimination and prejudice against Ainu prompted the Hokkaidō Ainu Association to alter its name to the Hokkaidō Utari Association to avoid the negative image of the Ainu label (*utari* in the Ainu language means comrades, intimates, and kin). Against the backdrop of the rise of ethnic consciousness around the world since the late 1960s, Ainu groups became involved in international exchanges with ethnic minority groups in similar plights in other countries, including North American Indians and Eskimos. In 1994, the Year of Indigenous Peoples, Ainu groups organized an international conference in Nibutani in Hokkaidō, paving the way for increased international exchanges between such groups.

In its 1984 general assembly, the Hokkaidō Utari Association called for the abolition of the former Savage Natives Law, adopted a document entitled "A Proposed Ainu Law," and demanded its passage as legislation at the national level. This historic charter urged the Japanese public to recognize the existence of the Ainu ethnic community and its distinctive culture within Japan. The paper also pressed for respect for the ethnic dignity and rights of the Ainu population.

The Japanese government has not yet recognized the Ainu as an indigenous people of Japan, or given them the level of financial and moral support indigenous peoples receive in other industrialized societies. Ainu activists take the view that government reluctance is attributable to the fear that it would not have a leg to stand on against their land claims.[32] However, an Ainu representative who ran on a socialist ticket gained a seat in the Upper House of the Japanese parliament in 1994 – the first Ainu to do so – and made a speech there partly in the Ainu language. While few high-school social studies and history textbooks give an account of the contemporary life of the Ainu,[33] their voices at the parliamentary level have both made them visible to the Japanese public and given some hope for its better understanding of Ainu issues.

VI Immigrant Workers from Overseas

Foreigners resident in Japan increased dramatically in the 1980s and early 1990s. An influx of workers from the Philippines, China, Brazil, Peru, Thailand, and other developing countries boosted the total number of foreign residents in Japan to over 1.32 million in 1993, more than 1 percent of the total population,[34] including long-term Korean and Chinese residents. In addition, more than three hundred thousand undocumented foreign workers are believed to be working in the margin of the Japanese economy. This situation has produced a significant diversification in the composition of the foreign population, with new migrants forming the fourth minority group in Japan.

The unprecedented flow of foreign workers into Japan stemmed from the situations in both the domestic and foreign labor markets. "Pull" factors within Japan included the ageing of the Japanese workforce and the accompanying shortage of labor in unskilled, manual, and physically demanding areas. In addition, the changing work ethic of Japanese youth has made it difficult for employers to recruit them for this type of work, which is described in terms of the three undesirable Ks (or Ds in English): *kitanai* (dirty), *kitsui* (difficult), and *kiken* (dangerous). Under these circumstances, a number of employers found illegal migrants, in particular from Asia, a remedy for their labor shortage.

The overwhelming majority of employers who hire foreign workers are themselves on the bottom rung of the subcontracting pyramid in construction and manufacturing, or are in the most financially shaky sectors of the service industry. These employers generally manage very petty businesses which involve late-night or early-morning work, and which must weather economic fluctuations at the lowest level of the occupational hierarchy. Male immigrants who work as construction laborers usually perform heavy work at construction sites. Most of those who are employed in manufacturing work in metal fabrication, operate presses and stamping machinery, make car parts, or work for printers and binders. In the service sector, migrant workers are employed in restaurants and other establishments to do much of the dirty work.[35] Many female foreign workers are hired as bar hostesses, stripteasers, and sex-industry workers. Without Japanese language skills and knowledge of Japanese culture, these new immigrants form the most marginalized cluster within the marginalized population in Japan.

The influx of undocumented foreign workers has led to unfounded fear in the public that they are potential criminals contaminating an allegedly safe, crime-free society. Media tend to play up crimes committed by foreigners, fueling xenophobic apprehensions in the community. Considerable evidence suggests that crime statistics on foreigners in Japan are distorted and inflated.[36] Yet the Japanese authorities tightened the Immigration Law in 1990 and made employers of undocumented foreign workers liable for up to three years' imprisonment or a maximum fine of two million yen. These workers have difficulty in accessing legal means, and the tightened police control has compelled some of them to go "underground" and enabled Japan's criminal and semi-criminal elements to manipulate them more easily.

The Ministry of Justice instituted special treatment for the descendants of overseas Japanese, allowing second- and third-generation Japanese from foreign countries to work as residents in Japan regardless of skill level. Consequently, the number of young Japanese Brazilians, for instance, has increased drastically in Aichi, Kanagawa, and Shizuoka prefectures where the car plants of Toyota, Nissan, Suzuki, and Honda operate. Observers attribute the preferential treatment of Japanese offspring to the Japanese authorities' belief that those of Japanese extraction are more dependable, trustworthy, and earnest than other foreigners.

In addition, a program to train foreign workers in Japanese firms was established. It was supposed to provide foreign workers with residence permits and enable them to learn techniques and skills and to gain experience which they would use in their home countries. For many small firms suffering labor shortages, the trainee program serves as a practical way of recruiting cheap labor, because of ambiguities regarding the distinction between real training and disguised labor. For large multinational corporations with plants overseas, the program is a way to train future core employees for their branch firms and solve their labor problems within Japan.[37]

Two stances compete regarding the ways in which Japan should accept non-Japanese as part of the nation. One position contends that the country should admit only skilled workers, already well-educated and well-trained in their home countries. Underlying this argument is the obvious concern that unskilled workers will lower the standard of Japan's workforce, and that the nation will have to bear the cost of their training and acquisition of skills. There is also tacit fear that, uneducated and undisciplined, they may "contaminate" Japanese society, leading to its destabilization and disintegration.

The opposing position, which argues for the acceptance of unskilled workers, is partly based on the pragmatic consideration that the Japanese economy simply cannot survive without unskilled foreign workers filling the lowest segment of the nation's labor force. The pro-acceptance position also maintains that how Japan addresses its minority issues will perhaps prove the most critical test of its globalization; the nation can hardly claim to have a cosmopolitan orientation while it fails to accept ethnic and racial diversity within.[38]

The notion of internationalization propels some segments of the Japanese population toward more open, universalistic and global orientations. A considerable number of citizens' groups devote themselves to assisting and protecting foreign residents in Japan. Across the country many individuals of various ages attend study sessions on Japan's ethnic issues, perform voluntary work in support of workers from overseas, and participate in political rallies for the human rights of minority groups.

With the international collapse of Cold War structures and the domestic realignment of labor union organizations, minority movements too have shifted their ideological framework away from the orthodox model of class struggle in which links with the working class were given prime importance. Instead, minority-group activists have moved towards international cooperation with ethnic and other minority groups abroad.[39]

There is perhaps much truth in minority groups' claims that their problems are the product of distortion and prejudice on the part of a majority of Japanese. Until 1995 Japan was among the few nations which had not ratified the International Convention on the Elimination of All Forms of Racial Discrimination, which the United Nations brought into effect in 1969. Even after ratification, the Ministry of Foreign Affairs does not consider the buraku discrimination problem as an area covered by the Convention, on the grounds that it is not a racial issue. Challenging this view, buraku liberation movements argue that their minority status derives from community prejudice based upon lineage or pedigree, precisely the realm of discrimination which the Convention attempts to eliminate. Japan's peculiarity lies not in its freedom from minority problems, but in its lack of recognition and admission that it has such problems.

VII Japan *Beyond* Japan

The globalization of Japanese society has produced considerable numbers of three types of Japanese who live *beyond* Japan's national boundary. The first of these are Japanese business people and their families who are stationed abroad to manage company business under the direction of corporate headquarters in Japan. With ample financial backing from their head office, these Japanese nationals enjoy lavish lifestyles far above those of the middle class of their country of residence. In most cases, they live in residences larger than their houses in Japan and relish the good living which the strong yen allows them. Since their lives are tied to Japanese corporate and state interests, their notion of internationalization is often coupled with a concern to maintain smooth business relations with foreign countries and foreign nationals, to conduct peaceful diplomatic negotiations, and to present abroad favorable images of Japanese society. To that extent, the *tatemae* of internationalization advocated by these overseas business representatives is tinged with the *honne* of nationalism.

The second type comprises Japanese citizens who choose of their own volition to live overseas semi-permanently. Many are "refugees from Japan" who have expatriated themselves from the corporate world, the education system, or the community structure of Japanese society.[40] These people differ from previous Japanese emigrants who fled economic hardship. The new breed of emigrants attempt to establish themselves abroad to escape what they regard as Japan's rigid social system. They find satisfaction in living beyond the confines of the *uchi* world of Japan and interacting with the *soto* world in a liberated fashion. By and large, the new "life-style emigrants" intend to stay in the country of their choice for a reasonably long period, though they may not plan to settle there permanently.[41] They have one foot outside and the other inside Japan, and endeavor to find some balance between the two worlds. To that extent they live cross-culturally. Some go as far as to savor the pleasure of "cultural schizophrenia". Others choose to forfeit Japanese citizenship and become non-Japanese nationals.

The third type consists of an increasing number of foreigners who have acquired fluency in the Japanese language and are "Japan literate," being capable of understanding not only the *omote* side of Japanese society but the *ura* side as well. These people are Japanese linguistically and culturally. Their subculture provides a significant input to Japanese society.

With an increasing number of Japanese going beyond Japan's geographical boundaries and more foreigners entering Japan, there is no single answer to the vexed questions of who the Japanese are and what Japanese culture is. While conventional analysis of the Japanese and Japanese culture focusses upon the comparison between "straight Japanese" and "straight foreigners," knowledge of globalized Japan will not improve without thorough investigation into the mixed categories, some of which Table 7.2 displays.[42] Japan *beyond* Japan sensitizes one to the viability of conceiving of Japanese society both inside and outside the Japanese archipelago.

Notes

1   Oguma 1995 presents a detailed analysis of how Japan's cultural elites have formulated and propagated this thesis.
2   Conscious of the extent of support for racist ideology of this type, the Japanese establishment has often resorted to the argument that mono-ethnic Japanese society has no tradition of accepting outsiders. Exploiting this, the government accepted only a small fraction of refugees from Vietnam and other areas of Indochina into Japan in the 1970s and 1980s, although the nation had brought millions of Koreans and Chinese into Japan as cheap labor before and during World War II. The ideology of mono-ethnic Japan is invoked or abandoned according to what is expedient for the interest groups involved in public debate.
3   Tsurumi 1987.

4 Kawamura 1980.
5 Russell 1991a and 1991b.
6 See Russell 1991b for the interpretation of this statement in a wider context.
7 *Sankei Shinbun*, December 19 1987, morning edition, p. 1.
8 MM August 4 1988, p. 5; *Shūkan Gendai* September 3 1988, p. 44.
9 See Russell 1991b.
10 At the community level, racist sentiment is manifest in everyday situations. For instance, foreigners with obviously non-Japanese physical complexions apparently pique the curiosity of many Japanese. Some Japanese, particularly in the countryside, stare rudely at them in streetcars, subways, parks, and shops. In the street children often are to be seen pointing their fingers at passing foreigners, chanting "*gaijin, gaijin* (foreigner, foreigner)," and shouting a few simple English words such as "hello" and "please." While ill-mannered, this type of behavior is perhaps not so much ill-intentioned as reflective of the extent to which the ideology of mono-racial, mono-ethnic Japan has penetrated into the psyche of the Japanese at grassroots level.
11 For example, the conceptual boundary of the Japanese race remains an unresolved question, though this table relies on the conventional racial classification. Language fluency is also a variable. Here it is defined as native or near-native competency in Japanese.
12 The following discussion follows Sugimoto and Mouer 1995, pp. 296–7; Mouer and Sugimoto 1995, pp. 7–8.
13 Buraku Kaihō Kenkyūsho 1988.
14 Buraku Kaihō Kenkyūsho 1992, p. 2.
15 A widespread myth is that burakumin are ethnically different from majority Japanese. A version of this fiction insinuates that the ancestors of burakumin came from Korea, an account that reflects Japanese prejudice against Koreans.
16 A 1985 survey of 9,164 couples resident in buraku communities, conducted by the Prime Minister's Office.
17 Buraku Kaihō Kenkyūsho 1988, pp. 142–3. AM May 21 1996, p. 30.
18 Buraku Kaihō Kenkyūsho 1992, p. 90.
19 Ikeda 1987.
20 Osaka-fu Kagaku Kyōiku Center's study (1974–82) reported in Ikeda 1987.
21 As a consequence of these attempts to correct discriminatory language, self-discipline by major cultural organizations has often verged upon self-censorship. Some novelists, comic writers, and popular magazines voice concern over what they regard as the minority groups' nitpicking and witch-hunting tendencies. These critics maintain that minority charges regarding "language correctness" have become so excessive and trivial that they now put freedom of expression in jeopardy. Some complain that they cannot use even such expressions as "blind" and "one-handed" for fear of being accused of prejudice towards the physically disadvantaged. Others complain that the language correctness argument suppresses various forms of humorous or comic conversation and writing. Countering these arguments, activists and representatives of minority groups maintain that freedom of expression exists not to defend the powerful and the status quo but to bolster the human rights of the weak and the deprived.
22 Min 1994, pp. 337–8; AM July 28 1994, p. 2.
23 A study of the attitude of real estate agencies in Osaka on this issue revealed that 48 percent made it a rule to reject non-Japanese applicants on the grounds of nationality (AE, Osaka edition, February 22 1990, p. 14).

24 Tanaka 1991, pp. 164–6.
25 Min 1994, pp. 253–64.
26 Min 1994, p. 272.
27 The discussion here is based on Fukuoka 1993, pp. 89–107.
28 This group (Type A) is cautious about the movement of the multiculturalist group (Type C) that demands voting rights for Koreans and other foreigners in Japan. Type A Koreans tend to regard such a move as assimilationist.
29 Hokkaidō-chō 1988.
30 There are a number of place names of Ainu origin in the eastern and northern parts of Honshū island. This is testimony to the fact that the Ainu lived in these areas in ancient Japan and a reminder that Japanese military power pushed the Ainu to the north after a series of military conquests.
31 Emori 1987, p. 219. None of the major English-language textbooks on Japanese society (Nakane 1970, Reischauer 1978 and Fukutake 1981) refer to the Ainu.
32 AM January 3 1993, p. 3.
33 AM December 21 1993, p. 29.
34 MM June 12 1994, p. 26.
35 Komai 1990; Ballescas 1992.
36 Herbert 1996.
37 Komai 1992.
38 See Komai 1995.
39 AM March 5 1994, p.3.
40 Sugimoto 1993, pp. 73–85.
41 Satō 1993.
42 On this point, see Mouer and Sugimoto 1995, p. 31; Mori 1993, p. 250.

8

Collusion and Competition
in the Establishment

Japan's establishment comprises three sectors – big business, parliament, and the national bureaucracy – which some commentators say are at a three-way deadlock. The economic sphere overseen by the leaders of big corporations is subordinate to the public bureaucracy which controls the private sector through its power to license companies, regulate their activities, and decide upon the implementation of publicly funded projects. However, officials in the bureaucracy are subservient to legislators, especially those of the governing parties, who decide upon the bills that bureaucrats prepare for the National Diet and whose ranks many officials join after they have climbed to a certain career level. Politicians, in turn, remain submissive to the leaders of the private sector because they require pecuniary contributions to individual and party coffers to maintain their political machines. Figure 8.1 summarizes mutual dependence and competition among these three power blocs at the helm of Japanese society.

The three-way structure of Japan's establishment resembles the tripartism of politics, business, and labor which collectively coordinate the policy-making process in some European and Australasian countries. However, the Japanese pattern is characterized by the conspicuous absence of labor union representatives. While the largest national labor confederation, *Rengō*, has some influence upon the state decision-making process, its level of representation is hardly comparable to that of union organizations in other countries. The public bureaucracy enjoys strong influence over both the economy and the politics of the entire nation.

Since chapter 4 has examined the operation of the business community, this chapter focusses upon the bureaucracy and Japan's political circles, touching upon the business world only when relevant and in terms of its relations to the other two power centers. The discussion also

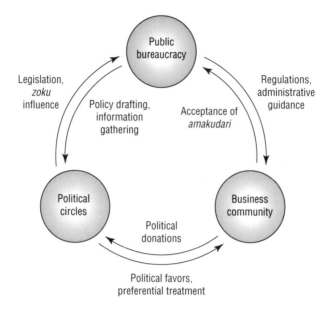

Figure 8.1 Three-way rivalry among power centers

covers some aspects of establishment media, both print and electronic, which have significant influence over the formation of public opinion.

I Dominance of the Public Bureaucracy

It is widely acknowledged that the state, particularly the government bureaucracy, holds supreme authority over private-sector companies in Japan. Throughout Japan's industrialization, the central government was the engine of economic transformation. To optimize this process the national bureaucracy has recruited talented university graduates as career officials chosen for management ability and provided with high prestige and official status. Able, dedicated, and often arrogant, these bureaucrats are believed by many to be the real power-holders in the nation. The perception is consistent with some state practices relating to the private sector. Government ministries hold the power of licensing, permitting, authorizing, and approving a wide range of production, distribution, and sales activities, thereby regulating the private sector even in trivial details. Furthermore, without statutory grounding, public officials are empowered to provide relevant companies in the private sector with administrative guidance (*gyōsei shidō*) on levels of production, pricing, and quantities of imports and exports, in the name of national interests. Career bureaucrats often retire from officialdom in the late stages of their careers to take up executive positions in large corporations, a practice referred to as *amakudari* (landing from heaven). These three conventions exemplify the power and privilege of elite bureaucrats in Japan.

1 Control and Regulation

The public bureaucracy imposes legal controls on institutions and individuals in any society. Japanese officialdom, however, stands out in several respects.

(a) Degree of Control

The Japanese bureaucracy exercises control over an extremely wide range of activities. It regulates more than ten thousand areas of economic activity, corresponding to about 40 percent of the gross national product.[1] National government ministries can restrict the number of producers and stores in certain spheres, and control the prices and shapes of some commodities. Regulation extends to individual lives. The Ministry of Transport requires car owners to have their cars inspected annually. Because the inspection covers dozens of items, car owners must normally rely upon the expensive and often excessive services of private car-inspection firms which the Ministry designates.

(b) Jurisdictional Sectionalism

Ministries compete with each other to maximize their spheres of regulation. Because different ministries try to place their domains of influence under their own jurisdiction, national economic activity is partitioned along ministry lines. Jurisdictional sectionalism impedes communication between different ministries and thwarts coordination.

In center-region relationships, the corresponding departments of prefectural and municipal governments serve as the local arms of national ministries, which delegate nationally funded projects to them while attempting to control them from above. Since prefectural and municipal governments have only limited rights to impose taxation, they must rely upon subsidies from the national government. This provides national bureaucrats with the power to oversee and influence local governments. Furthermore, national career officials are routinely sent from their base ministry to serve terms in key posts in prefectures and municipalities. The Ministry of Construction, for example, may dispatch elite-track officials to head the civil engineering department of a major city. The Ministry of Agriculture, Forestry, and Fisheries might regularly fill a post in the livestock industry division of a prefecture with a career ministry bureaucrat. Most of these officials move between the two spheres of government several times as part of the promotion process. This vertically partitioned structure of sectionalism intensifies inter-ministerial competition and makes bureacrats obsessed with their departmental vested interests.

(c) Partitioned Free Market

Ministries wield immense, informal power in regulating the entry of new corporate players into the market. Each ministry places the utmost importance on the maintenance of stable, long-term relationships between itself and the industries under its jurisdiction. This means that a ministry tends to see the admission of a new element into its field as potentially destabilizing. Thus, for example, with numerous, strict rules regulating the establishment of banking institutions, no new city banks have been established since 1953, though mergers and realignments have taken place. However, once companies are admitted into the regulated sphere, the government normally attempts to ensure that uniform rules apply without prejudice. As long as companies abide by the rules, the public bureaucracy is inclined to be non-interventionist and ensure so-called free market competition.[2]

2 Amakudari

The bureaucracy's power of regulation is linked with the ways in which elite officials secure posts in public corporations and private companies when their official careers have ended. High-ranking bureaucrats normally find executive positions in semi-government or private enterprises in the industry which they used to supervise. This practice is known as *amakudari*, "descent from heaven" appointment, which gives rise to collusive links between official circles and large companies.

The career track of elite bureaucrats has several phases. Initially, university students who aspire to the national public bureaucracy must pass a national examination before applying for admission to a particular ministry. The examination, which covers a range of subjects including some areas of law, is highly competitive, and the majority of successful applicants are from Tokyo University. For career bureaucrats selected in this way, year of entry to the ministry constitutes a prime index of promotion. Though they move across different sections and departments during their career, those who joined in the same year are promoted to positions at more or less the same level. However, because higher posts are fewer, a certain number must drop out of the race every year, and this elimination process continues until someone gets the position of bureaucratic vice-minister, the highest position in a ministerial hierarchy. Officials eliminated in this process must retire from the ministry and find a job outside government through the *amakudari* arrangement.

The business world finds it beneficial to have ex-bureaucrats in upper managerial positions because they have in-depth knowledge of, and personal networks within, the powerful national officialdom. The Japan Shipbuilding Industry Association, for instance, routinely imports high-ranking officials of the Ministry of Transport to fill its top positions. The Japan Association of Pharmaceutical Organizations makes it a rule to have former officials of the Ministry of Health and Welfare as its leaders. These "old boys" are valuable assets for an industry; through them the business world can maneuver officialdom into the directions it prefers. The other side of the coin is that the "young boys" in the bureaucracy know that they will be likely to end up occupying important positions in the corporate world, so see no harm in developing and maintaining congenial relations with representatives of the business world.

These posts assure former bureaucrats of high incomes, authority, and prestige in their fifties and sixties. According to a survey of the situation in 1991,[3] ex-bureaucrats occupy 71.2 percent of a total of 354 executive posts in sixty-one government corporations, such as the Japan Highway Public Corporation, the Smaller Business Finance Corporation, and the Japan International Cooperation Agency. Many former officials move from one corporation to another, collecting large retirement allowances. In the decade up to 1991, about two-thirds of the former Ministry of Finance officials who "descended from heaven" found jobs in financial institutions in the private sector, in securities companies, banks, credit unions, and so on. Most of the ex-officials were in executive positions and a considerable number were in charge of internal audit and inspection. Given that the financial sector provides employment for retired bureaucrats, it comes as no surprise that the Ministry of Finance often dithers about implementing a full investigation into financial scandals involving banking institutions in the private sector. This environment gives rise to a back-scratching alliance between the national bureaucracy and the business community.[4]

Politics is another significant career route for high-ranking bureaucrats who leave the public service. Some go into national politics by standing as candidates for parliament. More than a third of prime ministers after the end of World War II were ex-bureaucrats. Others end up winning governorships in prefectures.[5] The Ministry of Home Affairs is a breeding ground for top local politicians. Seconded to a prefectural government as section or department head from the Ministry during their career, many national bureaucrats cultivate ties in the political and business networks in the region and act as a pipeline between the locality and the national center. Some of these career officials are chosen for vice-governorship and make preparations for future gubernatorial elections. Such strong influence in prefectural politics stems in part from the prewar practice where governors were appointed by the national government, not elected by popular vote. In recent years, candidates for gubernatorial and mayoral elections are often chosen by a group of major political parties after horse-trading among themselves. The inter-party collusion tends to favor candidates who have high technocratic skills and no direct prior party affiliations, a condition which national elite bureaucrats tend to satisfy.

3 Administrative Guidance

The practice of administrative guidance (*gyosei shidō*) provides another illustration of the power of the national bureaucracy over the business world. Both institutionalized and amorphous, the practice takes the form of a ministry giving advice, suggestions, instructions, and warnings to business confederations; these are without statutory basis and are frequently made behind closed doors without written records being kept. In the absence of firm documentation, outsiders have virtually no means of acquiring detailed information concerning it.[6]

The business world is often a willing partner to administrative guidance and benefits from it. The practice leaves the task of coordinating competing interests in the business world to the overseeing ministry, thereby minimizing the cost of such activities to the private sector.[7] Making use of the third-party mediation expertise of the public bureaucracy, the business community can rely on administrative guidance to inexpensively resolve its internal disagreements.

Moreover, many managing directors and other key figures in major industrial associations are themselves ex-bureaucrats. They have landed from heaven and been hired by industry to deal with the bureaucrats offering administrative guidance. Although administrative guidance has the appearance of bureaucracy instructing the private sector, it is often the case that officials and business representatives have thrashed out the substance of guidelines before they are officially proposed. In these instances, the industrial world, as the object of ministerial guidance, is involved in its formulation and therefore becomes the source of guidance to itself.[8] Collaborations of this kind raise the question of who in fact determines the content of administrative guidance.

On the whole, administrative guidance and other forms of government intervention rely on manipulation rather than coercion. To impose their recommendations and advice, government ministries dangle such carrots as preferential treatment with regard to taxation and finance, public works contracts, and government subsidies. Since companies must obtain authorization for licenses and registration from ministries, ministries can use this power to induce businesses to comply with ministerial policies. Because administrative guidance has no statutory basis, the government has little scope for resorting to coercion.

Regulation, *amakudari*, and administrative guidance enable national bureaucratic elites to manage the state with enormous privilege and to run the economy with long-term planning of a bureaucratic nature. The webs of influence they weave are so extensive and entrenched that they are unwilling to abandon their vested interests even though politicians repeatedly attempt to implement administrative reform programs to downsize the bureaucracy. By definition, bureaucrats' positions are hardly affected by election outcomes. A change in government does not result in changes in the occupants of bureaucratic posts whose own rules and conventions govern their promotions, transfers, and retirements, with only a very limited number of cases of intervention by politicians. Neither subject to popular elections nor responsive to changes in parliamentary situations, national bureaucratic elites operate in an empire of their own, far from being "public servants."

II Parliamentarians and Money Politics

The conservative Liberal Democratic Party held government for nearly four decades until the middle of 1993 when it lost its parliamentary majority after a series of graft cases had revealed the extent of corruption in the party. The collapse of LDP rule ushered in a period of political realignment and instability. Initially, a new coalition of eight political groupings was formed under the leadership of conservatives who had defected from the LDP. Then came a grand alliance between the LDP and the Social Democratic Party of Japan, the largest parliamentary opposition party for forty years. The SDPJ gained the prime ministership, while abandoning almost all its previous ideological positions in exchange. In early 1996, three major political formations competed with each other. Two of these power blocs were made up of conservatives, one mainly of LDP politicians with the conventional power base of business and agrarian interests, and the other of ex-LDP neo-conservative reformists centering on the New Frontier Party (*Shinshintō*), with a similar power base. The third bloc comprised the so-called social democratic liberals, who include socialists and some reform-minded politicians inclined to press for social equity and the maintenance of the constitution, and who are concerned about conservative dominance in Japanese politics.

However, the political style of the LDP, which governed uninterrupted for so long, has left a lasting mark upon Japanese politics. Despite the changes in government, the fundamental features of Japanese politics have not altered.

1 Heavy Reliance on the Bureaucracy

Japanese parliamentarians rarely draw up their own bills for considera-tion in the Diet. Public bureaucrats draft, formulate, and finalize an over-whelming majority of bills, which the Cabinet submits to the legislative body. By and large, the bureaucracy is the virtual legislation-maker of the nation, and the Diet simply endorses or rejects the proposed laws pre-pared by bureaucrats. Some observers even suggest that bureaucrats determine 80–90 percent of each policy proposed and politicians the rest.[9]

The Fiscal Investments and Loans Program (zaisei tōyūshi keikaku) best exemplifies the dominance of bureaucratic executive power. The pro-gram relies upon funds raised through such government channels as postal savings, postal life insurance, welfare annuity insurance, and national pension systems. Through the Development Bank, Export and Import Bank, and various public finance corporations, government ministries provide low-interest loans to a wide range of priority areas in housing, construction, small business, education, key industries, local development, transportation and communication, trade and economic cooperation, and so forth. The program, which observers call the "second budget," amounts to one-third of the national budget, and much of it does not require parliamentary approval. Figure 8.2 displays the flow of the FILP.

Interest-group lobbyists consider the executive branch of government the most crucial political target, with the legislative branch nearly as important, and the judicial branch almost insignificant.[10] On the whole, business and agricultural organizations, most of which have well-established links with the policy-making processes, tend to direct their demands towards the public bureaucracy in order to maximize their chances of influencing policy formation. Even when they approach politicians and political parties, their final target remains the decision-making process within the bureaucracy. A national survey indicates that, while only 71 percent of organizations approached politicians for consultation and solicitation, 97 percent approached bureaucrats for the same purposes.[11] With frequent changes in government and intensified

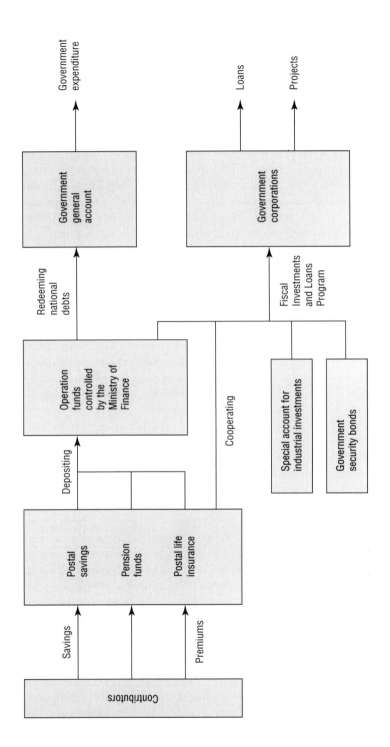

Figure 8.2 The flow of the Fiscal Investments and Loans Program
Source: Adapted from AM December 17 1993, p. 4.

competition between parliamentary parties, the national bureaucracy remains stable and consolidates its power over daily policy formulation.

2 Investment-driven Development and Zoku Politics

Successive conservative governments adopted the strategy of giving priority to industrial and technological development, at the expense of social welfare. The dearth of welfare programs induced households to save as much as possible to prepare for post-retirement life, and to ready themselves for rising costs in education and housing. Depositors directed their savings not only to commercial banks but to the colossal governmental postal savings system, which attracts a large number of depositors because its interest rate is higher than those of private banks. The industrial policy-makers invest the postal savings funds in target industries and enterprises. The key mechanism for this process is the FILP, through which the government can support selected areas of development for what it regards as national interests.

Such a heavy emphasis on investment-driven development paved the way for "money politics." In return for electoral support, members of parliament are expected to bring government-supported construction projects, railways, and trunk roads into their constituencies and expand their *jiban* (solid blocs of voters) buttressed by supporters' associations for politicians (*kōenkai*), which play a dual role. On one hand, the associations function as election committees. On the other, they act as informal grassroots units for distributing the benefits their parliamentarians have acquired for them.

Against this background, an increasing number of politicians, especially LDP parliamentarians, have become so-called *zoku* parliamentarians who represent special interest groups and exercise much political influence over the process of governmental and bureaucratic policy formulation. They have specialist knowledge of particular sectors of the economy: agriculture, construction, commerce, telecommunications, transport, or education. In return for serving as spokespersons of particular interest groups and swaying the law-making process in their favor, these politicians secure enduring financial support bases in influential business communities. This mutual support structure has consolidated the vast foundations of the LDP's hold on government power. Most of the recent prime ministers have acted as *zoku* politicians to rise in the LDP ranks and to expand their spheres of influence within the party hierarchy.[12]

The Ministry of International Trade and Industry sits at the hub of the political–industrial–bureaucratic complex of industrial policy formation. Because the Ministry has the power to grant and reject licenses and the authority to offer administrative guidance to the private sector, politicians attempt to influence its decision-making process for the benefit of corporate contributors to their political funds. In turn, they expect those beneficiaries to make continued and increasing donations to their political coffers.

Undoubtedly, their financial transactions put *zoku* politicians in precarious situations. In order to protect themselves against possible legal complications, they often have private secretaries deal with any pecuniary matters. These aides do not normally formulate policies or draft bills. Instead, they spend much time receiving and entertaining local bureaucrats, business people and other lobbyists who visit Tokyo to entreat their parliamentary representative for political assistance. The secretaries also frequently use their position to find employment or arrange introductions to influential people for children and relatives of voters in their master's constituency. Beneficiaries are expected to return these favors during elections.

3 Corruption and Electoral Reform

Many consider the source of political corruption in Japan to be partly the electoral system. After the collapse of the LDP government, the first act of the new coalition government was sweeping electoral reform. In the past, there were many multiple member constituencies in which two or more MPs were elected. This intensified the tradition of vote buying. Under this system, each political party had to calculate how many candidates it should field in those constituencies; if it put up too many candidates all of them might lose; if too few, some candidates might receive far more votes than necessary for successful election. This calculation exacerbated intraparty competition for party endorsement. For winning party nomination to candidacy, the size of a candidate's *jiban* is the prime determinant. To extend their *jiban*, candidates need extensive financial support from their faction bosses, who in turn look to business circles for political donations.

The national electoral system was revised in the legislation enacted in 1994 in a bid to remove the multi-seat constituency system. The new law provides that five hundred parliamentarians constitute the House of Representatives, three hundred of whom are elected from single-seat constituencies. With the nation being divided into eleven separate regional blocs, the remaining two hundred members are chosen by the regional proportional representation system where voters cast their votes for the political parties of their preference. All political parties nominate and rank-order their candidates, successful candidates being elected on the basis of their party's share of total votes.

The new electoral system prohibits individual politicians from receiving political donations personally. Each politician can establish a single fund-management organization to which enterprises, groups, and individuals can donate up to half a million yen per annum. Each political party is entitled to receive an annual grant-in-aid from public coffers. The amount which a party is granted depends upon its number of elected national parliamentarians and votes received in the previous national election. Furthermore, the guilt-by-association system has been strengthened so that, when the chief campaign manager, campaign treasurer, and other electoral leaders are arrested and found guilty of election irregularities, the elected politician is supposed to be forced from office.

While the new electoral system was established as part of the reform package to put an end to gerrymandering, the discrepancy in the value of votes between the least populated area (the third district of Shimane prefecture) and some sixty populous electoral districts (20 percent of all districts) is still greater than two to one,[13] the maximum allowable disparity in the judgment of the Supreme Court.

Moreover, the reform does not apply to the House of Councilors, the upper house composed of 252 members whose term of office is six years, half of the seats being up for election every three years. While one hundred seats are allocated to councilors elected through the national proportional representation system, the remaining seats are filled by local representatives voted in through the conventional multi-member constituency system.

4 The Social Basis of Corruption

Pecuniary scandals rife at the highest levels of the Japanese political hierarchy reflect the popular practice of gift-giving on private occasions. Gift-giving is regarded as an expression of intimacy and affection. This social custom sometimes blurs the line between illegal acts and accepted informal exchanges. For many Japanese it is an established custom to bring a gift when making a visit. Formal gift-giving is an institutionalized practice in summer and winter.[14] Gifts and gift certificates are sent, either directly or through department stores and shops, to acquaintances, friends, and relatives as *chūgen* in the middle and as *seibo* at the end of each year. Taking advantage of this convention, those who wish to acknowledge, or who seek, a favor from superiors or business connections send expensive presents to them.

Cash gifts are normal on ceremonial occasions. At marriage receptions, well-wishers are expected to donate the yen equivalent of a few hundred dollars to the marrying couple as an expression of congratulations. That family keeps meticulous records of who gave, and returns in kind a few weeks later. At funerals, mourners usually make monetary offerings to the family of the deceased. A majority of employees in large corporations find it socially necessary to make sizeable cash gifts of congratulation and condolence not only to members of their own families but also to senior and junior company colleagues. On New Year's Day, children collect monetary gifts from parents, relatives, and other adults. In temples and shrines, the names of large donors and the amounts of their gifts are listed conspicuously.

In this environment, it is accepted that powerful individuals make lavish cash contributions on such occasions as wedding ceremonies, funerals, and community festivals.[15] To maintain the continuing support of their electorate, politicians require a constant flow of cash. Surveys[16] show that funds legally received by legislators do not cover the costs of operating their offices. On average, they rely upon corporate donations for approximately 40 percent of their office incomes. They manage 1.3 offices in Tokyo and 3.1 in their own constituencies, hire 13.1 secretaries, attend seventy-nine wedding ceremonies per annum, 318 funerals, and about one hundred New Year and year-ending functions.

When conclusively tainted, politicians often resign from ministerial posts and party positions but rarely quit the Diet or leave politics. The object of resigning is to seek and obtain sympathetic indulgence. In most areas, pragmatic judgments override ethical considerations, and the electorate usually re-elects disgraced politicians. The re-elected parliamentarians then resort to Shintoist metaphors and claim that re-election implies the completion of the purification ceremony for their past blemish. Since they have performed absolutions, they maintain that they are qualified to make a fresh start. Using this type of logic, all the discredited prime ministers of the 1980s, including Nakasone and Takeshita, have made successful comebacks as powerbrokers in national politics. To some degree, such community tolerance reflects the daily reality of electors who themselves see nothing wrong in seeking favors by giving expensive gifts to those who may aid them. The practice of those at the helm of the establishment corresponds with the social habits of many people at the grassroots.

III Pluralistic Competition

While patterns of collusion and control figure in the relations between the three pillars of the Japanese establishment, these relations are also characterized by competition and confrontation. In view of the conspicuous dominance of the national bureaucracy, three areas of challenge within the establishment structure deserve particular attention. The first is the way in which the business world fights against bureaucratic regulation. The second is the degree to which politicians attempt to streamline the bureaucracy and government corporations, and the third is the extent to which local governments contest the national power of the central bureaucracy.

1 The Business Community's Push for Deregulation

The interests of most sections of business circles conflict with the regulatory power of the bureaucracy. Concerned for the efficient operation of their business ventures, private enterprises increasingly find its intervention frustrating as their activities become diversified, more sophisticated, and multinational. These circumstances contrast with the past where the Japanese business world needed national coordination to make a comeback from World War II and to establish an export-orientated high-growth economy. The obstructive nature of bureaucratic regulation has become more evident in the 1990s with the prolonged recession, the appreciation of the yen, and the increased domestic demand for relatively cheap imported goods. Furthermore, the multinationalization of Japanese corporations poses a threat to the system of government intervention, inasmuch as the national bureaucracy finds it difficult to oversee off-shore operations. As corporate Japan expands beyond national boundaries and embraces much more than geographical Japan, it is inevitable that powerful business groups press for deregulation.

However, while supporting the *tatemae* of deregulation, some industries are reluctant to facilitate it at the *honne* level, to protect their vested interests. Agricultural organizations which have much political clout make every attempt to defend Japan's uncompetitive agriculture. Some wholesale, retail, and other distribution outlets which have complicated *uchi* networks resist the participation of newcomers from outside. Many construction companies which have enjoyed a number of collusive arrangements have concerns about opening the market to outsiders who do not know much about the *ura* side of the industry.

Yet four dominant national centers for corporate interests are united in demanding speedy deregulation, though they differ in their internal composition. The *Keidanren* (Federation of Economic Organizations) acts as the public face of the business community and wields considerable power as the central body which collects political donations from business. The leaders of the manufacturing industries are the elite of the Federation. The *Nisshō* (Japan Chamber of Commerce and Industry) represents nearly five hundred chambers of commerce and industry in major cities across the nation, and therefore to a considerable extent reflects the interests of small businesses. The *Nikkeiren* (Japan Association of Employer Organizations) focusses its activity upon industrial relations and acts as a principal body to strengthen employer solidarity against unions. Finally, the *Keizai Dōyūkai* (Business Friendship Society) draws its membership from individual business people and aims to assess the national economy from a broad perspective without directly dealing with the specific interests of particular sectors or industries. While these four major organizations remain separate, each performing different functions, there is overlap in their leadership. The big four have on occasion issued joint statements on crucial national issues. For instance, in 1960 they collectively denounced nationwide demonstrations over the ratification of the security treaty between the United States and Japan. At time of the oil crisis in 1974, the four organizations warned the business community against taking advantage of opportunistic price rises. During the 1984 budget compilation, they opposed an increase in corporation tax and proposed a radical reduction in government expenditure. In the 1990s they collectively challenge the bureaucracy with a chorus of calls for deregulation.

2 Political Attempts at Administrative Reform

Politicians have made a series of attempts to curtail the public sector dominated by national officialdom and government corporations. Some administrative reforms in the 1980s proved relatively effective, with the successful privatization of the Japan National Railways, the Nippon Telegraphic and Telephone Corporation, Japan Tobacco Inc., and many other public enterprises.

However, ministries remain reluctant to abandon their vested interests, resisting and sabotaging various administrative reform programs. Specifically, government bureaucrats have frustrated politicians' undertakings to slim down government corporations, which are the major recipients of FILP funds under the direct control of the ministries. These corporations are managed mainly by *amakudari* officials who have landed from heaven. Some *zoku* politicians who have cultivated links with these corporations also dither about rationalizing their spheres of vested rights.

However, only two options are available to lessen the chronic deficit of national finance: an increase in government revenue and a reduction in government expenditure. In the late 1980s, the government introduced a sales tax, against strong public opposition, in an attempt to follow the first route. In the long run, the state machinery has little choice but to choose the second alternative, given that the first path would involve additional taxation measures which would be electorally unpopular. How far politicians can push administrative reform against the resistance of bureaucrats is a test of their relative power.

3 Local Politics Against the National Bureaucracy

Local governments in Japan have considerable autonomy in some areas in spite of Japan's highly centralized political and bureaucratic structure. Pluralistic competition exists between the central and local governments with the latter having two tiers: forty-seven prefectural governments, and within each prefecture, municipal governments of cities, towns, and villages. Muramatsu and other political scientists point out that this competition has several aspects.[17]

(a) Project Implementation

National ministries provide subsidies to prefectural and municipal governments and have the final decision-making power over crucial elements of their finance. However, every local government has its own regional demands and requirements and attempts to reflect them in the lobbying process. The central government does not uniformly impose its strategy upon local governments, which have the right to request and lobby for the subsidized projects they prefer. They have day-to-day know-how regarding a number of social welfare programs which are practically their business rather than that of the state. These programs include the establishment and operation of day-care centers, homes for the aged, public housing for the poor, and other welfare institutions. Unsatisfactory implementation of these programs sometimes means the loss of electoral support for local politicians, who thus have reason to press for their successful management and expansion. In most projects of this kind, significant input by local government into the process is inevitable, making it a two-way traffic between the state and localities. The central government formulates the general direction according to what it regards as the national interest; municipal governments implement the projects, and prefectural governments perform mediating functions.

(b) Routine Lobbying

Prefectural governors, municipal mayors, local legislators, and provincial business representatives visit Tokyo from time to time to negotiate with ministry bureaucrats to win as large a share as possible of the national government's budgetary and project allocations. Members of parliament who represent the constituencies of these lobby groups play vital roles in bringing political pressure to bear upon the decision-making process of ministries. Year in, year out, the prices at which agricultural producers sell rice to the national government are a matter for intense political negotiations. National parliamentarians from rural areas exercise great

influence as representatives of the agricultural community. On the
eve of national budget formulation, it is routine for a variety of local
lobbyists to fill the corridors of ministry buildings where national officials
hold a series of hearings with local representatives concerning their
situations.

(c) Inter-regional Competition

Ministerial sectionalism which filters through local governments has
taken its toll, but represents only one side of the coin. There is also
lateral rivalry between municipalities and between prefectures to maximize their performance in local politics and administration. In the early
1960s, many local governments entered into relentless competition and
mobilized all available means of political influence at the national level
in a bid to be designated as "new industrial cities" where public investments were to be provided as a matter of national priority. Local governments are conscious of their position in the national ranking and are
keen to compete with those of comparable size and status to obtain
subsidies, projects, and other preferential treatment. Neighboring
municipalities and adjacent prefectures insist on similar deals in view of
their proximity to favored regions. Appealing to regional identities, local
politicians run campaigns to raise the standard of their area, a demand
that national bureaucrats cannot easily ignore, for political reasons.
Local bureaucrats, too, often succeed in gaining salary levels and working conditions similar to those in comparable prefectures or municipalities. Relatively poor prefectures and municipalities actively seek large-
scale projects as a means of redressing the inter-regional balance. Local
initiatives have been essential to such major projects as the establishment
of nuclear energy plants, extension of the bullet-train lines, provision of
super-highways, development of resort centers, and so forth. Inter-
regional rivalry of this kind puts pressure on national bureaucrats in
their decision-making.

(d) The Legacy of Socialist Local Governments

The balance of power between the central and local governments was
tipped by the electoral victories of socialists in urban prefectures and
major cities in the 1960s and 1970s. Using such catchphrases as "advent
of the age of local autonomy" and "dialogue with local citizens," governors and mayors backed by the Japan Socialist Party, often in alliance
with the Japan Communist Party, got full political mileage out of
confrontation with the conservative national government. Since the late
1970s, this pattern has changed to an arrangement whereby all major

political parties, both conservative and reformist, agree to field a single gubernatorial or mayoral candidate. The system of joint candidates, called *ainori* (sharing a ride), became a dominant pattern throughout Japan in the 1980s and the early 1990s. While this lessened the chances of open electoral competition for top local government positions, the legacy of increased prefectural and municipal power against the center has gained strength.

(e) Strength of Resident Movements

Locally based resident movements prove sturdy buffers against state power. Nationwide social movements based on clear ideological causes have waned since the 1970s, but conflicts between state development programs and tenacious local community groups have become common throughout the country. Japan's spectacular economic growth produced a wide range of environmental victims and triggered two types of local protest.

At one end of the spectrum, community residents stood up against development projects which they regarded as detrimental to their vested interests. The construction of high-rise condominium buildings in densely populated urban centers provoked objections from neighboring residents who lost the "right to enjoy sunshine." The extension of highways and roads was opposed by residents who might suffer from noise and air pollution. By and large, these protestors enjoyed a reasonably comfortable standard of living and feared the possibility of losing what they had already gained. They were not necessarily politically radical; many in fact were conservatives who wished to maintain the status quo. Most resident movements of this type have been clustered in urban areas.

At the other end of the scale, there was a smaller number of rural resident movements which often adopted more extreme forms of dissent and focussed on the basic human rights of local inhabitants. Some movements arose in situations where residents of a particular area became ill or died as a direct consequence of water and air pollution. An example is Minamata disease, which crippled and killed a number of fishermen and their families around Minamata Bay in Kyūshū. This tragedy was caused by a chemical company which knowingly discharged mercury waste into the sea. Some rural development programs orchestrated by technocrats in government ministries in the name of national interests also triggered fierce, long-running protests. Cases include such large-scale national projects as the construction of the New Tokyo International Airport, the bullet-train networks, and nuclear plants across the country. Protest movements of this type often involve the participation of articulate city radicals alongside local residents.

Though different in styles, both types of resident movements gave power-holders in the center a lesson; bureaucrats, politicians, and business leaders became aware that they could not impose their development projects, but must first consult with the communities potentially affected. The influence of these movements has not only been felt in connection with pollution issues, but has been significant in a range of urban problems including city planning, environmental protection, and the preservation of cultural assets. Thus, policy-makers now have to calculate both benefits and social costs of programs, making resident movements a kind of local counterweight against the central establishment.

(f) The Rise of Anti-party Swinging Voters

Since the mid 1990s, a large proportion of the electorate have refrained from commitment to any political party and have become non-partisan swinging voters.[18] A series of political scandals, mergers, and party splits, and changes in party platforms without principles contributed to a mass desertion of the party faithful. Cynical and skeptical, these floating voters find political expression through candidates who are unaffiliated with political parties and take a strong anti-establishmentarian stance. Tired of political cliches and bored with interparty horse-trading, these voters regard themselves as the audience of a political playhouse, who expect surprise performances from politicians. In gubernatorial elections in 1995, for example, a TV personality and a comedian won the governorships of Tokyo and Osaka, the two urban centers of the nation, marking a new phase in Japanese politics. The anti-party swinging voters have much political information and knowledge. They have begun to form a formidable force which established political parties can no longer ignore.

Table 8.1 locates the major players on two axes. One dimension is that of competition between centralized and decentralized power structures. The other contrasts orientations in favor of bureaucratic regulation with those favoring deregulation. While the three power blocs displayed in Figure 8.1 exist in the centralized sector, their activities and orientations are influenced and constrained by various local forces.

IV The Media Establishment and the Knowledge Industry

Japan's fourth estate, the world of the mainstream media, is an influential bloc which exists separately from, but closely linked with, the three centers of power.[19] It has several distinctive characteristics. Media organizations exhibit a high degree of centralization and *keiretsu* arrangements similar to those in the corporate circles of manufacturing and trading.

Table 8.1   Orientations of major power players

	Structural Makeup	
Orientation	Centralized	Decentralized
Bureaucratic regulation	National bureaucracy; some national business organizations	Local governments; some resident movements
Deregulation	Most national business organizations; national political parties	Local business community; local political interest groups; some resident movements

They enjoy close links with establishment institutions through exclusive "reporters' clubs." Furthermore, the educational and social backgrounds of journalists in large media firms resemble those of elites in other spheres.

1 High Degree of Centralization

Japan's print media establishment is highly centralized; the concentration of major media industries in Tokyo facilitates ideological centralization, as discussed in chapter 3. Five nationally distributed dailies, *Asahi*, *Mainichi*, *Yomiuri*, *Nikkei*, and *Sankei* collectively claim about half the market. All have their headquarters in Tokyo, maintaining major editorial offices and printing facilities in Osaka and a few other large Japanese cities. These newspapers enjoy mammoth circulations, with the *Yomiuri*, printing some ten million copies daily, being the most widely circulated newspaper in the world.

On the whole, these newspapers remain politically neutral so as to maintain their large readership and avoid antagonizing subscribers. The *Asahi* and the *Mainichi* tend to be critical of the government and the *Yomiuri* and the *Sankei* are regarded as more pro-government, but none of them editorially supports any political party in elections.

These newspapers appear in both morning and evening editions, and stories in the morning edition are continued in the evening edition. Each edition has several sub-editions distributed to different regions. The contents of each sub-edition differ substantially to cater for local interests. Each morning edition has local news pages which staff writers at prefectural bureaus write and edit.

The book industry is also highly centralized, with some 80 percent of publishers operating in Tokyo. There is at least one bookshop in every shopping area and near almost every railway station, with some twenty-five thousand bookshops operating throughout the country as the community outlets of the knowledge industry. Most editors and writers are Tokyo-based because of the high concentration of book and magazine publishers there.

Two book-sales agents based in Tokyo, Tōhan and Nippan, together nearly monopolize distribution networks; bookshops purchase books through them, not directly from publishing houses. Thus a bookshop in Nagano, for example, cannot normally buy books directly from Nagano publishers, who must ship them first to the agents of the Tokyo-based distributors who in turn sell them to the bookshop. This is one of the reasons why so many publishers are concentrated in Tokyo; those who publish news and current affairs magazines are unwilling to operate outside the metropolis because they cannot afford to make such a detour in marketing their magazines.

In electronic media, the NHK networks, which are partly funded by the government, occupy a special place and are in the strongest position with regard to funding, prestige, and ratings. Broadcasting since 1925, NHK has a long history, and monopolized nationwide radio networks until the early 1950s when commercial radio stations were given licenses. NHK began television broadcasting in the late 1950s, well before commercial networks entered the field. It has two nationwide radio networks, two nationwide television networks, and two satellite TV channels beamed across the nation. NHK may be considered partly a pay-TV organization, as its budget is comprised not only of government subsidies but also fees that television viewers are supposed to pay to it.

2 Similarities with Other Large Corporations

The internal structure of Japan's mainstream media organizations resembles that of many other large business corporations. For commercial operations, major media organizations use *keiretsu* arrangements similar to those of large industrial and trading companies. In the distribution market, *keiretsu* principles prevail: of over twenty-three thousand newspaper distribution agents around the country, about two-thirds are exclusive outlets of major dailies. The big three newspapers, *Asahi*, *Mainichi*, and *Yomiuri*, have their own chains of distribution agents across the nation and compete fiercely for subscribers. *Asahi* paperboys deliver *Asahi* and its associated newspapers only, not *Mainichi* or *Yomiuri*, and vice versa. The sales division of each major newspaper sends sales agents to households across the nation to persuade them to subscribe to it. Newspapers frequently give away various commodities – detergents, towels, watches, washing machines, and even refrigerators – to expand their long-term market share. In this respect, Japanese newspapers epitomize the market expansion strategy of Japanese corporations. Their blatantly intrusive methods of soliciting for subscription have attracted public criticism, revealing a discrepancy between the high moral principles they advocate in their publications and the manipulative tricks they use in order to increase sales.

Major newspapers established commercial radio stations in the early 1950s and commercial television stations in the late 1950s. Five key television stations in Tokyo and Osaka are directly connected with five national dailies.

Journalists in major media organizations stay with the same company for their entire working lives. While some exceptionally high-profile star journalists permit themselves to be head-hunted, moving from one organization to another, the overwhelming majority resemble the salarymen and salarywomen in other large firms, remaining loyal to their corporation for some thirty-five years.

Multiskilling and lateral promotion are also part of the training of print-media journalists. Reporters beginning their careers with major national dailies commence work in a local bureau. Usually, they are first assigned to a police newsbeat, covering cases of homicide, suicide, robbery, embezzlement, fire, traffic accidents, natural disasters, and other incidents in which police are involved. This initiation is aimed at developing general skills in young journalists. In this way it resembles the training of employees in other large enterprises and of officials in the public bureaucracy.

Newspaper companies and television networks rely upon the same labor supply as other major corporations in recruiting prospective graduates from universities. Thus journalists and members of the bureaucratic and business establishment in Japan have quite similar social backgrounds, with a majority of news writers being male graduates of high-ranking universities. While they may be a countervailing force to Japan's establishment, their sociological attributes are similar to those of Japanese power elites and differ vastly from those of the majority of the population.

3 Institutional Linkage with the Establishment

Japan's mass media tend to be docile because of the way in which information-gathering units are based in government and business establishments. Government ministries, prefectural and municipal governments, police headquarters, and business and union organizations all provide reporters of major print and electronic media with office space called *kisha kurabu* (reporters' clubs). These clubrooms are normally equipped with telephones and other communication machines, service personnel, and other facilities. Media organizations use them free of charge. In almost all cases, club membership is restricted to the reporters of major news organizations and is not open to journalists from minor presses or to foreign journalists. In return, government officials, politicians, and business and union leaders use these clubs as venues for prepared public announcements which the reporters write up as news stories. By constantly feeding information to reporters in this environment, representatives of the institutions which provide club facilities can obliquely control the way in which it is reported to the public. Reporters cannot risk being excluded from their club because they would then lose access to this regular flow of information. The sentiment of mutual cooperation among all parties involved runs deep, and club members at times agree to place reporting embargoes on sensitive issues. The media establishment is also involved in the policy-making process of government by sending their representatives to its advisory councils.

Media organizations occasionally exercise excessive self-control over issues related to the imperial family. They neither discuss its problems nor criticize its activities with candor. When the Shōwa Emperor was on his deathbed in 1988, for example, the media refrained from airing jovial programs and merry commercials, but did not explicitly report that the Emperor was suffering from terminal cancer. The "chrysanthemum taboo," as it is often referred to, exists mainly because the media fears right-wingers' violent attacks on their organizations; modern Japanese history abounds with cases where ultra-nationalists have made brutal assaults on individuals and institutions that have been publicly critical of the imperial family.

With regard to the coverage of the Crown Prince's selection of a bride, both the Federation of Newspapers and the Association of Commercial Broadcasting Stations acceded in 1992 to the request of the Imperial Household Agency that the matter not be reported and that the Crown Prince's privacy be protected. Despite the fact that he was a public figure, the collusive relationship between the media and the imperial bureaucracy, together with journalists' fears of being expelled from reporters' clubs, drove the powerful media organizations to a collective agreement. The Federation of Magazines followed suit in imposing a ban on the Prince's "bride news."

Japan remains a country where freedom of the press is generally ensured and established. Yet the relationship between major media organizations and political and economic institutions contains elements of congenial rivalry and cordial coordination. Such affinities derive from the media's reliance on Japanese business practice and from the information-gathering infrastructure of exclusive reporters' clubs.

V Five Rifts in the Elite Structure

At the national level, rifts in the Japanese establishment led to the realignment of the political parties in the 1990s. Various elements within Japan are poised to contend against each other.

There is, first, a sharp rivalry between the nationalistic, racist, and particularistic elites on the one hand, and the more internationally minded, purely profit-orientated and universalistic elites on the other. The symbolic embodiment of the former type is *tennō*, the Emperor in particular and the imperial institutions in general. The latter type is exemplified by *shōsha*, the well-known Japanese trading houses which propelled the accumulation of trade surpluses and contributed to the international stature of the Japanese economy. *Tennō* capitalism and *shōsha* capitalism were compatible as long as the economy was not fully incorporated into the international market. With Japan becoming a global economic superpower, however, *shōsha* capitalism has become increasingly multinational, locating both its production bases and consumption outlets beyond Japan's national boundaries on a massive scale. For multinational organizations, domestic considerations are only part of a broad international strategy. In contrast, *tennō* capitalists find it difficult to accept encroachment upon Japan's domestic priorities; they vigorously oppose the liberalization of agricultural imports and the acceptance of Asian workers in the domestic labor market. They favor moral education and strict discipline in schools, defend Japan's activities during World War II, and attack foreign criticisms of Japan.

The second rift appears between economic superpower expansionists and strategic power-seekers. Economic superpower expansionists believe that the nation must continue to give priority to the economy-first policy of postwar Japan, make efforts to further strengthen its economic superpower status, and refrain from taking political and strategic leadership in the international context. According to these advocates, the constitution should be maintained, and chauvinism and jingoism should be avoided in favor of the economic well-being of the nation. In contrast, strategic power-seekers take the view that Japan must explore the possibility of assuming international responsibilities in political and strategic areas in accordance with its economic position in the world. These contenders stress the importance of the Japanese Self-Defense Forces participating in UN peacekeeping operations, suggest the possibility of amendments to the constitution, and recommend all-out efforts to acquire a permanent seat in the UN Security Council.

The third division appears to be emerging between US-orientated and Asia-oriented capitalists. While the United States remains the single most important country for Japan's exports, the increasing trade friction between the two countries left the Japanese business world little choice but to look towards Asia. The rapid appreciation of the yen against the dollar has forced Japanese companies to expand their off-shore production in Asia, where cheap labor and facilities are available. Japanese business finds vast and attractive markets in the booming economies of East and Southeast Asia. In this context, economic pragmatism overpowers ideological dogma. It is not surprising that Asia-orientated business elites find it helpful for the Japanese political establishment to make public apologies for, and to engage in self-criticism over, Japan's wartime atrocities in Asia. This helps smooth the way for Japanese business in the region. In the long run, the conciliatory stance of some leaders towards Asian countries will pay dividends.

The fourth area of competition is between rural and urban interests. For a long time, the National Federation of Agricultural Cooperative Unions has delivered votes to the Liberal Democratic Party, which in return refused to open the agricultural market to imports. The export-orientated urban manufacturing and service sectors of the economy, however, see the possibility of such protectionism backfiring and making it difficult for them to export their goods and commodities overseas on a reciprocal basis. In view of the fact that the farming population is now a small minority in comparison with the workforce in export industries, there are indications that the business hierarchy of Japan is about to desert rural interests.

The fifth contest, between those who give top priority to economic competition and those who emphasize the importance of political protection of the weak, underlies arguably the most fundamental ideological cleavage in contemporary Japan. On the whole, the economic efficiency argument seems to have the upper hand, given the obvious economic performance of the nation. Since the collapse of socialist systems around the world, economic indices have become universally regarded as the most significant measures of national status. Economy-first principles have become established more firmly than ever as the dominant ideology of Japanese society. However, Japan's very prosperity has now sensitized its public to the quality of life, ecology, and the environment, and to democratic representation and other fairness issues that the nation's elites cannot ignore.[20] Those who press for the protection of the weak regard contemporary Japan as a society whose concern with social justice has become tenuous in favor of economism.

All these rifts seem to have emerged as a consequence of Japan acquiring economic superpower status in the international community and undergoing profound cultural changes domestically. It is also noteworthy that different groups in the dominant segment of Japanese society have different interests on each issue. At one end of the continuum, there are groups staunchly committed to the status quo. At the other end are those advocating major reforms on all fronts. In between, diverse groups form complex networks of alliance and rivalry, thereby creating an increasingly pluralistic structure of power competition.

Notes

1 Yoda 1993, p. 12.
2 Murakami 1984a, pp. 103–8.
3 *Amakudari hakusho* (White paper on bureaucrats descending from heaven) compiled by Seirōren, unions organized by employees of public corporations, as reported in AM April 19 1992, p. 3.
4 For example, the Fair Trade Commission (*Kōsei Torihiki Iinkai*), which is supposed to enforce the anti-monopoly law and protect the operation of a fair and free market, is not an independent body uninfluenced by the government ministries closely connected with industrial and financial interests in the private sector. On the contrary, among the past thirteen Chief Commissioners, eight were former Ministry of Finance officials and two were from the Bank of Japan. Since early 1992, the five-member committee has been composed of former high-ranking officials, including two from the Ministry of Finance and one from the Ministry of International Trade and Industry. It is no accident that when the supposedly semi-judicial Commission laid criminal charges of illegal cartel formation against the wrapping-plastic industry in 1991, they were the first charges laid in the eighteen years since the oil industry was indicted on similar charges in 1973.
5 As of 1993, some twenty-five governors in forty-seven prefectures are ex-bureaucrats (ME October 5 1993, p. 2).
6 There are two other types of administrative guidance. One of these is addressed to local governments. In the 1980s, for example, the Ministry of Education repeatedly issued instructions to prefectural and municipal education committees, directing schools to hoist the national flag and students to sing the national anthem on ceremonial occasions. Likewise, the Ministry of Local Governments advised local governments to reduce the salary scales of local public servants to the levels of national bureaucrats, and to streamline the size and organizational structure of local government. Another type of administrative guidance is that which local governments give to private developers in the form of guidelines regulating their projects.
7 Shindō 1992, p. 105.
8 Shindō 1992, pp. 105–13. In the 1989 allocation of oil production and import levels for each oil company, for example, the Petroleum Department of the Agency of Natural Resources appeared to be taking charge of formulating the petroleum supply program, but in reality the demand estimation committee had worked out detailed figures in cooperation with Agency officials. The committee was comprised of some eighty business representatives from oil and electricity companies.
9 Itagaki 1987, p. 31.

10 Tsujinaka 1988, pp. 119–20.
11 Muramatsu, Itō, and Tsujinaka 1986. According to Tsujinaka 1988, this pattern contrasts sharply with the US situation where lobby groups and pressure organizations give the highest priority to persuading legislators in Congress and the Senate.
12 The late Nobusuke Kishi (Prime Minister from 1957 to 1960) was widely regarded as the boss of the *zoku* group in control of commerce and industry and wielded enormous power in the key industries under the guidance of the Ministry of International Trade and Industry. Zenkō Suzuki (1980–82) was influential in the Ministry of Agriculture, Forestry, and Fishery, and had strong links with agricultural cooperatives throughout the nation. Toshiki Kaifu (1989–91) was a leader of the education *zoku* group influential in the Ministry of Education. This coterie has expanded its coffers by procuring political donations from nationwide networks of the owners of private schools and kindergartens.
13 AM January 12 1996, p. 4.
14 The Daiichi Kangyō Bank survey of five hundred salarymen in Tokyo and Osaka, conducted in 1990, indicates that most married male employees in urban areas find find these practices "empty formalities" (*kyorei*) and burdensome customs.
15 These occasions are collectively called *kankon sōsai*.
16 AM April 4 1989, p. 1.
17 The discussion here follows Muramatsu 1988.
18 In the mid 1990s, about half of eligible voters fall into this category (AM January 10 1996, pp. 1 and 7).
19 Akhavan-Majid 1990.
20 The members of the House of Representatives are almost equally split between those who favor economic competition and those who endorse the political protection of the weak (AM January 5 1996, p. 1).

9

Popular Culture and Everyday Life

I Elite Culture and Popular Culture

Japanese society embraces a rich variety of cultural forms which reflect its tradition, stratification, and regional stretch. As in any society, the primary bearers of high and popular forms of Japanese culture can be differentiated along class lines. In the main, a small number of elites relish such traditional cultural styles as classic literature, flower arrangements, tea ceremonies, *noh* and *kyōgen* plays, *koto* music, *bunraku* puppet shows, and classic Japanese *buyō* dancing. They also enjoy Western classic music, opera, art exhibitions, and theatrical performances.

These images tend to mirror the elite culture, which is not that of most Japanese. Ordinary citizens of Japan adopt much more informal, vulgar, unassuming, ostentatious, and down-to-earth cultural styles. In contrast to the organized subculture of companies and schools, Japan's city life abounds with hedonism, intemperance, and overindulgence. The Japanese also enjoy various forms of traditional grassroots culture, ranging from colorful agrarian festivals to local folk dances. Further, Japan has a range of countercultural groups even though their public visibility may be limited.

Though Japan's popular culture is multifarious, it represents the ways of life the common people enjoy and share. For analytical purposes, this chapter divides popular culture into three categories: mass culture, which has spread with the expansion of the consumer market and the development of mass communication; folk culture, which has been based upon conventions, mores, and customs of the indigenous tradition; and alternative culture, which a small number of ordinary citizens generate spontaneously as counterculture challenging the cultural status quo. Table 9.1 provides a conceptual map of these three classes of popular

Table 9.1 Comparative dimensions of three types of popular culture

Comparative criteria	Mass culture	Folk culture	Alternative culture
Historical origin	Recent/contemporary	Traditional	Contemporary/traditional
Mass means of communication	Essential	Minimal/absent	Minimal/absent
Considerations of marketability	Imperative	Peripheral	Minimal
Consumption orientation	High	Limited	Low
Durability of contents	Subject to consumer popularity	Relatively durable	Subject to internal group cohesion
Geographic basis	Diffusion from urban areas	Both rural and urban	Variable
Concentration pattern	Tendency towards centralization	Regionally diversified	Tendency towards decentralization
Producers	Mostly specialists	Some specialists, mostly amateurs	Mostly amateurs, some specialists
Basis of sharedness	Shared media information	Shared historical memories	Shared defiance against established order
Size of the population involved	Large	Large	Small (though many people may be attracted, they have no means to practice)
Emic category of people	Taishū, shōshū, or bunshū	Jōmin	Jinmin and shin-jinrui

culture and their characteristics. The brief descriptions which follow sketch something of its diversity.

II Mass Culture

Mass culture in contemporary Japan is a lively and potent force that affects numerous people through mass media. It relies upon its market-ability because it cannot survive unless it is consumed by a large number of people; it is consumer-orientated because the size of the market determines its viability. Japan's mass culture today includes:

1 television and radio entertainment culture which is the most pervasive vehicle of mass entertainment;
2 the popular press, which appeases the mass appetite for gossip, scandals, and other grubby realities of life;
3 fashion and trend culture, where mass-produced and mass-distributed goods are accepted and rejected;
4 the entertainment culture that develops around theaters, restaurants, amusement facilities, and sex shops;
5 high-tech culture, where computers and computer-based information networks serve as the major intermediaries; and
6 commercialized traditional elite culture, in which masters of flower arranging, tea ceremonies, and the like instruct in traditional cultural practices for high fees.

With these dimensions overlapping, Japan's mass culture flourishes in di-verse forms and styles, all of which use channels of mass information dis-tribution such as television, advertisements, computers, or other forms of large-scale publicity, to generate a sense of doing things together. This section surveys Japan's mass culture by first browsing the world of electronic and print media and then scanning four phenomena peculiar to contemporary Japan: *manga, pachinko, karaoke,* and love hotels and other products of the love industry. Finally, it takes a brief look at the ways in which traditional elite culture is commercialized and popularized at the community level by the masters of various schools of traditional art.

1 Entertainment Media

(a) Television and Radio

With more than 90 percent of Japanese watching television every day, for about three hours on average,[1] the television industry has the most powerful homogenizing effect on the public, who share the same visual information across the country. This pattern occurs around the world. Many Japanese television programs, like television programs elsewhere, are designed to incite curiosity, envy, and anger. For instance, most major commercial stations televise morning entertainment shows filled with scandal, gossip, and other sensational stories about which a panel of self-styled and complacent social commentators makes moralizing comments. Many afternoon programs targetting housewives have a similar format. Even newscasters openly make evaluative comments between news stories, taking one side and accusing the other. With high ratings, these shows contribute greatly to the formation of homogeneous social views.

As is the case with many other societies, Japan's prime-time television is filled with nonsense and funny programs, because television stations' ratings determine their annual profits. In a bid to win the largest slice of the audience, major commercial stations' programs are full of slapstick comedies, knockabout competition games, and voyeuristic shows. Many families have developed the habit of watching television during dinner, losing the sphere of family conversation and subjecting themselves nearly exclusively to what television programs feed them.

The centralized organization of mass media in general, and television in particular, makes it easy for central image-makers to capture the nation's curiosity. This contributes to Japan's frequent nationwide crazes, including those for tea mushrooms in 1975, UFO searching in 1978, Rubik's cubes in 1980–81, and family computers in 1985–86. In the middle of the oil shock in 1973, toilet-paper sold out in supermarkets around the country because of the unfounded but widely circulated rumor that Japan might face a paper shortage. In 1994, when the government imported rice because of a poor rice crop the previous year, some sections of the nation went into near hysteria and attempted to buy up domestic rice from rice dealers. In 1995, the discovery of a number of poisonous redback spiders in the Osaka area led to a nationwide search for them, with rumors of venomous spiders hiding in every community. In all these cases, mass media, especially television, played a major role in stirring up a feeling of insecurity and inciting national panic.

Radio listeners have declined in number with the arrival of television. Only about one in five Japanese tunes into radio, yet those who do listen for more than two hours a day.[2] Among occupational groups, a markedly high proportion of self-employed persons listen to radio while doing their work. For carpenters, noodle-shop owners and hairdressers, radio is an important source of information and entertainment during work. More than a dozen radio stations operate in major city areas and each has a different group of listeners. While young fans tune into FM music stations, some late-night radio programs are important to many older people. Unlike television, radio thus addresses segmented audiences with differing needs and requirements.

(b) Tabloid Press and Weekly Magazines

Japan has many sensationalist, scandal-hungry, and exposé-orientated tabloid newspapers and weekly magazines whose approaches contrast sharply with those of the established and sanitized broadsheet newspapers. *Fuji* and *Nikkan Gendai* are the two leading tabloids. This category of publications also includes scandalous photographic weeklies such as *Focus* and *Friday*. In addition, some seventeen sports newspapers cover mainly baseball, sumō wrestling, and general entertainment news, selling a total of more than six million copies per day.[3] All major newspapers and established publishing houses produce these papers and magazines, cashing in on the public's desire for non-sterilized stories.

In contrast to the sanitized and balanced major newspapers and television networks, weekly magazines unashamedly publish muck-raking stories, sex scandals, and revelations of trickery, often at the risk of being sued for defamation. Because mainstream media produce stories only in socially correct ways, readers who are interested in "dirty *honne* and *ura* realities" turn to these yellow magazines. *Shūkan Posuto*, *Shūkan Hōseki*, *Shūkan Bunshun*, *Shūkan Shinchō*, *Shūkan Gendai*, and many others compete in the weekly magazine market. The vitality of these publications suggests that a large proportion of the Japanese public identifies with popular culture at this level. Their contents differ depending upon their readership. A majority of the weeklies – notably *Shūkan Posuto* and *Shūkan Gendai* – target salarymen, running sexist, nationalist, and anti-government stories. Some weeklies regularly feature color pictures of nude girls and sex-life confessions of movie stars and television personalities. Other magazines such as *Sapio* have followers among anti-establishment youngsters and offer behind-the-scenes stories written in sensational language. Various weeklies for women, such as *Josei Jishin* and *Shūkan Josei*, focus on stardom, royal families, and female sexuality.

These papers and magazines target the commuting public in addition to general readers, selling in large quantities at newsstands and kiosks at railway and subway stations. Because many company employees in major metropolitan areas must travel long distances between homes and the workplace, reading is common on commuter trains.

These publications reveal a deviant but real side of Japanese society, as opposed to its legitimate aspects which the mainstream mega-media are inclined to emphasize. Editors run bluntly sexist and violent cartoons in publications oriented to the male readership. Some magazines for young women highlight stories about how to look feminine and how to please and seduce men. The market for the popular press is highly differentiated and is catered to by a wide variety of magazines, including magazines for career women, established businessmen, teenage girls, leisure-oriented men, and housewives. Their diversity also demonstrates that the types of aspirations, frustrations, and grievances they publish reflect the social locations of their readers.

2 Four Japanese Phenomena

Even casual observers of Japan's mass culture cannot overlook four obvious phenomena. One, pertaining to reading taste, is that so many Japanese, including adults, are avid readers of cartoons (*manga*). Another, in the area of solitary amusements, is the obsession of many Japanese with playing *pachinko* pinball games in *pachinko* parlors. The third, in the sphere of collective entertainment, is the nationwide popularity of *karaoke* singing. The fourth is the commercialization of love and sex in ways which have given rise to several unique Japanese institutions.

(a) Manga

Manga (literally, funny pictures) is a generic term that covers cartoons, comic strips, funnies, and caricatures. *Manga* books and magazines comprise nearly one-third of publications in Japan, a pattern that does not exist in any other industrialized society. The weekly *manga* magazine for young boys, *Shūkan Shōnen Jump*, sells some four million copies per week and is the best-selling magazine in Japan. The five most widely sold magazines are all *manga* publications, and more than three thousand comic books are published every year. Many of these books and magazines are story *manga* where dramas have clear themes. Osamu Tezuka's work, internationally known as *Astro Boy*, is a semi-classic example.

While *manga* are generally designed to provoke laughter in their readers, a genre known as *gekiga* (dramatized pictorial stories) is a *manga* form which depicts the dark side of human existence. Like long novels, *gekiga* have complex story lines, mostly with an undertone of malice, hostility, and bitter sarcasm towards the established order. *Gekiga* initially won popularity in the 1960s among youngsters uprooted from rural areas to become blue-collar workers in factories in large cities. Uneducated and exploited, at the bottom of Japan's high-growth economy, these young workers empathized with the *gekiga* figures who resisted and challenged their powerful rulers and moral authorities, often through illegitimate and unconventional means. A series of peasant uprisings during the feudal period formed the central theme of seventeen volumes of *Ninja bugei-chō* (Ninjas' martial arts notebooks), the landmark *gekiga* that established the genre. The solidarity of dissident groups also provided a theme for some *gekiga* which had a wide readership among student rebels during campus turmoil in the late 1960s and early 1970s.

Female cartoonists have played significant roles in *manga* production. The best-known postwar Japanese cartoonist, Machiko Hasegawa, was a female who penned the comic strips that centered on the everyday life of a housewife named *Sazae-san*, and her family members. Serialized in the morning edition of the *Asahi* newspaper for more than three decades, *Sazae-san* became a household name and popularized a housewife's perspective on Japanese society throughout the postwar period. Since the 1970s, an increasing number of talented female cartoonists have published *manga* specifically addressed to teenage girls. Attracting a wider range of readers, some of these authors have moved beyond the genre of girls' *manga* and become the engine of contemporary *manga* culture.

Manga enjoy great popularity across a wide range of age groups. Some observers attribute this to increasing social pressures of compliance brought to bear upon the school, work, and community lives of many Japanese. In a world of intense *tatemae* conformism, readers of *manga* find freedom in the peculiar and often iconoclastic fantasies, often laced with sex and bloody violence, in boys' *manga*. Other analysts see the popularity of *manga* against the background of the increasingly visually oriented lifestyles of the high-tech age, and regard the Japanese as trailblazers. Analysts are divided on whether *manga* popularity reflects immaturity in Japanese adults or represents an indirect form of popular dissatisfaction with and dissent against the established order.

(b) Pachinko

Pachinko pinball, a nationwide pastime which some 20 percent of the population enjoy,[4] allows players to divert their minds from their cares. In a *pachinko* saloon with hundreds of computer-operated pinball machines, filled with cigarette smoke and resounding with popular music, many people spend hours attempting to put pinballs into holes on the board. When a ball goes into a hole, the *pachinko* machine returns a large number of balls to the player, who can exchange them not only for such prizes as chocolates and cigarettes, but also for cash. Though cash prizes are prohibited, the reality is that an overwhelming majority of winners cash their acquired pinballs at backstreet cashing shops. In this sense, *pachinko* is a very accessible form of gambling; the annual sales figure of the *pachinko* industry far exceeds the yearly total turnover of the more visible forms of gambling as horse, bicycle, speedboat, and car races. *Pachinko* parlors outnumber middle schools in Japan.

While there is controversy over the international birthplace of *pachinko*,[5] there is little dispute that in Japan it originated immediately after World War II in Nagoya, where the many military aircraft manufacturing firms clustered in the region had to find a profitable way of using countless surplus ball bearings. Resourceful entrepreneurs devised a simple *pachinko* machine, which provided the masses with cheap amusement and spread across the country. The machine became more sophisticated as technological innovations were added.

Some mass culture observers attribute the popularity of *pachinko* in Japan, particularly among blue-collar workers, to its affinity with the pattern of their work, in which they compete with each other in finger dexterity on assembly lines in the same noisy surroundings.[6] These workers entertain themselves as an extension of their work environment. This is why the number of *pachinko* parlors increased most rapidly during Japan's economic growth and in the areas where the working environment became quickly mechanized. One may also argue that *pachinko* attracts so many Japanese partly because it is essentially detached from direct human interaction. Playing *pachinko* does not require players to interact face-to-face with others. To the extent that mass culture points to daily realities which the masses wish to evade, the non-interactive quality of *pachinko* games indirectly testifies to the intensity of group pressures and constraints on the working and community lives of the Japanese.

(c) Karaoke

Karaoke (singing to a taped accompaniment) became a popular form of mass entertainment relatively recently. It is believed[7] to have originated in a snack bar in Kobe, where management recorded a tape for use at practice sessions of professional singers. In 1976 an electronics company commenced selling a machine called "Karaoke 8," which selected an eight-track cartridge tape containing four tunes. This prototype developed into laser-disk *karaoke*, VHD *karaoke*, CD *karaoke*, and so on, as these sorts of equipment became standard in entertainment establishments popular with salarymen. Many customers had a good time diverting their minds from their cares by drinking and singing with a microphone in hand. The taped accompaniment of *karaoke* gave them the fantasy of singing like a professional singer on stage. As various types of family *karaoke* equipment came onto the market, the vogue begun in amusement areas spread to some well-to-do households.

Although *karaoke* singing takes place in the apparently collective environment of bars and pubs, singers face a television screen which displays lyrics and song-related pictures, while those waiting to sing busily scan the song list to choose a song, without listening to the present singer. But the singer's co-workers usually clap loudly in appreciation. In this ambience meaningful conversation is impossible, which appears to give a sense of relaxation to Japanese *karaoke* participants.[8] It is no wonder that so-called *karaoke* boxes where singers can behave more audaciously have become widespread in Japan since the late 1980s.

Proliferating in the streets of busy quarters, they provide small, self-contained, soundproofed rooms where anybody can sing to the tune of *karaoke* music. These *karaoke* boxes enable song lovers to give vent to their emotions, and have gained popularity among housewives, young female workers, and students. It may not be beside the mark to speculate that the mass culture of *karaoke* has established itself, like *pachinko*, as a way ordinary people can escape the stringent realities of Japanese working and community life.

(d) The Love Industry

Japan's sex industry reflects the underside of Japanese society. For instance, the "love hotels" that thrive in Japanese cities reflect the resourcefulness of pragmatic hotel operators. These hotels provide rooms openly to couples who would like to have sex. Some spend a few hours and pay hourly rates. Others stay overnight, generally at a reasonable rate. These hotels do not have a lobby, a restaurant, or even a coffee room. For obvious reasons, lodgers are not required to register their names and addresses. Establishments of this kind flourish partly because of the high frequency of premarital sex and adultery and partly because of the unfavorable housing conditions in Japanese cities.

The prostitution industry prospers despite the Prostitution Prevention Law implemented in 1965. Illicit underground groups arrange "lovers' banks" and "date clubs" and play cat-and-mouse with police. "Soap land" joints, which offer private rooms, each with a bath, are virtually brothels where "massage girls" work as sex workers. Called "Turkish baths" in the past, these houses of ill-repute which exist in almost all cities testify to the uninhibited flourishing of the sex industry.[9]

On the other side of the equation, the marriage industry has played up images of romantic love and luxurious wedding receptions to manipulate the aspirations of the prosperity generation. As a result, marriage ceremonies and receptions of young, upper-middle-class Japanese have become so lavish that their cost often exceeds their participants' annual salaries. Hotels and ceremonial halls display advertisements in subways and trains, Japanese urban scenery indicating the sizeable market. The marriage industry makes wedding receptions into lavish performances. In a standard package, the couple appear in a gondola and in the dark, with candles, dry ice "smoke", laser lights and other stage effects being used to dramatize the occasion.

3 Commercialization and Popularization of Elite Culture

Mass culture depends upon its market. Once the consumers of mass culture weary of it, it must change to maintain its appeal. Thus, popular songs come and go. Fashion is by definition temporary and changing. The *pachinko* industry changes its machine format to satisfy players' appetite for change and high technology. Fluidity, variability, and transformability characterize contemporary mass culture.

Against this background, the high art forms often serve as frames of reference for ordinary masses and filter through as models to emulate. School curricula include some of these artistic activities, thereby facilitating the process; most Japanese pupils learn about parts of high culture by studying Chinese classical literature (called *kanbun*), practicing calligraphy and playing Western musical instruments. Mass media have also popularized it: in major cities, major media organizations manage "culture centers" where ordinary citizens can study high culture; national daily newspapers have regular columns to which readers can contribute *tanka* poems; from time to time, the educational network of NHK broadcasts high culture performances. Companies and community organizations often call upon Shintoist and Buddhist priests to educate and vitalize their members with their esoteric teachings. Thus, most Japanese are more or less familiar with high cultural activities though only a small segment of the population actually practice them.

The popularization of high culture has led to the sphere of activities which can be labelled popular elite culture. Though emanating from the elite sector, it has many followers. Some high cultural forms have been propagated by the system in which *iemoto*, the head family of a school of an established art form, oversees its nationwide hierarchical networks of followers with various levels of teachers as middle managers. In the case of tea ceremonies, two major schools exist, each having its *iemoto*. In flower arranging, several schools compete with each other with similar *iemoto* structures. Under the authorization of *iemoto*, most teachers in these disciplines run teaching sessions at their homes and receive tuition fees from students. When students finish the course, they are entitled to acquire shingles from the *iemoto* to certify that they have acquired required skills. When obtaining these certificates, students must pay considerable sums to the *iemoto* through their teacher, who retains some of the money. After arriving at a certain level, students can become qualified teachers. This licensing system ensures the *iemoto* households not only social prestige but also material gains, with some of them managing vocational schools and junior colleges of their own. They prosper with the successful proliferation of the notion that middle-class women must have some knowledge of tea ceremonies and flower arranging before marriage.

In addition, numerous literary coterie magazines edited, distributed, and read by avid composers of poems and novels exist around the nation. Many contributors to these magazines are amateur writers from various walks of life who find satisfaction in creative writing. The Chinese chess, *go*, which a small circle of elites enjoyed in the past, is so popular that some communities have parlors where enthusiasts play against each other. Lovers of Japanese, Western, and Chinese painting, brush calligraphy, and woodblock printing attend private tutorial sessions by experts, with some devotees forming clubs with regional and national networks.

The popularized elite culture does not really reach the bottom of the social scale and remains the pastime of the relatively well-off, if not the very rich. Its influence may decline in future as a result of the changing cultural taste of younger generations, who are less inclined than older ones to enjoy these cultural forms in favor of more commercialized mass culture. Yet contemporary Japanese society has solid layers of local intelligentsia and grassroots artists who are popular practitioners of high culture. To a certain degree, this pattern reflects the teaching qualities of some cultural elites in Japan. It also perhaps partially accounts for a large proportion of the Japanese who consider themselves as members of the middle class regardless of their economic status.

III Folk Culture

Folk culture is the type of popular culture that has been conventionalized in the everyday life of the populace. It includes local festivals, seasonal holidays, and traditional playful art. Having taken root over decades or centuries, the content of folk culture differs from place to place and relies upon the historical memories of people in a region. Folk culture requires neither mass products nor mass media, and while it does not have to be mass-consumed it normally involves a large number of people in a locality or region, or even throughout Japan.

1 Local Festivals as Occasions of Hare

Japan's ethnographers and ethnologists have long regarded three Japanese *emic* concepts – *hare, ke,* and *kegare* – as fundamental categories for understanding Japanese folk culture. *Hare* represents situations where formal, ceremonial, and festive sentiments prevail. On these occasions (*hare no hi*), people dress in their best clothes (*haregi*) and eat gala meals (*hare no shokuji*). In contrast, *ke* stands for routine life in which people do things habitually, conventionally, and predictably. As they consume energy in *ke*-based daily lives, they arrive at a condition of *kegare* in which their vitality withers. Some analysts argue that *hare* occasions are organized to animate, invigorate, and restore vivacity.[10] Others suggest that the characteristics of a given folk society are determined by whether it regards opposite types as being *hare* and *ke* or *hare* and *kegare*.[11] Japanese folk-culture researchers also debate the extent to which these concepts correspond to the conventional sociological distinction between the sacred and the profane.

Local festivals which represent important *hare* affairs are closely linked with the tradition of community Shintoism, Japan's indigenous religion, understanding which requires knowledge of the ways in which religion is practiced in Japan. To begin with, sociologists estimating the distribution of individual religious affiliation in Japan encounter difficulties because the total membership of all religious groups, sects, and denominations appears to exceed the population of Japan. This apparent anomaly derives from the fact that many Japanese belong to two or more religious groupings without feeling inconsistent. A number of Japanese families have both a household Shinto shrine and a Buddhist altar. Most Japanese find it quite acceptable to visit Shinto shrines on festive days, have a marriage ceremony in a Christian church, and worship the souls of their ancestors at a Buddhist temple. In this sense, the Japanese religious system is non-exclusivist, eclectic and syncretic.

Shintoism has no scriptures; it developed a mythology that the Japanese nation was created by the Goddess of the Sun, who emerged from a rock hut where a strip dance was being performed in front of it. The Japanese term *kami*, which corresponds to "god" in English, originally meant "that which excels in its act, be it good or bad." Belief in *kami* therefore does not imply faith in a single God. Instead, the most native of Japan's religions is based upon worship of mana, the supernatural or mystical power that resides not only in human beings but also in animals, plants, rivers, and other natural things. Most Shintoist shrines deify human figures who excelled in some way. Thus, for example, Tenjin shrines in many parts of the country enshrine Michizane Sugawara, a ninth-century politician and scholar, as the god of scholarship. The Izumo Shrine in Shimane prefecture is well-known as a shrine dedicated to a mythological character, Ōkuninushi no Mikoto, a figure believed to have excelled in medical and magical matters and worshipped as a god who presides over marriage. Meiji Shrine in the heart of Tokyo enshrines Emperor Meiji, the first emperor of modern Japan. Inari shrines across Japan venerate foxes and their allegedly supernatural power.

Shintoism also includes elements of animism, the veneration of spirits which are believed to dwell in people and in non-human beings such as trees and rocks. The animistic tendency in Japanese thinking manifests itself on ceremonial occasions. At the commencement of construction work, even some mega-scale multinational corporations will organize a purification ceremony to appease the "god of earth." While animism is often accompanied by superstition, some ecologists and environmentalists in Japan observe that the tradition of animism must be seriously studied and selectively revitalized as a system of values for the protection of nature, to counter the scientific industrialism that has brought about the worldwide environmental crisis.

Traditionally, those who live near a Shinto shrine are called *ujiko*, children under the protection of the community deity, and contribute to the organization and proceedings of their community festivals. As the most momentous *hare* occasions, these celebrations provide *ujiko* with the opportunity to energize themselves by happily abandoning daily routines. They shoulder portable shrines together, dance in the street collectively, and enjoy the sense of liberation and rapture. In agrarian Japan, community festivals have been connected with the timing of harvest.

In the everyday life of most Japanese, Buddhism has lost visible significance except at most funerals, in which Buddhist priests play a major role. Although some Buddhist temples are tourist attractions and many care for family graves and tombs, they have only limited relevance in the area of popularized elite culture such as tea ceremonies, flower arrangements, and calligraphy. Still, the Buddhist heritage is evident in the short period in August during which ancestors' souls are supposed to return to their native locality. In this mid-summer interval known as *bon*, many city-dwellers take holidays to visit their home villages and towns, where their relatives still reside. This is also the season when many communities organize various kinds of *bon* dances, communal dances which local residents perform in streets, playgrounds, and other public areas to the accompaniment of traditional folk songs. Like other Japanese folk dances, *bon* dancing involves no physical contact; participants dance in a circle or advance in rows. Each locality has its own style, perhaps the most famous being the Awa dance in Tokushima prefecture where people dance through one street after another. Even in some housing complexes in Tokyo, children and adults dance to the relatively recent tune of the Tokyo Song. On the last day of the *bon* festival, some communities organize a colorful event at which drawings are made on paper lanterns, which are floated on a river to carry away the spirits of the dead.

Many Japanese families celebrate certain festival days that reflect the rhythm of changing seasons. On New Year's Day, arguably the most significant national holiday, most households enjoy eating *zōni* (rice cakes boiled with vegetables), herring roe, dried young anchovies, and other festive delicacies. During the New Year season, people fly kites on which they have painted unique pictures. On the day before the beginning of spring, in February, some families scatter parched beans to drive evil spirits out of their houses. March 3, when peach blossoms are at their best, is the day of the Girls' Festival, when girls and their parents display dolls on a tiered stand. In various parts of the country, large parks are full of people who come to view the cherry blossoms, some drinking, eating, and singing on a mat spread on the ground under cherry trees in full bloom. Many Japanese write their wishes on strips of paper that they hang on a bamboo tree on July 7, the day of the Festival of the Weaver when two lover stars, Altair and the Weaver, on opposite sides of the Milky Way, are believed to meet by crossing it. On the vernal and fall equinoxes, people follow the custom of visiting their family tomb, cleaning and washing it, and dedicating flowers to it. They fold their hands in front of the grave to pray that the departed souls of their ancestors will protect them from misfortune and lead them to prosperity. Most Japanese engage in such activity at least once a year,[12] visits to the family grave ranking highest among the religious and quasi-religious activities of the Japanese.

2 Regional Variation of Folk Culture

Folk culture exhibits much regional diversity. As discussed in chapter 2, different areas have different folk songs, folk dances and folk crafts. The plurality of folk culture across Japan can be seen in Okinawa, the southernmost prefecture, and in Hokkaidō, the northernmost major island.

In Okinawa, neither Shintoism nor Buddhism has been influential. Across Ryūkyū islands, each village has a *utaki* shrine where the souls of village ancestors are worshipped and gods descend from heaven. The prevailing belief is that the gods who bring happiness to people visit on festive occasions from utopias that exist beyond the ocean. Many annual festivals on these islands are related to the sea. Ryūkyū dance, which is performed on festive occasions, is well known for the wave-like movement of the dancers' fingers, similar to that found in dances in Southeast Asia. The Okinawan system of musical scales differs from those in other parts of Japan, resembling those of Indonesia, Malaysia, and the Philippines. Since Okinawa was occupied by the United States until 1972, the American influence remains more pervasive than in other parts of Japan.

Folk culture in some areas of Japan is on the verge of extinction because of the penetration of more dominant cultural forms. Ainu folk culture is a conspicuous example. Before the invasion of the Japanese pushed them from the northern parts of Honshū island into a small corner of Hokkaidō, Ainu communities had a different language, a distinct tradition of festivals, and a separate belief system. Traditional Ainu clothes are furs or dresses made of lindens with special embroidery. Ainu used to engage in hunting and fishing and have special techniques of carving, tattooing, and extrasensory perception. Ainu hold highly

animistic beliefs, deeming every physical object to contain a kind of
spiritual being which puts it in motion. According to Ainu folk belief,
good and bad supernatural beings exist, and positively or negatively
influence the object in which they have landed. Hence, the everyday life
of the Ainu community includes a variety of religious ceremonies and
practices which are presumed to propitiate these invisible divine forces.
In the house, various gods are supposed to reside underneath a fireplace,
at the rear, and near the entrance. *Ianu*, pieces of shaved wood, are put
in appropriate places to serve as intermediaries with gods. The bear
festival, regarded by Ainu as the most important ceremony for praying
for a successful hunting season, was celebrated until recently. Some Ainu
communities are making attempts to preserve their folk *yukar* – lyric
poems which will otherwise sink into oblivion.

These cultural practices are all parts of Japan's folk culture, though
some are less visible or are dying out. It would be erroneous to assume
that all grassroots cultural traditions have been cast in the same mold.
Commercially organized events have to a large extent supplanted folk
festivals in recent years. At the community level, local shopping areas
stage parades, fairs, and galas with the explicit aim of improving business
turnover. City and prefectural governments hold one exhibition after
another, and are often involved in musical, sporting, and other planned
events. In collaboration with the mass media, large corporations sponsor
such festival-like events as ladies' marathons, music concerts, machine
shows, and trade fairs. On the whole, these manufactured events acquire
the characteristics of mass culture and lose those of folk culture.

3 Marginal Art

In classifying art forms, Tsurumi, an analyst of popular culture, distinguishes between three analytical categories – pure, mass, and marginal
art types – and argues that the third type deserves serious examination.[13]
In what he calls pure art, producers are professional artists and those
who appreciate it are specialists with some degree of expert knowledge.
Its concrete forms include *noh*, symphonies, and professional paintings.
Mass art, whose modes include television shows, popular songs, posters,
and detective stories, is often regarded as pseudo-art or vulgar art, inasmuch as its production is based upon collaboration between professional
artists and media organizations, and its recipients are non-specialist
masses. In contrast, marginal art is seen as a domain at the intersection
between everyday life and artistic expression. Its forms range from
graffiti, to gestures in daily interaction, New Year cards, song variations,
building blocks, and room decorations. Even the ways in which people
interact in communal baths (*sentō*) and hot springs would be a kind of

marginal art; people of different backgrounds meet naked, engage in unpretentious conversation, and thereby generate an artistic form of communication in the space of a mini-democracy. Marginal art is based on amateur activities to the extent that both its producers and consumers are laypersons without specialist or professional expertise. Although such art forms have existed since ancient times, the development of mass media and democratic economic and political systems have paved the way for the dichotomy between pure and mass art, and have removed marginal art from the sphere of legitimately recognized art. Once one accepts the realm of marginal art thus conceptualized, one can see many popular activities as reflections of Japan's folk culture, as in Table 9.2.

IV Alternative Culture

Alternative culture is composed of indirect devious, and not necessarily overtly political forms of mass dissent against the institutionalized order. Some are reformist or even radical, while others are simply troublesome and threatening. All are located at the margin of Japanese society and challenge the patterns of the routine lives of ordinary citizens in various ways.

Japanese history abounds with so many activities of this type that only a few illustrations would suffice. Many Buddhist religious sects which today enjoy established status initially started as alternative culture with a charismatic leader who had enthusiastic followers ready to defy the social order of the day. This is true, for example, of Shinran, the priest who established the Jōdo Shinshū sect in the thirteenth century as a kind of protestant movement in defiance of established Buddhist sects. He attracted peasants and the urban populace as firm believers. The same applies to Saint Nichiren who started the Nichiren sect in the thirteenth century, vigorously attacked other Buddhist groups, and was condemned by the government to exile on Sado island. Many newer religions in modern Japan, including Sōka Gakkai, Ōmotokyō, and Konkōkyō, resisted the military government's attempts to unite the public into supporting Japan's war activities during World War II. In the area of literature, Bashō, the seventeenth-century poet who established *haiku* (a mode of Japanese poems with seventeen syllables) as a respected literary field, challenged the existing circles of *haiku* poets with serious alternative artistic styles, travelled extensively around the nation in solitude, and won the admiration of devoted followers who were dissatisfied with the literary status quo. At a more popular level, urban residents in feudal Japan enjoyed writing poems called *senryū*, which are similar to *haiku* in style but more sarcastic and wittier in substance, mocking the ways of the world and the rulers of the day. Even today, most newspapers have *senryū*

Table 9.2 Specific cases of marginal art

Type of action	Concrete examples
Moving one's body	Gesture in everyday life; rhythm in work; the New Year's parade of fire brigades; play; courting; applause; *Bon* festival dance; walking on stilts; bouncing a ball; *sumo* wrestling; *shishimai* (ritual dance with a lion's mask)
Constructing, making, living, using, and watching	Housing; the appearance of houses lining the street; miniature garden; *bonsai* (dwarf tree in a pot); straps of a *geta* thong; paper flowers that open when placed in a glass of water; knot making; building blocks; cocoon balls; tombs
Singing, talking, listening	Calls used to enliven physical labor; speaking in a singsong tone; tongue twisters; variations of a song; humming a tune; nicknaming; *dodoitsu* (Japanese limerick); two-person *manzai* comic acts; mimicry
Writing and reading	Graffiti; votive tablets of a horse; battledores; picture painting on kites; New Year cards; picture drawing on paper lanterns floated on a river
Writing and reading	Letters; gossip; calligraphy; conventional *haiku* poem writing; decorations on the day of the Festival of the Weaver
Performing	Festivals; funerals; *miai* meetings; family albums; family videos; *karuta* (Japanese playing cards); *sugoroku* (a Japanese variety of parcheesi); *fukubiki* lotteries; visits to a family tomb; political demonstrations

Adapted from Tsurumi 1967, p.70.

sections in which avid amateurs contribute satirical observations on world affairs in the form of short poems.

Contemporary Japan is full of alternative culture. The following sections delineate only a few aspects of it.

1 "Mini-communication" Media

Despite the immense power of mass media, small-scale publications flourish in grassroots Japan. Community newsletters, consumer group pamphlets, voluntary association magazines, ecological newspapers, and many other types of "mini-communication" publications thrive throughout the country. Maruyama lists some 750 titles of this kind,[14] although this inventory is only the tip of a substantial iceberg. Called *mini-komi*, these publications proliferated especially from the mid 1960s to the mid 1970s in the context of the collapse of social movements opposing the US–Japan Security Treaty and the rise of those against the Vietnam War and university authorities. This was a time when politically committed citizens consciously developed a counterculture with networks of small groups in deliberate opposition to the mass media's depictions of the world. The waves of small communication media subsided with the good performance of the Japanese economy and the decline in open political confrontations. Nonetheless, mini-communication media play significant roles in environmental movements, notably those against nuclear electricity plants. Groups concerned about the safety of food are active in the publication of newsletters, pamphlets, and mini-magazines. Other alternative groups, in their *mini-komi*, question the Japanese quality of life, which seems not to reflect the nation's apparent material wealth.

Using feeble radio transmissions that do not require legal authorization, mini-FM stations have proliferated since the 1980s. These small, community-based "free radio" stations try to mirror the needs and views of small groups of listeners not catered to by the major radio stations. Since 1992, more substantial community FM radio stations have commenced operation throughout the country. Staffed by small groups of employees and volunteer workers, these stations reflect the voices of marginalized groups much more than large commercial radio stations, and open the possibility that they might become significant grassroots media.

The development of high technology by the Japanese corporate world has provided these small groups with efficient modes of communication. With the advent of online networking, alternative group activists are now able to exchange and disseminate information about their movements. With the expansion of personal-computer communication systems throughout the country, an increasing number of youngsters participate in discussions on various issues on these networks. While this type of "high-tech conversation" is available only to those with sufficient money and technical knowledge, it does provide a new mode of social intercourse which enables people to have democratic access to electronically controlled but open conversations with strangers, often cutting across national boundaries.

2 Countercultural Events and Performances

Alternative theaters figure in the countercultural scenery in urban Japan. They challenge the formalist styles of drama performed in established theaters and seek to offer independent, intentionally scandalous and "non-routinized" entertainment in show tents, small playhouses, and underground halls. These theaters reject the convention of following prepared scripts and defy the formal division between the actors (as players on stage) and the audience (as spectators). They involve both in interactive situations, use non-verbal symbols including human bodies and physical objects on stage to the maximum extent, and invite spontaneity in a bid to "demolish" time and space. The flesh, dreams, emotions, and "alien substances" play major symbolic roles in these theaters, where primitive sentiments are to be revitalized against the background of the modern, technological, and mechanical environment. These small theaters have been gradually absorbed into the mainstream since their heyday in the 1960s and 1970s, but still function as dissonant voices against the increasing influence of mass media.

At a more spontaneous level, new waves of pop art, street performance, and stylish fashion come and go in urban centers, where lavish shops, postmodern buildings, and high-technology screens abound. In Tokyo, for instance, railway terminals such as Shinjuku and Shibuya and entertainment districts such as Harajuku and Roppongi provide a milieu where trendy youth culture bubbles and talk-of-the-town groups flourish. A case in point is the so-called bamboo shoot tribe,[15] teenagers who regularly appeared in the 1980s in unconventional clothes in Tokyo's Harajuku-Yoyogi area on Sundays when the streets were closed to vehicular traffic. These youngsters danced in the streets, wearing a variety of richly colored and eye-catching clothes, including Japanese happi coats, Chinese dresses and Hawaiian muumuus. They worked as ordinary company employees during the week but at the weekend liberated themselves in this manner from daily routine. Though temporary and tentative, these street performances provided youngsters with self-expression and self-actualization.

3 New Religions

New religions come and go, capturing marginalized individuals and giving them some fantasies of salvation. In the immediate postwar decades when Japan was in both material and spiritual turmoil, established religions were challenged by new religious groups, including *Sōkagakkai*, a Buddhist sect with a political grouping called *Kōmei* at both national and local politics, and *Seichō no Ie*, a right-wing religious organization with a nationalist ideology and an anti-abortion commitment. They lost their initial populist fervor and became institutionalized over time. In their place, small but rapidly expanding fresh religious groups came to the fore after the nation gained stability and affluence in the 1970s. Though relatively small in membership, they make their presence felt by energetic campaigns, and forming subcultures which differentiate them from the prevailing patterns of life in contemporary Japan. These new religious subcultures display a few distinct characteristics.[16]

First, many of the new religions engage in occultism and mysticism, and use magic and necromancy in contradiction to the rationalist approach of modern religion. *Shinreikyō* (God-Soul Sect), *Mahikari Kyōdan* (True Light Sect), and *Kiriyama Mikkyō* (Kiriyama Esotericism) fall into this category. They all set forth a doctrine of various types and worlds of souls in an invisible space, and elaborate on the ways in which both good and bad souls govern the happiness, health, and life of each individual. These sects also claim to have secret exorcist rituals to remove deleterious souls from possessed people. Adherents seem to be interested primarily in participating in the acts of incantation and enchantment.

Second, the tenets of most new religions are based upon spectacular images of the cosmos, labelled as the solar system; there is a ring of souls, and other groups of souls form star constellations. The teaching is that the apocalyptic dramas that unfold in such a vast universe with souls, angels, and demons as main actors influence the everyday life of individuals in this world. Some of these new religions are also orientated to eschatological fundamentalism, which teaches that the end of the earth is drawing close. Stirring fear and anxiety and smacking of science fiction, these grandiose visions appear to captivate those who feel profoundly alienated in the automated, predictable, and regulated environment of the modern world. Some of the religions make maximum use of mass media. The founder of *Kofuku no Kagaku* (Science of Happiness), for example, published some one hundred books with a total of several million copies sold. These organizations also hold spectacular mass religious performance sessions in baseball stadiums and large halls.

Finally, believers in these religions take much interest in developing what they regard as supernatural capacities such as extrasensory perception and psychokinesis. Followers engage in ascetic practices in an attempt to acquire these abilities. Leaders of *Aum Shinrikyō*, the group which in 1995 was suspected of releasing deadly nerve gas in the Tokyo subway system, became the focus of nationwide criticism for giving followers chemical drinks and injections of dangerous doses of drugs, allegedly to induce a high level of enlightenment. On the pretext of enabling followers to elevate their spiritual capacities, the group confined adherents to its precincts, arrested deserters by force, and compelled new participants to offer all their personal assets and belongings to the sect. In these ways, followers were forced to give total loyalty to the guru in return for the supposed acquisition of supernatural skills.

The absence of firm political ideology after the end of the Cold War provides a breeding ground for new religious groups. Growing frustrations, particularly among youngsters, with regimented school life and stern company life pave the way for commitment to irrational alternatives.

4 Socially Deviant Groups

Deviant groups are countercultural in their defiance of authorities. "Bikies" or motorcycle freaks, for instance, form countercultural youth gangs.[17] Clad in singular costumes, they ride their motorcycles in groups, generate much noise pollution (often at night), and cause a public uproar from time to time. Many of them live at the fringe of society, having dropped out of school and taken menial jobs. They despise and resent the stability of middle-class culture and find satisfaction in disturbing it.

At a more serious level, *Yakuza*, Japan's mafia groups, construct a particular pattern of anti-social culture, engaging in all sorts of illegal activities from blackmail, extortion, and fraud to murder. Their groups have a strict hierarchical order, demand total devotion from members, and require each new member to have his little finger cut off at an initiation ceremony. Many members come from the bottom of society and have a unique sense of bonding, unity, and comradeship among themselves. Their marginal background sometimes makes them side with the powerless and the poor despite their generally parasitic existence in society. These outlaw groups developed the moral code of *ninkyō*, a kind of chivalrous spirit with which each member is supposed "to assist the weak and resist the powerful," "to help others with total disregard for his own life," and "not to be ruled by avarice despite being a ruffian." These formulae do not represent the realities of the toughs, but constitute expected standards for their behavior in some areas and under some circumstances. These elements of their subculture have been portrayed with some sympathy in novels and films which have attained wide circulation.

5 Sexually Alternative Life-styles

Japanese lesbians and gays gradually and openly formed homosexual groupings in the 1990s.[18] Some of them run gay magazines such as *Adon*, *Za Gei*, *Sabu*, and *Barazoku*, some of which sell tens of thousand of copies. Lesbian newsletters like *Regumi Tsūshin* provide forums for organizing dance parties and establishing networks for homosexual females. Some groups organize local meetings and discuss their own issues and agendas, often in open defiance of the general community. It is public knowledge that there are gay bars and saunas where gay men have casual sex. While operating less conspicuously, some lesbian couples have come out of the closet.[19] Both steady, monogamous homosexual relationships and multiple sexual contacts between homosexuals form significant alternative cultures in Japan today, though they remain relatively undetectable in public in comparison with their counterparts in Western societies, a situation attributable to the harsher ideological reality that homosexuality is still rigidly taboo in Japan.

A small number of empirical studies of homosexual subculture in Japan[20] have shown that both gay men and lesbian women expect household chores to be equally divided between partners, while heterosexual men and women tend to be less egalitarian in this respect. Homosexual people are more open to experimenting with relationships and role patterns. They also appear to value *omoiyari*, the Japanese sense of empathy, very highly in friendships and relationships, more than those who criticize gays and lesbians as immoral. Troubled by the duality of female and male, some advocates of alternative culture in this area maintain that the public should accept, or at least tolerate, transvestism (cross-dressing) and transsexuality (sex change by operation) as legitimate life-styles, and redefine femininity and masculinity more liberally.[21]

The moral norm of "proper marriage" as the only acceptable life-style lingers, making it difficult even for de facto heterosexual relationships and remaining unmarried to be recognized as alternatives. Yet an increasing number of women and men choose to live as singles and prove to be happy and confident. A number of books have popularized the notion of "liberated single culture" in a positive light.[22] Such groupings as *Dokushin Fujin Renmei* (Single Women's League) provide networks for women who do not marry either by circumstance or by choice. More and more youngsters appear to choose *jijitsu-kon* (de facto relationships) as their way of life. These life-styles are deeply discordant with Japan's narrow and marriage-based definition of sexuality, thereby shaking the dominant ideology of fixed gender roles.

6 Political Activism

Politically charged alternative culture has emerged during radical protest movements against the state. In Minamata, Kyūshū, a series of anti-pollution protests, lasting for nearly four decades, developed a distinctive dissident culture: many members of the fishing community there were crippled after eating fish poisoned by a large quantity of mercury which a chemical company in the area knowingly discharged into the sea. The victims were supported by political activists from city areas, who joined forces with them in demanding both apologies and material compensation from the company and the state, whose negligence contributed to the spread of the problem.[23] Another case in point is a long-lasting protest movement against the construction of the New Tokyo International Airport in the rural town of Narita. Farmers in the area mounted a series of violent confrontations in the 1970s and 1980s together with student radicals and other supporters from Tokyo and other urban centers, protesting against the state expropriation of farmers' land.[24]

In these and similar cases, the fusion between local protesters and outside radicals generated a particular type of alternative culture; a kind of "magnetic field" of cultural creativity was generated when permanent local residents who constituted the "subjectivity of the movement" formed a tie with volunteer support groups which drifted into the local community from outside.[25] This kind of alternative culture is characterized by a strong sense of defiance against the state which destroyed the peaceful lives of local residents, using police to protect the expansionary programs of the business or the state. This type of dissident culture has a sharp moral tone, denouncing development programs as vicious and claiming that it is essential for their promoters to engage in sincere self-criticism and apologize.

7 Communes and the Natural Economy

Alternative culture finds radical expression in communes based upon the natural economy and the abolition of private ownership. Cases in point include *Atarashii Mura* (New Villages) in Saitama and Miyazaki prefectures, *Shinkyō Buraku* in Nara, and *Ittō-kai* in Kyoto. *Yamagishi-kai*, founded by Miyozō Yamagishi in the 1950s, is arguably the best-known and largest in Japan. Originating with a small group of mainly farmers in Mie prefecture, it is now a nationwide network of small-scale communes espousing a philosophy of symbiosis with nature and total pacifism. Renouncing private property and income, commune dwellers make a life-time commitment to the movement, adopt simple life-styles, and remain entirely non-religious. While many of its communes manage poultry farms and engage in agricultural production, the group's headquarters publishes newsletters, runs schools, and organizes special courses at which outsiders lodge together for a week to discuss the communes' philosophy. *Yamagishi-kai* has attracted ex-student political activists, environmentalists, and other disenchanted reformist types.

In a broader context, networks of ecologists are formed across the country to provide organically produced agricultural goods to the public, using the symbols of cooperation and coexistence with nature. In rural communities, they challenge mechanized mass-production of produce contaminated by agricultural chemicals, and turn their attention to the traditional wisdom of environmentally sound methods. In distribution processes, the "life-club cooperatives" based in urban communities collectively purchase organic foods directly from growers. A few take the form of "worker collectives" in which participating members promote the establishment of distribution networks based on principles of direct democracy and flexible organization. They look for ways of recycling and exchanging unwanted goods, establishing collective children's nurseries, and developing a kind of counter-economy among themselves.[26] Several hundred cooperatives and collectives of this kind operate throughout Japan.[27]

Table 9.3 Characteristics of four types of culture

Population size of appreciators	Economic resources of producers	
	Plentiful	Limited
Small	Elite	Alternative
Large	Mass	Folk

V The Plurality of Popular Culture

This chapter has surveyed three types of popular culture which derive from different social formations. Mass culture is constantly produced as a process of modern society in which the populace is atomized and susceptible to mass-produced merchandise and information propagated by mass media. The Japanese analytical category for this type of mass is *taishū*, though it is increasingly segmented into small units such as *bunshū* and *shōshū* – masses which have particular requirements for certain goods, services and information, as discussed in chapter 1.

Folk culture has been nurtured in the soil of what Japanese ethnographers call *jōmin*, those ordinary persons who may not engage in the production of pure or mass art but who express themselves in various forms of marginal art. Folk culture has its origin mostly in the non-literary world, having little to do with written forms of communication.

Alternative culture mirrors the dissatisfaction, grievances, and disenchantment of some sections of the community but remains small and marginal. Located at the fringe of Japanese society, alternative culture groups present images and world views that are discordant with or go beyond the frameworks of both mass and folk culture. As such, they are invariably exposed to the danger of being extinguished or assimilated into mass or folk culture.

Each person embodies all three cultural elements, though their relative importance may differ between individuals. A committed commune activist may enjoy reading *manga* magazines and singing traditional folk songs. An avid Shinto believer may participate in countercultural *mini-komi* publications and spend a few hours playing *pachinko* every week. Looking at the entire cultural scene at a macro level, one might be able to classify elite and popular culture in terms of the magnitude of the economic resources that producers of culture require and possess, and the proportion of the population which appreciates it. As Table 9.3 indicates, elite culture is appreciated by comparatively few but is amply supported economically, while alternative culture tends to be both small and in economic terms relatively deprived. The four types are respectively majority and minority cultures, depending upon the criteria used.

Notes

1 NHK 1992, pp. 347–8.
2 NHK 1992, pp. 238–41.
3 AM April 20 1994, p. 29.
4 The Leisure Development Center's 1988 edition of the Leisure White Paper.
5 Pierre Baudry maintains that *pachinko* originated in the late nineteenth century in France (*Nihon Keizai Shinbun*, December 13 1994, morning edition, p. 36).
6 Tada 1978, pp. 42–51.
7 AE July 25 1992, p. 5.
8 Satō 1994, p. 114.
9 At the beginning of the 1990s, there were over 1,400 Japanese "soap lands" where some 15,000 "soap girls" worked.
10 Sakurai 1982.
11 Namihira 1979.
12 NHK 1991, p. 93.
13 Tsurumi 1967, ch. 1.
14 Maruyama 1985.
15 The term is attributable to the fact that the youngsters wore clothes that they bought at the boutique known as *Takenoko*, meaning "bamboo shoots."
16 Nishiyama 1979.
17 See, for example, Kersten 1993.
18 Lunsing 1995a represents the most extensive ethnographic study in English on this form of alternative culture.
19 See, for example, the special edition of the magazine *Bessatsu Takarajima*, no. 64, published in 1991 by JICC Shuppan under the title of *Onna-tachi o aisuru onna-tachi no monogatari* (*The Stories of Women Who Love Women*). It reported the stories of 234 lesbian women.
20 See, for example, Lunsing 1995a and 1995b; Fushimi 1991.
21 See Lunsing 1995a, ch. 7.
22 Ebisaka 1986; Yoshihiro 1987 and 1988.
23 See Huddle and Reich 1987.
24 See Apter and Sawa 1984.
25 Irokawa 1989, pp. 80–1.
26 Furusawa 1988, especially part IV.
27 Shimogō 1990.

10

Friendly Authoritarianism

Two ostensibly contradictory forces operate in Japanese society, as they do in other industrialized societies. On the one hand, it is subject to many centrifugal forces that tend to diversify its structural arrangements, life-styles and value orientations. On the other hand, a range of centripetal forces drive Japanese society towards homogeneity and uniformity. While this book has examined both forces, its chapters are organized in terms of the ways in which centrifugal forces operate in such key spheres as work, education, gender, and ethnicity. This chapter concentrates on the centripetal forces, locating a variety of forms of control in an analytical framework.

Japanese society has various forms of regimentation that are designed to standardize the thought patterns and attitudes of the Japanese and make them toe the line in everyday life. While these pressures exist in any society, in Japan they constitute a general pattern which one might call friendly authoritarianism. It is authoritarian to the extent that it encourages each member of society to internalize and share the value system which regards control and regimentation as natural, and to accept the instructions and orders of people in superordinate positions without questioning. As a system, friendly authoritarianism:

1 uses small groups as the basis of mutual surveillance and deterrence of deviant behavior. A kind of lateral control within a small group compels each member to compete with the others to comply with the expected norms and standards;
2 institutes an extensive range of mechanisms in which power is made highly visible and tangible;
3 legitimizes various codes in such a way that superordinates can use ambiguities to their advantage. Arrangements couched in vague terms allow power-holders to reinterpret them as the occasion requires; and

4 inculcates various forms of moralistic ideology into the psyche of every individual with a particular stress upon minute and trivial details. Spontaneous expressions and free actions of individuals are generally discouraged.

Japan's authoritarianism does not normally exhibit its coercive face, generally dangling soft incentives of various kinds.[1] It is "friendly" to the extent that:

1 it resorts, wherever possible, to positive inducements rather than negative sanctions – "carrots" rather than "sticks" – to encourage competition to conform;
2 it portrays individuals and groups in power positions as congenial, cordial, and benevolent, and uses socialization channels for subordinates to pay voluntary respect to them;
3 it propagates the ideology of equality and the notion of a unique national homogeneity, ensuring that images of class cleavage are as blurred as possible; and
4 it relies upon joyful, amusing, and pleasant entertainments such as songs, visual arts, and festivals to make sure that authority infiltrates without obvious pains.

When ineffective, these friendly elements are abandoned, and recourse is had to more coercive controls.[2] While Japan's formal institutions are no doubt organized in accordance with democratic principles, there lingers a suspicion that the Japanese system is not really arranged to give first priority to the human rights that are regarded as the cornerstone of democracy.[3]

1 Mutual Surveillance Within Small Groups

The first element of Japanese friendly authoritarianism relies upon the capacity of small groups to evoke from members maximum compliance with the dominant norms of society. These groups are often pitted against each other to achieve intragroup mutual surveillance by dint of intergroup competition. The most prevalent form of this method is *han*, a small unit composed of five to ten individuals. All children in Japan learn the *han* system in primary school, where each class is subdivided into *han* units.[4] They are expected to compete with each other in conforming to such school norms as high academic achievement and good behavior. On classroom walls, teachers and pupils often display the outcomes of daily, weekly, or monthly competition among *han* groups, ranging, for example, from mathematics test results, the number of pupils who failed to complete homework assignments, and scores for tidiness, to the number of pupils who forgot to clip their nails. As each *han* is praised or blamed as a collective unit, there is constant intragroup pressure on members to comply with the expected standard.

The total quality control (TQC) movement to which Japanese economic success is often attributed perhaps best epitomizes the Japanese technology of human control through mutual surveillance. The initial version of quality control in the United States was statistical quality control, where a random sample of commodities was checked thoroughly so as to decrease the number of defective goods shipped out of the firm. After the importation of this method from the United States, Japanese management expanded its application to the workers themselves.

The basic unit of the QC movement in Japanese firms is a group of ten to fifteen members in the same section or division. Each group is expected to present as many proposals as possible to improve both the quality of products and the efficiency of work arrangements, in order to maximize productivity and marketing efficiency. Since the number of proposals per group is the crucial index of competition, each group member is under constant pressure to think of ways to improve his or her company. In this process, employees often unconsciously conceptualize their work setting not from the worker's but from the manager's point of view. While the primary function of this movement is quality improvement and it does not involve physical coercion, it tends to produce employees highly devoted to the company. In some firms, the TQC movement is called JK (*jishu kanri*) activity (literally, voluntary control). The phrase epitomizes latent aspects of the activity, drawing attention to the extent to which employees are controlled under the guise of voluntary commitment.

The ideology that the members of a collective unit are jointly responsible for its performance places restraints upon each member. When one or a few members of a unit indulge in culpable behavior, all members bear the blame collectively. When one pupil plays a mischievous trick or disobeys the rules, teachers sometimes punish the entire class by making all pupils stay late, organizing a soul-searching session, or, as in one controversial case, ordering all boys in the class to cut their hair short.[5] If a member of a promising high-school baseball team engages in delinquent behavior, the principle of shared responsibility can force the entire team to withdraw from a national tournament. The whole group assumes collective responsibility (*rentai sekinin*) for the wrongdoings of each member.

Every community has a *han* network. In the lowest reaches of government, Japanese communities have neighborhood associations composed of several to a few dozen households.[6] These associations are variously called *chōnaikai* or *chōkai* (town-block associations). They are called *jichikai* (self-government associations) or simply *han* in some areas, and *burakukai* or *kukai* (hamlet associations) in rural localities. There are only seven municipalities in Japan without such associations.[7] Once formed, they normally involve an overwhelming majority of households in a community. Only a small fraction of Japanese, mostly resident in metropolitan areas, are not members of such a group.

Neighborhood associations are characterized by several features.[8] First, they engage in a wide range of activities and function as all-purpose organizations. At a social level, their members organize and take part in community gatherings, fetes, outings, and festival dances. Once in a while they are called upon to clean gutters, engage in activities for the prevention of crime and fire, and collect donations for community causes. Many associations manage and maintain a community hall. Almost all of them serve as distribution networks for circulars, fliers, and information leaflets from their municipal government.

Second, the unit of association membership is the household, not the individual. This means that associations tend to be male-dominated because the head of the family, who is usually male, attends association meetings and participates in association activities as the household representative. The directory of an association's membership normally lists the names of family heads only.

Third, it is semi-compulsory for a household to join a neighborhood association. When a family moves into a locality, its neighborhood association automatically enlists the family as a member and requests its subscription. Association membership is not voluntary, as the family is given little choice. Furthermore, because only one neighborhood association exists per area, residents do not have alternative options.

Chōnaikai associations function as the grassroots *han* units which transmit governmental and semi-governmental programs at community level in a variety of ways. One of them is the practice of vertical quota allotment typical of nationwide fund-raising campaigns. In a community-chest drive, for example, the semi-governmental National Community Chest Organization first sets the national target of the total amount of funds to be raised and allocates an amount to each prefecture on the basis of its population. Each prefectural government then divides its allocated figure among all municipal governments in proportion to their populations, and each municipal government issues quota figures to all *chōnaikai* on the same basis. The leaders of each association then normally send the exact amount to the municipal government. The donations thus raised flow to the national level after prefectural governments have collected them through municipal governments. Because of this system, community chest drives in Japan rarely fail to achieve their targets.

As community-based *han* units, neighborhood associations cooperate in many ways with various branches of local government and semi-governmental agencies. A section of a *chōnaikai* often collaborates with police in crime prevention programs in its area. *Chōnaikai* frequently act as the basic units in fire drills and other disaster prevention exercises organized by the local fire defense headquarters. Members of *chōnaikai* also come into close cooperative contact with government-backed associations concerned with local hygiene, social welfare, and compliance with tax laws.

A survey[9] suggests that an overwhelming majority of Japanese support the existence of *chōnaikai*, though there is much regional variation in the grounds for support. Residents in regional cities place the significance of neighborhood associations in their capacity to organize such social functions as local galas, entertainment gatherings, and *bon* festival dances. Those who live in Tokyo, however, regard crime prevention and sanitation as the prime functions of *chōnaikai*. To the extent that there is community support for grassroots state apparatus, the mechanism of mutual surveillance within each *han* group continues to operate, blurring the line between voluntary dedication and state manipulation.

The prototype of *han* ideology is discernible in Tokugawa Japan in the feudal regime's implementation of a nationwide network of five-family neighborhood units known as the *go-nin gumi* system. This served as a quasi-espionage organization. Families in a neighborhood were required to watch each other for any signs of deviant activities. During World War II, a similar system was devised under the name *tonari-gumi* (neighborhood watch) to promote conformity and solidarity at the community level in support of war activities. Even today, while this type of community network no longer serves as machinery for military propaganda, it is a significant channel through which the power of the state permeates into every part of Japanese society in the form of community voluntary cooperation.

The *han* system is effective in ensuring attitudinal and behavioral conformity among its members precisely because it is not predicated upon the imposition of authority from above. Instead of vertical control, the system counts upon a kind of horizontal control where the policing of people of the same status in a small unit – classmates, work colleagues, or neighborhood acquaintances – makes it difficult for them to diverge from the standard expected;[10] while higher status persons are connected to each *han*, those who control a person are not necessarily above but next to them.

2 Visible and Tangible Power

The second aspect of the Japanese style of friendly authoritarianism is the way in which power and authority are made visible and tangible in everyday life rather than being abstract and conceptual; attempts are made to ensure that the dominant moral order is reproduced at the level of face-to-face "existential" situations.

This tendency is most conspicuous in the area of law enforcement. The Japanese police system penetrates into every corner of society. More than half a million households, or about one in fifty, are organized as "households for crime prevention" and are closely associated with police stations. About 40 percent of Japanese police officers are stationed in small community-based police boxes known as *kōban*, or in substations called *chūzaisho*.

While this system has received international attention as a way of reducing crime rates, it imposes close surveillance on the private lives of individuals. Each *kōban* or *chūzaisho* policeman routinely visits households and business establishments within his jurisdiction to obtain information about them and to inquire whether any "suspicious figures" hang around the neighborhood. Though performed in the name of the maintenance of public safety, this practice, known as *junkai renraku* (patrol liaison), often verges upon invasion of individual privacy.

As an essential part of this exercise, police provide a liaison card to each household, requesting details such as its telephone number, the date of residents' settlement at that present address, the identification of the household head, each member's name, date of birth, occupation, place of work or school, and the address and telephone number of a contact person in emergency. For enterprises such as firms and shops, the card covers such items as the type of business, the person in charge, the number of employees, the hours which it is open for business, the days it is regularly closed, and whether the business owns a dog. Officially, the system is intended to make it easy for policemen in the community to show the way to visitors, make contact in emergencies, and facilitate other public services. Community residents are not legally required to fill out these cards and return them to police.

In reality, however, nearly all households do so. Many genuinely believe that the system prevents neighborhood crime and improves police services. Others accept it because they fear that declining to fill out the card might incur police suspicion that they are rebels or criminals, and police might bring them under close surveillance. Only a tiny minority of civil libertarians are willing to risk the likelihood of police suspicion. The practice serves to test the level of community cooperation with police activities. The performance of policemen who are placed in *kōban*, *chūzaisho*, and other small, community-linked police stations is evaluated in terms of the extent to which they have secured "voluntary cooperation" from the community under their jurisdiction. Such appraisal includes the number of households about which they have succeeded in acquiring information through *junkai renraku*.[11] While the system is based upon the voluntary cooperation of the public, most households are will-ing to expose themselves to police data-gathering machinery. Effective community control thus occurs even though its implementation takes the form of supposed individual voluntarism.

In the area of education, teachers actively present themselves as moral authorities in their school district. At primary-school level, home-room teachers routinely visit the home of every child under their charge to meet his or her parents at least once a year. The teachers are expected to discuss the child's scholastic and social development and exchange views with the parents. While this practice allegedly facilitates good communi-cation between schools and homes, it is virtually compulsory in the sense that parents do not have the option of welcoming or declining these visits. Teachers frequently perform policing functions, making parents serve as quasi-agents to control children at home in line with the school's ethos. It is not unusual for teachers, together with police and parents, to patrol amusement arcades and shopping areas to make sure pupils toe the line after school.

In community life, the Japanese encounter a steady flow of verbal and visual instructions from authorities about expected behavior. Japanese train conductors constantly announce what passengers should and should not do, saying, for instance, "Do not stand near the door," "Hold on to a strap," "Make room for other people," and "Let us offer seats to senior citizens." Railway stations broadcast such announcements as "Please stand behind the white line as a train is approaching the station," "Stand in two rows in an orderly manner until the train arrives," and "Would you kindly not jostle one another when you step into the train." Streets and public places are studded with signs with such instructions as "Keep out" and "No admittance."

These techniques softly control the populace by ensuring that the dominant moral order is reproduced in face-to-face situations. The power of the state does not remain an abstract concept but is brought into daily experience in a moralistic fashion.

3 Manipulation of Ambiguity

The third ingredient of Japan's friendly authoritarianism relies upon an ideology which encourages ambiguity in a variety of circumstances. This enables those in positions of authority to interpret various situations at their discretion.

In the sphere of law, police enjoy extensive discretionary power. A case in point concerns the supplementary jail system in which lockup cells at police stations are used as substitutes for prison. Police are supposed to send an arrested suspect to a house of detention under the jurisdiction of the Ministry of Justice within forty-eight hours of arrest. However, in reality, a majority of suspects are kept in police detention under the Jail Law, enacted in 1908 and still enforced. In an exception clause, this law allows police to use their lockup cells as an alternative to an official detention house. While the Ministry of Justice wishes to retain this practice, the Japan Federation of Bar Associations and human rights groups oppose it as an arrangement which allows investigators to question suspects for inordinately long periods, resulting in numerous false charges based upon groundless confessions wrung out of suspects under duress. A dubious exception clause of a law enacted nine decades ago has thus been used as a basis for modern, general police practice simply because it suits law enforcement authorities.

The interpretation of the constitution, particularly Article 9, has also been a locus of ambiguity. The article states:

> Aspiring sincerely to an international peace based on justice and order, the Japanese people forever renounce war as a sovereign right of the nation and the threat or use of force as means of settling international disputes.
>
> In order to accomplish the aim of the preceding paragraph, land, sea, and air forces, as well as other war potential, will never be maintained. The right of belligerency of the state will not be recognized.

When the constitution was promulgated in 1946, the spirit of the Article was that Japan would never again possess armed forces of any kind. With the Cold War escalating in East Asia, the Police Reserve Forces were established in 1950 without parliamentary approval, claiming that they were not military troops. Soon they changed their name, first to the Public Security Forces and then to the Guard Forces after the ratification of the peace treaty. In 1954 they became the Self-Defense Forces, and have since developed into armed forces of some quarter of a million troops equipped with sophisticated weaponry. While the Self-Defense Forces are organized to defend the country against acts of aggression from outside, some members have served as part of UN peacekeeping operations abroad, and as disaster relief units domestically.

These step-by-step shifts in the interpretation of the same text reflect what Japanese call *nashikuzushi*, the pragmatic strategy that many Japanese power-holders at various levels use to adapt gradually to changing circumstances. The term *nashikuzushi* originally meant payments by installment, but in this context it implies that players achieve their final goal by making a series of small changes in the meaning of key terms in a document. The technique does not call for alteration of the text itself. The point is not so much the validity of the changing interpretations as the almost imperceptible way in which they been brought about, little by little.

In all these circumstances, equivocation rather than articulation is promoted, allowing those in dominant positions to manipulate what is meant, what is right, and what should be done. In many companies, as suggested in chapter 4, fresh employees are not given formal contracts or job specifications and their supervisors can use their discretion in defining the tasks which subordinate employees should perform, a practice which partly accounts for the long working hours in Japan. As discussed in chapter 8, the practice of administrative guidance (*gyōsei shidō*) enables public bureaucrats to maneuver the private sector without clear statutory basis, because the representatives of companies are aware that the bureaucrats have the power to apply implicit sanctions against those who do not follow their instructions. The school textbook authorization system described in chapter 5 gives the Ministry of Education censors broad scope for subjective revisions of submitted manuscripts, enabling them to exercise unspecified control over textbook writers. In effect, ambiguity offers advantages to power-holders as they can use it to enforce their will upon subordinates at their discretion, in the absence of clearly documented rules and regulations.

4 Moralizing and "Mind Correctness."

The fourth element of Japan's friendly authoritarianism is the extent to which various moralizing techniques are used to appeal deeply to the psyche of individuals. A case in point is the way in which Japanese authorities require offenders against laws and rules to express total contrition for their wrongdoing. For even minor offenses such as traffic violations and unintended trespassing, the authorities regard it as insufficient for an offender to lose a license or pay a fine; they also demand that the offender write or sign a letter of apology (*shimatsusho*). It is usually a form letter containing such sentences as "I am very sorry for breaching a public regulation" and "I endeavor never to repeat the same error." The letter is normally addressed to the holder of a public office, such as the head of district police or the mayor of the municipality where the offense occurred. This practice has no statutory basis but is enforced with the reasoning that offenders need to cleanse their spirits completely to conform to social norms in the future. This thinking gives priority to "mind correctness" of citizens. Various means are supposed to achieve such attitudinal conformity.

(a) Physical Correctness

The first of these focusses on "physical correctness." Japanese schools make it a rule for pupils to clean their classrooms each day after school.

At every Japanese school, pupils do keep-fit exercises to the well-known tunes of a radio program broadcast at a set time every day through a national public radio network. At school, each Japanese child is taught how to bow correctly, how to stand correctly, how to sit correctly, how to walk correctly, and so on. At work, many companies train employees how to greet customers, how to address superiors, and how to exchange name cards in an appropriate fashion. With this type of repeated training, many Japanese acquire a disposition to attend to details. In controlled situations, they tend to give heed to such matters as how to wrap gifts, how to present meals, and how to blow their noses.

(b) Emotive Moralizing

The second focus is the notion that people should learn conformity through emotive means. In this respect, collective singing plays an important role in generating a sense of group solidarity. All schools, including primary schools, have their own school song which has many moralistic lines, and pupils sing it on such occasions as morning assemblies, athletic meets, and entrance and graduation ceremonies. Many companies also have their own enterprise song which exalts the virtues of hard work and job commitment. Employees are expected to sing it daily at a morning gathering and on ceremonial occasions. Cities and other municipalities have a song that, in most cases, glorifies the natural beauty and historical tradition of their locality. Given that singing is generally fun blended with sentimental emotion, the Japanese method of enhancing solidarity combines such gaiety with the inculcation of values which praise organizational dedication. This technique strikes a responsive chord in participants and so tends not to give them the impression that they are being psychologically steered in a certain direction. Conscious of the power of collective singing for mass mobilization, Japan's leaders observed during World War II that popular "songs are military commodities."[12]

Against the background of the widespread practice of collective singing, it comes as no surprise that *karaoke* singing has become common in Japan's entertainment quarters. As a combination of merriment and tension management, this new popular culture, which has become an epidemic since the late 1970s, reflects the extent to which emotive conformity and collective singing interact in Japanese society.

(c) A Community of Sanctions

The socially constructed images of a community that exercises sanctions against acts of deviance are a third means of generating psychological compliance. For this purpose, *emic* notions are often invoked as those

Table 10.1   Japanese *emic* conceptions of social relations

	Group size	Kinship relationship (either real or symbolic)	
		Absent	*Present*
Large		*Seken*	*Harakara*[a] (fraternity)
Small		*Nakama* (mates, fellows or comrades)	*Miuchi*[b] (relatives)

Source: Adapted from Yoneyama 1990, p. 98.
Notes
[a] This concept often is used to describe "we, the Japanese" (*ware ware Nihonjin*) as the largest imagined kinship unit.
[b] This notion refers to a small, fictitious kinship unit in which *oyabun* (patriarchal godfather figure) and *kobun* (his devoted followers) form family-like relationships.

which penetrate into the soul of the Japanese. A case in point is the concept of *seken*, an imagined community that has the normative power of approving or disapproving of and sanctioning individual behavior. *Seken* extends beyond primary groups such as immediate kin, workmates, and neighbors, but does not encompass the entire society of Japan, and still less overseas societies. As an intermediate network, *seken* makes its presence felt in the minds of many Japanese as the largest unit of social interaction which does not imply blood relations[13] (see Table 10.1). In reference to *seken*'s censuring functions, it is often said that if one deviates from social norms, *seken* will not accept one. If one does something shameful, one will not be able to face *seken*. One should not expect *seken* to be lenient and permissive. When an organization is found to be involved in an unacceptable practice, its leaders often make public apologies for disturbing *seken*. When one refers to *seken* accepting or renouncing a certain choice or behavior, one envisages *seken* not only as the standard gauge or rule but as those individuals who compel it. As an imagined but realistic entity, *seken* presents itself as a web of people who provide the moral yardsticks that favor the status quo and traditional practices.

(d) Ideology of Egalitarian Competition

Finally, the Japanese establishment has promoted an ideology of equality of opportunity and generally discourages ascriptive inequality based upon family origin. While the framework has not covered women and minority groups, it has nevertheless championed the meritocratic doctrine that every Japanese has an equal chance of achieving high status through persistent effort. In the world of secular symbols, this notion is translated into the phrase *risshin shusse*, the "careerism" in which one can get ahead in life and rise in the world through arduous endeavor and perseverance. Even if born in a deprived peasant family, a bright boy who studies hard is legitimately expected to get into a top university and eventually attain a high-ranking position in an important company. Prewar textbooks abound with legends of self-made men of this sort. Popular writings argue that one's success in life depends solely on the extent to which one mobilizes the spirit of *ganbari* (determination) which everyone possesses intrinsically and equally. Invoking the principle of fairness to all, most public and private universities in Japan accept or reject students exclusively on the basis of their scores at entrance examinations, without considering their other attributes. In this limited sense, Japan is an egalitarian, achievement-orientated society. In reality, those who have risen to the higher echelons of society from lower family backgrounds comprise only a small portion of the total population. Therefore, Japan is, on a mass basis, a pseudo-egalitarian society. Nevertheless, the illusion, and occasional reality, that everybody is given equal opportunities to succeed is sufficiently prevalent to drive many Japanese in a quest for educational, occupational, and material achievements.

This fantasy obscures the fact that opportunities are unevenly distributed across different social groups and strata. More importantly, it enables status-attainers to defend themselves as rightful winners of contests which have supposedly given everybody equal chances. It also makes it difficult for status-losers to hold grievances against successful achievers, because of the dominant myth that losers have been given an equitable opportunity but simply could not make it. Losers take the blame upon themselves and accept the supremacy and authority of those who have succeeded in climbing the ladder. Thus, the ideology of equality of opportunity leads to individualized and fragmented self-accusations by those who have failed, and blinds them to the structural inequalities they are subject to. In this sense, the Japanese experience appears to demonstrate that the ideology of equality of opportunity justifies the reality of the inequality of outcomes more plausibly than does the doctrine which rationalizes inequality of opportunities.[14]

These four aspects of moral indoctrination in Japan can be summarized schematically. Table 10.2 combines the two dimensions of inculcation. One dimension is whether the method in question emphasizes negative sanctions or positive inducements. For example, while *seken* imposes negative constraints (Cell B), singing songs relies upon the positive sense of releasing one's feelings (Cell C). The other dimension concerns

Table 10.2 Types of strategies for moral indoctrination

	Negative moral sanctions	*Positive moral inducements*
Behavioral	(A) Physical correctness	(C) Collective singing
Ideational	(B) *Seken*	(D) Equality of opportunity

Table 10.3 Some specific examples of friendly authoritarianism in Japan

	Type of control			
Sphere of control	*Mutual surveillance within small groups*	*Visible and tangible power*	*Manipulative ambiguity*	*Moralizing and mind correctness*
Law	Family registration; resident-card system	*Kōban* (police box)	Constitution; supplementary jail system	*Shimatsusho* (apology letters)
Community	Neighbor-hood associations	Police house-hold checks	Extensive gift-giving practices	Sanction of *seken*
Business	TQC movement	Long working hours; service overtime	Unaccounted expenses; *dangō*	Company songs; company mottoes
Education	*Han* groups in class	Corporal punishment; *katei hōmon* (teachers making calls at pupils' homes)	School textook authorization system	Classroom cleaning; military attention

whether mind correctness is achieved behaviorally or ideationally. For instance, while training through physical learning requires behavioral rectification (Cell A), the ideology of equality of opportunity is propagated in the ideational sphere (Cell D). The other combinations are self-explanatory. The Japanese system compounds these elements to ensure both behavioral and ideational compliance through both negative and positive pressures.

Both institutional and ideological systems manipulate the everyday life of the Japanese from a variety of angles in a wide range of spheres so as to maintain the moral order of Japanese society. Table 10.3 shows some examples of the control mechanisms discussed in this book.

A finely blended combination of these control pressures in Japanese daily life has yielded the friendly authoritarianism which counteracts the diversified and stratified realities of Japanese society. This constraining force operates unevenly in different sectors of Japanese society. A tug-of-war between centripetal and centrifugal forces remains an ongoing process which produces dissimilar outcomes at different times.

The characteristics of Japanese society cannot be fully determined without defining its population base. It would be one-sided to define Japaneseness in a unitary way on the basis of observations of the elite sector only, without thoroughly analyzing the characteristics of a wide range of subcultural groups. The recognition of internal variation in Japan has implications for recognizing possible international similarities with counterparts in other societies, and for subcultural group communications and interactions across national boundaries. Comparative studies based upon such awareness would underscore the ways in which forces of friendly authoritarianism produce conformity and order in Japan. As diversity counteracts uniformity and subcultural groupings countervail control and regimentation, "Japan literacy" requires an in-depth understanding of the ways in which a shifting balance is struck in Japan between economic efficiency and political equity, between social stability and cultural reform, and between collective integration and individual dignity.

Notes

1 Soft control in Japanese society has been discussed by such writers as Broadbent 1983 and forthcoming; Pharr 1989.
2 Some Japanese critics have characterized Japanese society as *kanri shakai* (a manipulative society) with some of these features in mind. See, for example, Hidaka 1984; Shōji 1989; Yoshida 1989.
3 Some who accuse the Japanese system of being undemocratic have been adversely criticized as applying the Western yardstick of democracy to a different cultural context. Yet, unlike the leaders of some other Asian nations, most Japanese elites appear to accept democracy as a desirable goal even though they may neither articulate nor practice it.
4 Lewis 1988, especially pp. 168–70.
5 This case, which took place in a boys' high school in Fukuoka prefecture in Kyūshū in March 1995, generated much controversy. See AE March 3 1995, p. 15.

6 Bestor 1989 provides a detailed account of the ways in which these organizations function in Tokyo.

7 The national survey conducted by the Ministry of Home Affairs (Jichishō) in 1984.

8 Kurasawa and Akimoto 1990.

9 Iwasaki et al. 1989.

10 See Ashkenazi 1991 for a different interpretation of traditional, small group organizations and their functions in Japan.

11 AM June 3 1989, p. 30.

12 The comment of Navy Captain Ikuo Hirade of the Cabinet Information Bureau in 1941.

13 See Yoneyama 1971 and 1990, pp. 98–9.

14 Kumazawa 1993, pp. 105–20, shows how this process operates in workplaces.

References

Abbreviations

Newspapers

AM	*Asahi Shinbun*, morning edition.
AE	*Asahi Shinbun*, evening edition.
MM	*Mainichi Shinbun*, morning edition.
ME	*Mainichi Shinbun*, evening edition.

Books

SSM   Gendai Nihon *no kaisō kōzō* (Social stratification in contemporary Japan). Four volumes of the 1985 Social Stratification and Mobility study, published in 1990, University of Tokyo Press.

Japanese-language books in the following list were all published in Tokyo, unless specified otherwise.

Abegglen, James C. 1958, *The Japanese Factory: Aspects of Its Social Organization*. Bombay: Asia Publishing House.

Akhavan-Majid, Roya 1990, "The press as an elite power group in Japan," *Journalism Quarterly*, vol. 67, no. 4 (Winter): 1006–14.

Amanuma, Kaoru 1987, *"Ganbari" no kōzō: Nihonjin no kōdō genri* (Structure of "endurance": principle of Japanese behaviour). Yoshikawa Kōbundō.

Amino, Yoshihiko 1990, *Nihonron no shiza* (Perspectives on theories of Japan). Shōgakkan.

Amino, Yoshihiko 1994, *Nihon shakai saikō* (Reconsidering Japanese society). Shōgakkan.

Apter, David and Sawa, Nagayo 1984, *Against the State: Politics and Social Protest in Japan*. Cambridge, Massachusetts: Harvard University Press.

Arnason, Johann and Sugimoto, Yoshio (eds) 1995, *Japanese Encounters with Postmodernity*. London: Kegan Paul International.

Asada, Akira 1983, *Kōzō to chikara* (Structure and power). Keisō Shobō.

Asahi Shinbunsha (ed.) 1992, *Asahi kii waado '92–'93* (Asahi key words 1992–1993). Asahi Shinbunsha.

Ashkenazi, Michael 1991, "Traditional small group organization and cultural modelling in modern Japan," *Human Organization*, vol. 50, no. 4 (Winter): 385–92.

Ballescas, Ma. Rosario P. 1992, *Filipino Entertainers in Japan: An Introduction.* Quezon City: Foundation for Nationalist Studies.

Bandō, Mariko (ed.) 1992, *Zu de miru Nihon no Josei deeta banku* (Illustrated data bank on Japanese women). Ōkurashō Insatsu-kyoku.

Beardsley, Richard K., Hall, John W. and Ward, Robert E. 1959, *Village Japan.* Chicago: University of Chicago Press.

Befu, Harumi 1980, "A critique of the group model of Japanese society," *Social Analysis*, no. 5/6 (December): 29–43.

Befu, Harumi 1989, "The *emic–etic* distinction and its significance for Japanese studies," in Yoshio Sugimoto and Ross Mouer (eds), *Constructs for Understanding Japan.* London: Kegan Paul International, pp. 323–43.

Befu, Harumi 1990a, *Ideorogii to shite no Nihon bunka-ron* (Theories on Japanese culture as ideology), revised version. Shisō no Kagakusha.

Befu, Harumi 1990b, "Conflict and non-Weberian bureaucracy in Japan," in S. N. Eisenstadt and Eyal Ben-Sri (eds), *Japanese Models of Conflict Resolution.* London: Kegan Paul International, pp. 162–91.

Bellah, Robert 1957, *Tokugawa Religion: The Values of Pre-Industrial Japan.* New York: Free Press.

Benedict, Ruth 1946, *The Chrysanthemum and the Sword: Patterns of Japanese Culture.* Boston: Houghton Mifflin.

Berger, Peter L. and Hsiao, Hsin-Huang Michael (eds) 1988, *In Search of an East Asian Development Model.* New Brunswick: Transaction Books.

Bestor, Theodore 1989, *Neighborhood Tokyo.* Stanford: Stanford University Press.

Borthwick, Mark 1992, *Pacific Century: The Emergence of Modern Pacific Asia.* Boulder: Westview Press.

Bourdieu, Pierre 1986, *Distinction: A Social Critique of the Judgement of Taste*, trans. Richard Nice. London: Routledge.

Brinton, Mary C. 1988, "Social-institutional bases of gender stratification: Japan as an illustrative case," *American Journal of Sociology*, vol. 94, no. 2 (September): 300–34.

Brinton, Mary C. 1992, *Women and the Economic Miracle: Gender and Work in Postwar Japan.* Berkeley: University of California Press.

Broadbent, Jeffrey 1983, "Environmental movements in Japan: Citizen versus state mobilization." Paper presented at the annual meeting of the American Sociological Association.

Broadbent, Jeffrey forthcoming, *Environmental Politics in Japan: Networks of Power and Protest.* Cambridge: Cambridge University Press.

Buraku Kaihō Kenkyūsho (ed.) 1988, *Buraku mondai, shiryō to kaisetsu, dai 2-han* (Buraku problems: data and commentaries) 2nd edn. Osaka: Kaihō Shuppansha.

Buraku Kaihō Kenkyūsho (ed.) 1992, *Zusetsu konnichi no buraku sabetsu, dai 2-han* (Illustrated accounts of contemporary buraku discrimination) 2nd edn. Osaka: Kaihō Shuppansha.

Burenstam Linder, Staffan 1986, *The Pacific Century: Economic and Political Consequences of Asia-Pacific Dynamism.* Stanford: Stanford University Press.

Chan, Steve 1990, *East Asian Dynamism: Growth, Order and Security in the Pacific Region.* Boulder: Westview Press.

Cummings, William K. 1980, *Education and Equality in Japan.* Princeton: Princeton University Press.

Dale, Peter 1986, *The Myth of Japanese Uniqueness*. London: Routledge.

De Roy, Swadesh R. 1979, "A one-class society?," *Japan Quarterly*, vol. 26, no. 1: 204–11.

Deutschmann, Christoph 1987, "The Japanese type of organisation as a challenge to the sociological theory of modernisation," *Thesis Eleven*, no. 17: 40–58.

Deutschmann, Christoph 1991, "Working-bee syndrome in Japan: An analysis of working-time practice," in Karl Hinrichs, William Roche, and Carmen Sirianni (eds), *Working Time in Transition: The Political Economy of Working Hours in Industrial Nations*. Philadelphia: Temple University Press, pp. 189–202.

De Vos, George and Wagatsuma, Hiroshi 1966, *Japan's Invisible Race: Caste in Culture and Personality*. Berkeley: University of California Press.

De Vos, George and Wetherall, William O. (updated by Kaye Stearman) 1983, *Japan's Minorities: Burakumin, Koreans, Ainu and Okinawans*. London: Minority Rights Group.

Doi, Takeo 1971, *Amae no kōzō* (Patterns of dependence). Kōbundō.

Doi, Takeo 1973, *The Anatomy of Dependence*. Kodansha International.

Dore, R.P. (ed.) 1967, *Social Change in Modern Japan*. Princeton: Princeton University Press.

Dore, R.P. (ed.) 1973, *British Factory – Japanese Factory*. Berkeley: University of California Press.

Dore, R.P. (ed.) 1987, *Taking Japan Seriously: A Confucian Perspective on Leading Economic Issues*. London: Athlone.

Ebisaka, Takeshi 1986, *Shinguru raifu: Onna to otoko no kaihō-gaku* (Single life: liberation strategy for women and men). Chūō Kōronsha.

Eccleston, Bernard 1989, *State and Society in Post-War Japan*. Oxford: Polity Press.

Economic Planning Agency 1985, *Shakai katsudō sanka no jittai to kadai* (Realities and problems of participation in social activities).

Economic Planning Agency 1991, *Kokumin Seikatsu Hakusho* (White paper on national life).

Edwards, Walter Drew 1989, *Modern Japan Through its Weddings: Gender, Person and Society in Ritual Portrayal*. Stanford: Stanford University Press.

Eijingu Sōgō Kenkyū Sentā (ed.) 1993, *Kōreika shakai kiso shiryō nenkan, 1994-nen ban* (The 1994 yearbook of basic data on aging society). Eijingu Sōgō Kenkyū Sentā.

Eisenstadt, S.N. (ed.) 1987, *Patterns of Modernity*. London: Printer.

Emori, Susumu 1987, *Ainu no rekishi* (A history of the Ainu). Sanseidō.

Famighetti, Robert (ed.) 1994, *The World Almanac and Book of Facts 1995*. Mahwah, New Jersey: Funk & Wagnalls.

Forum Josei no Seikatsu to Tenbō (ed.) 1994, *Zuhyō de miru onna no genzai* (Graphic illustrations of women's situations today). Kyoto: Mineruva Shobō.

Fujita, Wakao 1984, *Sayonara, taishū* (A farewell to masses). Kyoto: PHP Kenkyūsho.

Fukuoka, Yasunori 1993, *Zai-nichi Kankoku Chōsen-jin* (Korean residents in Japan). Chūō Kōronsha.

Fukutake, Shoten 1992, *Monogurafu kōkōsei* (Monograph series: High-school students), no. 34.

Fukutake, Tadashi 1949, *Nihon nōson no shakai-teki seikaku* (Social characteristics of Japanese agricultural villages). University of Tokyo Press.

Fukutake, Tadashi 1981, *The Japanese Social Structure: Its Evolution in the Modern Century*, 2nd edn. University of Tokyo Press.

Furusawa, Kōyū 1988, *Kyōsei shakai no ronri* (The logic of co-habiting society). Gakuyō Shobō.

Fushimi, Noriaki 1991, *Puraibēto gei raifu: posuto ren'ai-ron* (Private gay life: A thesis on post-love). Gakuyō Shobō.

Gaimushō (ed.) 1995, *Sekai no kuni ichiranhyō, 1995-nen ban* (A list of countries in the world), 1995 edn. Sekai no Ugoki-sha.

Granovetter, Mark 1984, "Small is bountiful: Labor markets and establishment size," *American Sociological Review*, vol. 49: 323–34.

Hakuhōdō Seikatsu Sōgō Kenkyūsho 1985, *"Bunshū" no tanjō* (The emergence of segmented masses). Nihon Keizai Shinbunsha.

Hakuhōdō Seikatsu Sōgō Kenkyūsho 1989, *Kyūjū-nen-dai kazoku* (Families in the 1990s). Hakuhōdō.

Haley, John Owen 1978, "The myth of the reluctant litigant," *Journal of Japanese Studies*, vol. 4, no. 2 (Summer): 359–90.

Hamaguchi, Eshun 1985, "A contextual model of the Japanese: Toward a methodological innovation in Japanese studies," *Journal of Japanese Studies*, vol. 11, no. 2 (Summer): 289–321.

Hamaguchi, Eshun 1988, *"Nihon-rashisa" no sai-hakken* (Rediscovering "Japanese-like" qualities). Kōdasha.

Hamashima, Akira 1991, *Gendai shakai to kaikyū* (Contemporary society and class). University of Tokyo Press.

Hardacre, Helen 1989, *Shinto and the State: 1868–1988*. Princeton: Princeton University Press.

Hashimoto, Kenji 1990, *"Kaikyū shakai to shite no Nihon shakai"* (Japanese society as class society), *SSM*, vol. 1: 51–64.

Herbert, Wolfgang 1996, *Foreign Workers and Law Enforcement in Japan*. London: Kegan Paul International.

Hidaka, Rokuro 1984, *The Price of Affluence: Dilemma of Contemporary Japan*. Kodansha International.

Hofstede, Geert 1984, *Culture's Consequences: International Differences in Work-Related Values*. Beverly Hills: Sage Publications.

Hokkaidō-chō 1988, *Hokkaidō utari fukushi taisaku, dai 3-ji* (Welfare measures for the utari in Hokkaidō: the third round). Sapporo: Hokkaidō-chō.

Horio, Teruhisa 1979, *Gendai Nihon no kyōiku shisō* (Educational thought in contemporary Japan). Aoki Shoten.

Horioka, Charles Yuji 1995, *Household Saving in Japan: The Importance of Saving for Specific Motives*. Amsterdam: Elsevier Science.

Huddle, Norie and Reich, Michael 1987, *Island of Dreams: Environmental Crisis in Japan*. Cambridge, Massachusetts: Schenkman Books.

Huntington, Samuel P. 1993, "The clash of civilizations," *Foreign Affairs*, vol. 72, no. 3: 22–49.

Ide, Sachiko 1979, *Onna no kotoba, otoko no kotoba* (Female speech and male speech). Nihon Keizai Tsūshinsha.

Ikeda, Hiroshi 1987, "Nihon shakai no mainoritii to kyōiku no fubyōdō" (Minorities and inequalities of education in Japanese society), *Kyōiku Shakaigaku Kenkyū*, no. 42: 51–69.

Imada, Sachiko 1982, "Shokugyō keireki to rōdō shijō no kōzō," (The occupational background and structure of the labor market), *Koyō Shokugyō Kenkyū*, no. 19: 45–54.

Imada, Takatoshi 1987, *Modan no datsu-kōchiku* (Deconstructing the modern). Chūō Kōronsha.

Imada, Takatoshi 1989, *Shakai kaisō to seiji* (Social strata and politics). University of Tokyo Press.

Imada, Takatoshi and Hara, Junsuke 1979, "Shakai-teki chii no ikkan-sei to hi-ikkan-sei" (Status consistency and inconsistency), in Ken'ichi Tominaga (ed.), *Nihon no kaisō kōzō* (Stratification structure of Japan). University of Tokyo Press, pp. 161–97.

Imazu, Kōjirō 1991, "Kyōiku: Tōkō kyohi o chūshin ni" (Japanese education with a special focus on school-refusal cases), in Tsutomu Shiohara et al. (eds), *Gendai Nihon no seikatsu hendō* (Life-style changes in contemporary Japan). Kyoto: Sekai Shisōsha, pp. 71–89.

Inoguchi, Takashi and Iwai, Tomoaki 1987, *"Zoku giin" no kenkyū* (A study of *zoku* parliamentarians). Nihon Keizai Shinbunsha.

Inoue, Tadashi 1977, *"Sekentei" no kōzō* (Structure of "appearances"). Nihon Hōsō Shuppan Kyōkai.

Inoue, Teruko and Ehara, Yumiko (eds) 1991, *Josei no deta bukku* (Women's data book). Yūhikaku.

Inui, Akio 1990, *Nihon no kyōiku to kigyō shakai* (Education and corporation society in Japan). Ōtsuki Shoten.

Irokawa, Daikichi 1989, "Popular movements in modern Japanese society," in Gavan McCormack and Yoshio Sugimoto (eds), *The Japanese Trajectory: Modernization and Beyond.* Cambridge: Cambridge University Press, pp. 69–89.

Ishida, Hiroshi 1989, "Class structure and status hierarchies in contemporary Japan," *European Sociological Review*, vol. 5, no. 1 (May): 65–80.

Ishida, Hiroshi 1993, *Social Mobility in Contemporary Japan.* London: Macmillan.

Ishida, Hiroshi, Goldthorpe, John H. and Erikson, Robert 1991, "Inter-generational class mobility in postwar Japan," *American Journal of Sociology*, vol. 96, no. 4 (January): 954–92.

Ishida, Takeshi 1983, *Japanese Political Culture.* New Brunswick: Transaction Books.

Ishida, Yūzō 1996, *Yoko-shakai no riron* (The theory of horizontally structured society). Kage Shobō.

Ishikawa, Tsuneo (ed.) 1994, *Nippon no shotoku to tomi no bunpai* (The distribution of income and wealth in Japan). University of Tokyo Press.

Itagaki, Hidenori 1987, *"Zoku" giin no kenkyū* (A study of *zoku* politicians). Keizaikai.

Itō, Shuntarō 1985, *Hikaku bunmei* (Comparative studies of civilizations). University of Tokyo Press.

Iwai, Tomoaki 1988, *Rippō katei* (Legislative processes). University of Tokyo Press.

Iwasaki, Nobuhiko et al. 1989, *Chōnaikai no kenkyū* (Studies of neighborhood associations). Ochanomizu Shobō.

Iwata, Ryūshi 1981, *Gakureki shugi no hatten kōzō* (Development structure of educational credentialism). Nihon Hyōronsha.

Izumi, Seiichi and Gamō, Masao 1952, "Nihon shakai no chiiki-sei" (Regional characteristics of Japanese society), in Hiroshi Satō and Misao Watanabe (eds), *Nihon chiri shin-taikei* (New series in Japanese geography), vol. 2. Kawade Shobō.

Johnson, Chalmers 1982, *MITI and the Japanese Miracle.* Stanford: Stanford University Press.

Johnson, Chalmers 1990, "The Japanese economy: A different kind of capitalism." in S.N. Eisenstadt and Eyal Ben-Ari (eds), *Japanese Models of Conflict Resolution.* London: Kegan Paul International, pp. 39–59.

Josei Shokugyō Zaidan 1990, *Joshi kanrishoku chōsa kekka hōkokusho* (Report on the results of inquiries of female managers). Joshi Shokugyō Zaidan.

Josei Shokugyō Zaidan (ed.) 1991, *Wākingu ūman jiten* (Dictionary of working women). Tōyō Keizai Shinpōsha.

Kabashima, Ikuo 1988, *Seiji sanka* (Political participation). University of Tokyo Press.

Kamata, Satoshi 1984, *Kyōiku kōjō no kodomatchi* (Children in education factories). Iwanami Shoten.

Kanomata, Nobuo 1990, "Shisan kakusa no jidai wa kuruka?" (Will the age of asset-based stratification come?), *ESP*, no. 222 (October): 23–7.

Kariya, Takehiko 1991, *Gakkō, shokugyō, senbatsu no shakaigaku: Kōsotsu shūshoku no Nihonteki mekanizumu* (Sociology of schooling, work and selection: Japanese mechanism of transition from high school to work). University of Tokyo Press.

Karōshi Bengodan Zenkoku Renraku Kaigi (National Coordination Council of Defence Attorneys for Victims of Death from Overwork) 1991, *Karōshi* (Death from overwork). Mado-sha.

Karōshi Bengodan Zenkoku Renraku Kaigi (National Coordination Council of Defence Attorneys for Victims of Death from Overwork) 1992, Karōshi! (Death from overwork!). Kōdansha.

Kashima, Yoshihisa, Yamaguchi, Susumu, Kim, Uichol, Choi, San-Chin, Gelfand, Michele and Yuki, Masaki 1996, "Culture, gender, and self: A perspective from individualism-collectivism research," *Journal of Personality and Social Psychology*, vol. 69, no. 5: 925–37.

Kataoka, Emi 1987, "Shitsuke to shakai kaisō no kanren ni kansuru bunseki" (An analysis of relationship between family socialization and social class), *Ōsaka Daigaku Ningen Kagakubu Kiyō*, vol. 13: 23–51.

Kataoka, Emi 1991, "Shakai kaisō to bunka" (Social class and culture), in Yukio Shirakura (ed.), *Gendai no shakai shisutemu* (Contemporary social system). Gakujutsu Tosho Shuppansha, pp. 253–79.

Kataoka, Emi 1992, "Shakai kaisō to bunkateki saiseisan" (Social and cultural reproduction processes in Japan), *Riron to Hōhō*, vol. 7, no. 1: 33–55.

Kato, Tetsurō 1992, *Shakai to kokka* (Society and the state). Iwanami Shoten.

Kawahito, Hiroshi 1990, *Karōshi to kigyō no sekinin* (Deaths from overwork and corporate responsibilities). Rōdō Junpōsha.

Kawamura, Nozomu 1980, "The historical background of arguments emphasizing the uniqueness of Japanese society," *Social Analysis*, no. 5/6: 44–62.

Kawanishi, Hirosuke 1986, "The reality of enterprise unionism," in Gavan McCormack and Yoshio Sugimoto (eds), *Democracy in Contemporary Japan*. Sydney: Hale & Iremonger; New York: M.E. Sharpe, pp. 138–56.

Kawanishi, Hirosuke 1992, *Enterprise Unionism in Japan*. London: Kegan Paul International.

Kersten, Joachim 1993, "Street youth, bosozoku and yakuza: Subculture formation and societal reactions in Japan," *Crime and Delinquency*, vol. 39, no. 3: 277–95.

Kimura, Sakae and Baba, Ken'ichi 1988, *Boshi yuchaku* (Mother-child adhesion). Yūhikaku.

Kishimoto, Shigenobu 1978, *"Chūryū" no gensō* (The illusion of being "middle-class"). Kōdansha.

Kiyonari, Tadao 1985, *Chūshō kigyō* (Small businesses in Japan). Nihon Keizai Shinbunsha.

Kobayashi, Jun'ichi, Kanomata, Nobuo, Yamamoto, Tsutomu and Tsukahara, Shūichi 1991, "Shakai kaisō to tsūkon-ken" (Social stratification and marriage zones), in *SSM*, vol. 1, pp. 65–82.

Kohn, Melvin L. 1977, *Class and Conformity: A Study in Values*, 2nd edn. Chicago: University of Chicago Press.

Kohn, Melvin and Schooler, Carmi 1983, *Work and Personality: An Inquiry into the Impact of Social Stratification*. Norwood, New Jersey: Ablex Publishing.

Koike, Kazuo 1988, *Understanding Industrial Relations in Modern Japan*, trans. Mary Saso. London: Macmillan.

Komai, Hiroshi 1990, "On the fringes," *Journal of Japanese Trade and Industry*, no. 3 (May/June): 40–2.

Komai, Hiroshi 1992, "Are foreign trainees in Japan disguised cheap labourers?," *Migration World*, vol. 20, no. 1: 13–17.

Komai, Hiroshi 1995, *Migrant Workers in Japan*. London: Kegan Paul International.

Kosaka, Kenji (ed.) 1994, *Social Stratification in Contemporary Japan*. London: Kegan Paul International.

Koyasu, Masuo 1992, "Kyōiku shinrigaku kara gakkō itsuka-sei o kangaeru" (Considering the five-day week school system from the viewpoint of educational psychology), *Shosai no Mado*, April.

Kumazawa, Makoto 1993, *Shinpen Nihon no rōdōshazō* (Profiles of Japanese workers). Chikuma Shobō.

Kurasawa, Susumu and Akimoto, Ritsuo (eds) 1990, *Chōnaikai to chiiki shūdan* (Neighborhood associations and local groups). Kyoto: Mineruva Shobō.

Kusayanagi, Daizō 1990, *"Nihon-rashisa" no shin-dankai* (New stage of "Japanese-like" qualities). Rikurūto Shuppan.

Kyūtoku, Shigenori 1979, *Bogen-byō* (Mother-pathogenic disease). Kyōiku Kenkyūsha.

Lee, O-young 1984, *Smaller is Better: Japan's Mastery of the Miniature*, trans. Robert N. Huey. Kodansha International.

Lewis, Catherine C. 1988, "Japanese first-grade classrooms: Implications for U.S. theory and research," *Comparative Education Review*, vol. 32, no. 2: 159–72.

L'Hénoret, André 1993, *Le clou qui dépasse: Récit du japon d'en bas* (The nail that stands out: A narrative of Japan from below). Paris: Editions La Découverte.

Lincoln, James R. and Kalleberg, Arne L. 1990, *Culture, Control, and Commitment: A Study of Work Organization and Work Attitude in the United States and Japan*. Cambridge: Cambridge University Press.

Lunsing, Wim 1995a, *Beyond Commonsense: Negotiating Constructions of Sexuality and Gender in Japan*. PhD thesis submitted to Oxford Brookes University. A revised version will be published by Kegan Paul International in 1997.

Lunsing, Wim 1995b, "Japanese gay magazines and marriage advertisements," *Journal of Gay and Lesbian Social Services*, vol. 3, no. 3: 71–87.

Maruyama, Hisashi (ed.) 1985, *"Minikomi" no dōjidai-shi* (Contemporary history of "mini-communication" publications). Heibonsha.

Maruyama, Masao, Katō, Shūichi and Kinoshita, Junji 1991, *Nihon bunka no kakureta katachi* (Hidden shape of Japanese culture). Iwanami Shoten.

Matsumoto, Koji 1991, *The Rise of the Japanese Corporate System*. London: Kegan Paul International.

McCormack, Gavan and Sugimoto, Yoshio (eds) 1986, *Democracy in Contemporary Japan*. Sydney: Hale & Iremonger.

Min, Kwan Sik 1994, *Zainichi kankokujin no genjō to mirai* (The present and future conditions of Korean residents in Japan). Byakuteisha.

Minami, Ikuhiro 1989, "Chūnen dansei no seikatsu to ikikata" (Life conditions and life-styles of middle-aged Japanese men), in Ken'ichi Misawa et al., *Gendaijin no raifu kōsu* (The life-course of the contemporary Japanese). Kyoto: Mineruva Shobō.

Mitsuyoshi, Toshiyuki 1986, "Ikyo oyako kazoku ni okeru 'ie' no hen'yō: Oya kazoku to 'atotsugi' kazoku" (The transformation of *ie* structure in two generation families living separately: The parental family and the 'inheritance' family), *Shakaigaku Zasshi*, no. 3.

Mitsuyoshi, Toshiyuki 1991, "Kazoku (1): Shūren to kakusan" (The family, section 1: Convergence and divergence), in Sōkichi Endō, Toshiyuki Mitsuyoshi and Minoru Nakata (eds), *Gendai nihon no kōzō hendō* (Structural transformation in contemporary Japan). Kyoto: Sekai Shisōsha, pp. 123–42.

Miyajima, Takashi and Fujita, Hidenori (eds) 1991, *Bunka to shakai: saika, kōzōka, saiseisan* (Culture and society: distinction, structure and reproduction). Yūshindō.

Miyajima, Takashi and Tanaka, Yūko 1984, "Joshi kōkōsei no shingaku kibō to kazokuteki shojōken" (Educational aspirations of high-school girls and their family environment), *Ochanomizu Joshidaigaku Josei Bunka Shiryōkanhō*, no. 5: 41–59.

Miyake, Ichirō 1989, *Tōhyō kōdō* (Voting behavior). University of Tokyo Press.

Miyamoto, Masao 1994, *Straitjacket Society: A Rebel Bureaucrat Tells*. Kodansha International.

Mori, Atsushi 1993, "Nihonjin o tsuzukeru hōhō" (How to continue to be Japanese), commentary in Yoshio Sugimoto, *Nihonjin o yameru hōhō* (How to cease to be Japanese). Chikuma Shobō, pp. 249–53.

Morioka, Kiyomi and Aoi, Kazuo (eds) 1991, *Gendai Nihonjin no raifu kōsu* (The life-course of the contemporary Japanese). Nihon Gakujutsu Shinkōkai.

Morioka, Kiyomi and Mochizuki, Takashi 1993, *Atarashii kazoku shakaigaku, 3-teiban* (New family sociology), 3rd edn. Baifūkan.

Mouer, Ross and Sugimoto, Yoshio 1986, *Images of Japanese Society*. London: Kegan Paul International.

Mouer, Ross and Sugimoto, Yoshio 1995, "*Nihonjinron* at the end of the twentieth century: A multicultural perspective," *La Trobe University Asian Studies Paper – Research Series*, no. 4.

Mouer, Ross and Sugimoto, Yoshio (eds) 1980, *Japanese Society: Reappraisals and New Directions*, special issue of *Social Analysis*, nos 5/6 (December). Adelaide: University of Adelaide.

Mouer, Ross and Sugimoto, Yoshio (eds) 1987, *Kojin kanjin Nihonjin* (Individuals, interpersonal relations and society in Japan). Gakuyō Shobō.

Murakami, Yasusuke 1984a, *Shin chūkan taishū no jidai* (The age of new middle masses). Chuō Kōronsha.

Murakami, Yasusuke 1984b, "*Ie* society as a pattern of civilization," *Journal of Japanese Studies*, vol. 10, no. 2: 281–367.

Murakami, Yasusuke, Kumon, Shunpei and Satō, Seizaburō 1979, *Bunmei to shite no ie shakai* (*Ie* society as civilization). Chuō Kōronsha.

Muramatsu, Michio 1988, *Chihō jichi* (Local autonomy). University of Tokyo Press.

Muramatsu, Michio 1994, *Nihon no gyōsei* (Japanese public bureaucracy). Chuō Kōron.

Muramatsu, Michio, Itō, Mitsutoshi and Tsujinaka, Yutaka 1986, *Sengo Nihon no atsuryoku dantai* (Pressure groups in postwar Japan). Tōyō Keizai Shinpōsha.

Nagashima, Hironobu 1977, "Nihon-teki shakai kankei" (The Japanese mode of social relations), in Yoshio Masuda (ed.), *Nihonjin no shakai* (The society of the Japanese), vol. 6 of *Kōza hikaku bunka* (Series on comparative culture). Kenkyūsha Shuppan, pp. 185–213.

Nakamura, Hideichirō 1990, *Shin chūken kigyō-ron* (A new theory on middle-sized enterprises). Tōyō Keizai Shinpōsha.

Nakamura, Hideichirō 1992, *Nijū-isseiki gata chūshō kigyō* (Medium- and small-size businesses of the twenty-first century type). Iwanami Shoten.

Nakane, Chie 1967, *Tate shakai no ningen kankei* (Interpersonal relationships in a vertically structured society). Kōdansha.

Nakane, Chie 1970, *Japanese Society*. London: Weidenfeld & Nicolson.

Nakane, Chie 1978, *Tate shakai no rikigaku* (Dynamics of a vertically structured society). Kōdansha.

Nakano, Shūichirō and Imazu, Kōjirō (eds) 1993, *Esunishitii no shakaigaku: Nihon shakai no minzoku-teki kōsei* (Sociology of ethnicity: The ethnic composition of Japanese society). Kyoto: Seikai Shisōsha.

Nakano, Osamu 1992, *"Kazoku suru" kazoku* (Families which "do a family"). Yūhikaku.

Nakano, Yumiko 1974, "Kaisō to gengo" (Class and language), *Kyōiku Shakaigaku Kenkyū*, no. 29: 146–60.

Nakayama, Osamu 1982, *"Bokashi" no Nihon bunka* (Japanese culture of "ambiguity"). Arufaa Shuppan.

Namihira, Emiko 1979, "Hare to ke to kegare" (*Hare, ke* and *kegare*), *Nippon no minzoku shūkyō* (Japan's folk religion), vol. 1. Kōbundō.

Naoi, Atsushi 1989, "Kuzure hajimeta heijunka shinwa" (The myth of equalization begins to collapse), *Asahi Journal*, April 7: 14–19.

Nester, William 1990, "The development of Japan, Taiwan and South Korea: Ends and means, free trade, dependency, or neomercantilism?," *Journal of Developing Societies*, vol. 6, no. 2 (July–October): 203–18.

Neustupný, J.V. 1980, "On paradigms in the study of Japan," *Social Analysis*, no. 5/6 (December): 20–8.

NHK Yoron Chōsabu (ed.) 1991, *Gendai Nihonjin no ishiki kōzō* (The consciousness structure of contemporary Japanese), 3rd edn. Nippon Hōsō Shuppan Kyōkai.

NHK Yoron Chōsabu (ed.) 1992, *Zusetsu Nihonjin no seikatsu jikan*, 1990 (Patterns of time usage of the Japanese, 1990). Nippon Hōsō Kyōkai.

Nippon no Shachō Kenkyū-kai 1994, *Nippon no shachō-tachi* (Company presidents in Japan). Daiyamondosha.

Nishiyama, Shigeru 1979, "Shin shūkyō no genkyō" (The present situation of new religions), *Rekishi Kōron*, vol. 5, no. 7 (July): 33–7.

Nitoda, Rokusaburō 1987, *Tatemae to honne: Nihonjin no ura to omote* (*Tatemae* and *honne*: *Ura* and *omote* of the Japanese). Mikasa Shobō.

Noguchi, M.G. 1992, "The rise of the housewife activist," *Japan Quarterly*, (July–September): 339–53.

Ochi, Noboru 1980, "Chōnaikai no soshiki bunseki" (Organizational analysis of neighborhood associations), in Otohiko Hasumi and Michihiro Okuda (eds), *Chiiki shakairon* (On local communities). Yūhikaku, pp. 335–66.

Ochiai, Emiko 1989, "Gendai no nyūyōji to sono oyatachi" (Babies and their mothers today), in Ken'ichi Misawa et al., *Gendaijin no raifu kōsu* (Life course of the contemporary Japanese). Kyoto: Mineruva Shobō, pp. 1–53.

Odaka, Kunio 1961, "Nihon no chūkan kaikyū: Sono ichizuke ni kansuru hōhōron-teki oboegaki" (Japan's middle classes: methodological notes on their conceptualization), *Nihon Rōdō Kyūkai Zasshi*, no. 22: 4–27.

Oguma, Eiji 1995, *Tan'itsu minzoku shinwa no kigen* (The origin of the myth of the homogeneous nation). Shin'yōsha.

Ōhashi, Ryūken 1971, *Nihon no kaikyū kōsei* (Class composition in Japan). Iwanami Shoten.

Okamura, Chikanobu 1990, *Karōshi to rōsai hoshō* (Overwork death and industrial injury insurance). Rōdō Junpōsha.

Okano, Kaori 1993, *School to Work Transition in Japan*. Clevedon: Multilingual Matters.

Okano, Kaori 1994, "'Modern' Japan and social identity: Minority youth in school to work transition," in Albert Gomes (ed.), *Modernity and Identity: Asian Illustrations*. Melbourne: La Trobe University Press, pp. 206–31.

Okonogi, Keigo 1992, *Katei no nai kazoku no jidai* (The age of family-less families). Chikuma Shobō.

Okumura, Hiroshi 1991, *Hōjin shihonshugi* (Corporate capitalism), revised edn. Asahi Shinbunsha.

Organization for Economic Cooperation and Development 1973, *Manpower Policy in Japan*. Paris: OECD.

Ōsono, Tomokazu 1991, *Hitome de wakaru kigyō keiretsu to gyōkai chizu* (Enterprise groupings and the industry map at a glance). Nippon Jitsugyō Shuppansha.

Ōtake, Fumio and Horioka, Charles Yuji 1994, "Chochiku dōki" (Motives for savings), in Tsuneo Ishikawa (ed.), *Nihon no shotoku to tomi no bunpai* (Distribution of income and wealth in Japan). University of Tokyo Press, pp. 211–44.

Ōtsu, Tōru 1985, "Ritsuryō kokka to kinai: Kodai kokka no shihai kōzō" (The Kinki district in ancient Japan and its structure of domination), *Nihon shoki kenkyū*, vol. 13. Hanawa Shoten.

Ozawa, Masako 1989, *Shin kaisō shōhi no jidai* (New age of stratified consumption). Asahi Shinbunsha.

Parsons, Talcott 1951, *The Social System*. New York: Free Press.

Pharr, Susan J. 1989, *Losing Face: Status Politics in Japan*. Berkeley: University of California Press.

Ramseyer, J. Mark 1988, "Reluctant litigant revisited: Rationality and disputes in Japan," *Journal of Japanese Studies*, vol. 14, no. 1 (Winter): 111–23.

Reischauer, Edwin O. 1977, *The Japanese*. Cambridge: Belknap Press of Harvard University Press.

Rōdōshō, Kanbō Seisaku Chōsa-bu (ed.) 1991a, *Shisan kakusa* (Asset disparity). Ōkurashō Insatsu-kyoku.

Rōdōshō, Kanbō Seisaku Chōsa-bu (ed.) 1991b, *Tenkin to tanshin funin* (Transfers and company bachelorship). Ōkurashō Insatsu-kyoku.

Rōdōshō, Kanbō Seisaku Chōsa-bu (ed.) 1991c, *Zusetsu: Rōdō hakusho.* (1991 White paper on labor: An illustrated version). Shiseidō.

Rōdōshō, Rōdō Kijunkyoku 1991, *Rōdō jikan hakusho* (White paper on working hours). Nihon Rōdō Kenkyū Kikō.

Rohlen, Thomas P. 1983, *Japan's High Schools*. Stanford: Stanford University Press.

Rosenbaum, James E. and Kariya, Takehiko 1991, "Do school achievements affect the early jobs of high school graduates in the United States and Japan?," *Sociology of Education*, vol. 64, no. 2 (April): 78–95.

Rosenberger, N. 1987, "Productivity, sexuality, and ideologies of menopausal problems in Japan", in E. Norbeck and M. Lock (eds), *Health, Illness and Medical Care in Japan.* Honolulu: University of Hawaii Press, pp. 158–87.

Russell, John 1991a, "Race and reflexivity: The black other in contemporary Japanese mass culture," *Cultural Anthropology,* vol. 6, no. 1 (February): 3–25.

Russell, John 1991b, "Narratives of denial: Racial chauvinism and the black other in Japan," *Japan Quarterly,* vol. 38, no. 4 (October–December): 416–28.

Saha, Arunoday 1991, "Zen and Japanese economic performance," *International Journal of Sociology and Social Policy,* vol. 11, no. 4: 17–36.

Sakaiya, Taichi 1980, *Dankon no sedai* (The baby-boomer generation). Bungei Shunjū.

Sakaiya, Taichi 1991, *Nihon to wa nanika* (What is Japan?). Kōdansha.

Sakaiya, Taichi 1993, *What is Japan?* Tokyo: Kodansha International.

Sakakibara, Fujiko 1992, *Josei to koseki* (Women and the family registration system). Akashi Shoten.

Sakurai, Tokutarō 1982, *Nippon no minzoku shūkyō-ron* (On Japan's folk religion). Shunjūsha.

Sakurai, Tokutarō et al. 1984, *Kyōdō tōgi: hare, ke, kegare* (A collective discussion on *hare, ke* and *kegare*). Seidosha.

Sataka, Shin 1992a, *Nippon ni igi ari* (Dissenting from Japan). Kōdansha.

Sataka, Shin 1992b, "Hanran shite iru seishin shugi kenshū" (A flood of spiritualist training sessions for company executives), *AM* May 23, p. 8.

Sataka, Shin 1993a, *"Kaisha kokka" o utsu* (Denouncing Japan as a "corporation country"). Kyoto: Kamogawa Shuppan.

Sataka, Shin 1993b, *Kigyō genron* (An introduction to Japanese business practices). Shakai Shisōsha.

Satō, Bunmei 1991, *Koseki ga miharu kurashi* (Everyday life controlled by the family registration system). Gendai Shokan.

Satō, Machiko 1993, *Shin kaigai teijū jidai* (The new age of migrating and settling abroad). Shinchōsha.

Satō, Machiko 1994, *Gōrei no nai gakkō* (Schools without words of command). Chikuma Shobō.

Schoolland, Ken 1990, *Shogun's Ghost: The Dark Side of Japanese Education.* New York: Bergin & Garvey.

Seiyama, Kazuo 1990, "Chū-ishiki no imi" (The meaning of middle-class identification), *Riron to Hōhō,* vol. 5, no. 2: 51–71.

Seiyama, Kazuo 1994, "Intergenerational occupational mobility," in Kenji Kosaka (ed.), *Social Stratification in Contemporary Japan.* London: Kegan Paul International, pp. 54–77.

Sengoku, Tamotsu 1991, *"Majime" no hōkai: Heisei Nippon no wakamonotachi* (Japanese youth today: A generation no longer so serious). Saimaru Shuppan-kai.

Shibamoto, Janet S. 1985, *Japanese Women's Language.* Orlando: Academic Press.

Shibata, Kōzō 1983, *Hō no tatemae to honne* (*Tatemae* and *honne* in law). Yūhikaku.

Shikata, Hiroshi 1984, *Rikon no kōzu* (Perspectives on divorce). Mainichi Shinbunsha.

Shimizu, Hirokichi 1991, "Gakureki, kekkon, kaisō saiseisan" (Educational background, marriage, and class reproduction), in *SSM,* vol. 3, pp. 107–26.

Shimogō, Satomi (ed.) 1990, *Chikyū to ikiru gojūgo no hōhō* (Fifty-five methods of living together with the earth). Honnoki.

Shimono, Keiko 1991, *Shisan kakusa no keizai bunseki* (An economic analysis of asset disparity). Nagoya Daigaku Shuppan-kai.

Shimono, Keiko 1992, "Aratana kaikyū shakai no shutsugen" (The emergence of a new class society), *AE* March 21, p. 8.

Shindō, Muneyuki 1992, *Gyōsei shidō* (Administrative guidance). Iwanami Shoten.

Shōji, Kōkichi 1989, *Kanri shakai to sekai shakai* (Manipulative society and the world community). University of Tokyo Press.

Shufu to Seikatsusha 1992, *Todōfuken-betsu kankonsōsai daijiten* (Dictionary of prefectural variations in the ceremonies of coming of age, marriage, funeral, and ancestral worship). Shufu to Seikatsusha.

Sofue, Takao 1971, *Kenmin-sei* (Prefectural character). Chūō Kōron.

Sōrifu Tōkei-kyoku (Management and Coordination Agency, Bureau of Statistics) 1996, *Shakai seikatsu tōkei shihyō* (Statistical indices of social life), 1996 edn. Nihon Tōkei Kyōkai.

Steven, Rob 1983, *Classes in Contemporary Japan*. Cambridge: Cambridge University Press.

Stevenson, David Lee and Baker, David P. 1992, "Shadow education and allocation in formal schooling: Transition to university," *American Journal of Sociology*, vol. 97, no. 6 (May): 1639–57.

Stevenson, Harold W. 1992, "Learning from Asian schools," *Scientific American*, December: 32–8.

Stevenson, Harold W. and Stingler, J.W. 1992, *The Learning Gap: Why Our Schools are Failing and What Can We Learn from Japanese and Chinese Education*. New York: Summit Books.

Sugimoto, Yoshio 1993, *Nihonjin o yameru hōhō* (How to cease to be Japanese). Chikuma Shobō.

Sugimoto, Yoshio and Mouer, Ross 1995, *Nihonjinron no hōteishiki* (The Japanology equations). Chikuma Shobō.

Sugimoto, Yoshio and Mouer, Ross (eds) 1989, *Constructs for Understanding Japan*. London: Kegan Paul International.

Tachibanaki, Toshiaki 1989, "Japan's new policy agenda: Coping with unequal asset distribution," *Journal of Japanese Studies*, vol. 15, no. 2 (Summer): 345–69.

Tachibanaki, Toshiaki 1992, "High land prices as a cause of increasing inequality in wealth distribution and socio-economic effect," in J.O. Haley and Kozo Yamamura (eds), *Land Issues in Japan: A Policy Failure?* Society for Japanese Studies.

Tachibanaki, Toshiaki 1994, "Shotoku bunpai byōdō no 'shinwa' wa kuzureta" (The end of the 'myth' of egalitarian income distribution), *Sekai*, March: 72–5.

Tachibanaki, Toshiaki and Yagi, Tadashi 1994, "Shotoku bunpai no genjō to saikin no suii" (The present situation and the recent trend of income distribution) in Tsuneo Ishikawa (ed.), *Nippon no shotoku to tomi no bunpai* (The distribution of income and wealth in Japan). University of Tokyo Press, pp. 23–58.

Tada, Michitarō 1978, *Asobi to Nihonjin* (Play and the Japanese). Chikuma Shobō.

Tada, Michitarō 1988, "Osaka popular culture: A down-to-earth appraisal," in Gavan McCormack and Yoshio Sugimoto (eds), *The Japanese Trajectory: Modernization and Beyond*. Cambridge: Cambridge University Press, pp. 33–53.

Takahara, Kimiko 1991, "Female speech patterns in Japanese," *International Journal of the Sociology of Language*, no. 92: 61–85.

Takatori, Masao 1975, *Nihon-teki shikō no genkei* (The original pattern of Japanese-style thinking). Kōdansha.

Takeuchi, Kiyoshi 1993, "Seito bunka no shakaigaku" (Sociology of student culture), in Takahiro Kihara et al. (eds), *Gakkō bunka no shakaigaku* (Sociology of school culture). Fukumura Shuppan, pp. 107–22.

Takeuchi, Yo 1991a, "Myth and reality in the Japanese educational selection system," *Comparative Education*, vol. 27, no. 1 (March): 101–12.

Takeuchi, Yo 1991b, *Risshi, kugaku, shusse* (Achievement orientation, study under adversity, and advancement in life). Kōdansha.

Tanaka, Hiroshi 1991, *Zainichi gaikokujin* (Resident foreigners in Japan). Iwanami Shoten.

Tanigawa, Gan 1961, "Nippon no nijū kōzō" (Japan's dual structure), *Gendai no hakken* (Discovering contemporary Japan), vol. 13. Shunjūsha.

Tōkei Sūri Kenkyūsho (Institute of Statistical Mathematics) 1979, *Nihonjin no kokumin-sei* (National character of the Japanese). Shiseidō.

Tōkei Sūri Kenkyūsho (Institute of Statistical Mathematics) 1994, "Kokumin-sei no kenkyū: 1993-nen dai 9-kai zenkoku chōsa" (Studies of national character: the 9th national survey, conducted in 1993). *Tōkei Chōsa Kenkyū Report*, no. 75.

Tokugawa, Munemasa (ed.) 1979, *Nihon no hōgen chizu* (Maps of dialects in Japan). Chūō Koron.

Tokuoka, Hideo 1976, "Kakei no kyōdō to bunri" (Sharing and separation of the domestic budget), in Takeji Kamiko and Kōkichi Masuda (eds), *San-sedai kazoku: Sedai-kan kankei no jisshō-teki kenkyū* (Three-generation families: Empirical studies of intergenerational relations). Kakiuchi Shuppan.

Tokyo Daigaku Kōhō Iinkai 1991, *Gakunai Kōhō* (University of Tokyo Newsletter), no. 906–2, November 25.

Tominaga, Ken'ichi (ed.) 1979, *Nihon no kaisō kōzō* (Stratification structure of Japan). University of Tokyo Press.

Tominaga, Ken'ichi (ed.) 1982, "Problems of viewpoint in interpreting Japanese society: Japan and the West," Ostasiatisches Seminar, Freie Universität Berlin, *Occasional Papers*, no. 38.

Tominaga, Ken'ichi (ed.) 1988, *Nihon sangyō shakai no tenki* (Turning points of Japanese industrial society). University of Tokyo Press.

Tominaga, Ken'ichi (ed.) 1990, *Nihon no kindaika to shakai hendō* (Modernization and social change in Japan). Kōdansha.

Tominaga, Ken'ichi and Tomoeda, Toshio 1986, "Nihon shakai ni okeru chii hi-ikkansei no suusei 1955–1975 to sono imi" (Trend and significance of status inconsistency in Japanese society from 1955 to 1975), *Shakaigaku Hyōron*, vol. 37, no. 2: 20–42.

Tomoeda, Toshio 1989, "Kaisō kurasutā no torendo" (Trend of stratification clusters), *Shakai Bunseki*, no. 18: 151–64.

Toneri, Eiichi 1980, *Waga ken no jutsuryoku banzuke* (Rank-ordering the merits of prefectures in Japan). Shōdensha.

Tōyama, Kei 1976, *"Nōryoku shugi" to "joretsu shugi"* ("Ability orientation" and "hierarchy orientation"). Tarō Jirō-sha.

Tsujinaka, Yutaka 1988, *Rieki shūdan* (Interest groups). University of Tokyo Press.

Tsunoda, Tadanobu 1981, *Migi-nō to hidari-nō* (Right brain and left brain). Shōgakkan.

Tsurumi, Shunsuke 1967, *Genkai geijutsu-ron* (On marginal art). Chikuma Shobō.

Tsurumi, Shunsuke 1986, *An Intellectual History of Wartime Japan, 1931–1945*. London: Kegan Paul International.

Tsurumi, Shunsuke 1987, *A Cultural History of Postwar Japan, 1945–1980*. London: Kegan Paul International.

Twu, Jaw-yann 1990, *Tōyō shihon-shugi* (Oriental capitalism). Kōdansha.

Ueno, Chizuko 1988, "The Japanese women's movement: The counter-values to industrialism," in Gavan McCormack and Yoshio Sugimoto (eds), *The Japanese Trajectory: Modernization and Beyond.* Cambridge: Cambridge University Press, pp. 167–85.

Ueno, Chizuko 1990, *Kafuchōsei to shihonsei* (Patriarchy and capitalism). Iwanami Shoten.

Ueno, Chizuko 1991, "Josei no henbō to kazoku" (Women's transformation and the family system), in Sōichi Endo, Toshiyuki Mitsuyoshi and Minoru Nakata (eds), *Gendai Nihon no kōzō hendō* (Structural transformation in contemporary Japan). Kyoto: Sekai Shisōsha, pp. 141–65.

Ueno, Chizuko 1992, "The position of Japanese women reconsidered," *Current Anthropology*, vol. 28, no. 4 (August–October): S75–S82.

Umehara, Takeshi (ed.) 1990, *Nihon to wa nannanoka* (What is Japan?). Nihon Hōsō Shuppan Kyōkai.

Umesao, Tadao 1967, *Bunmei no seitai shikan* (An ecological view of the history of civilizations). Chūō Kōronsha.

Umesao, Tadao 1986, *Nihon to wa nanika* (What is Japan?). Nihon Hōsō Shuppan Kyōkai.

Umesao, Tadao 1987, *Nihon santo-ron* (On three Japanese cities: Tokyo, Osaka, and Kyoto). Kadokawa Shoten.

Vogel, Ezra F. 1979, *Japan as Number One: Lessons for America.* Cambridge: Harvard University Press.

Watanabe, Osamu 1987, "Gendai Nihon shakai no ken'i-teki kōzō to kokka" (Authoritarian structure and the state in contemporary Japanese society), in Isamu Fujita (ed.), *Ken'i-teki chitsujo to kokka* (Authoritarian order and the state). University of Tokyo Press, pp. 181–228.

Watanabe, Osamu 1990, *"Yutakana shakai" Nippon no kōzō* (The structure of "affluent Japanese society"). Rōdō Junpōsha.

Watanabe, Shōichi 1989, *Nihonshi kara mita, Nihonjin, Kodai-hen, "Nihon-rashisa" no gensen* (The Japanese in Japanese history: Ancient period. The origin of "Japanese-like" qualities). Shōdensha.

White, Merry 1987a, *The Japanese Educational Challenge: A Commitment to Children.* New York: Free Press.

White, Merry 1987b, "The virtue of Japanese mothers: Cultural definitions of women's lives," *Daedalus*, vol. 116, no. 3 (Summer): 149–63.

White, Merry 1992, "Home truths: Women and social change in Japan," *Daedalus*, vol. 121, no. 4 (Fall): 61–81.

White, Michael and Trevor, Malcolm 1984, *Under Japanese Management: The Experience of British Workers.* London: Heinemann Educational.

Wolferen, Karel Van 1990, *The Enigma of Japanese Power.* New York: Vintage Books.

Yamamoto, Shichihei 1989, *Nihonjin to wa nanika* (What are the Japanese?). Kyoto: PHP Kenkyūsho.

Yoda, Kaoru 1993, *Hitome de wakaru Nihon no kyoninka seido no subete* (All about the system of government regulation in Japan). Nihon Jitsugyō Shuppansha.

Yonekawa, Hideki 1978, "Kōkō ni okeru seito kai-bunka no sho-ruikei" (Various types of high-school student subculture), *Osaka Daigaku Ningen Kagaku-bu Kiyō*, no. 4: 183–208.

Yoneyama, Toshinao 1971, "Nihon-teki shakai kankei ni okeru 'kihon-teki gainen gun'" ('Basic conceptual clusters' in Japanese social relations), *Kikan Jinruigaku*, vol. 2, no. 3: 56–76.

Yoneyama, Toshinao 1976, *Nihonjin no nakama ishiki* (The Japanese sense of mateship). Kōdansha.

Yoneyama, Toshinao 1990, *Ima, naze bunka o tounoka* (Why do we examine culture, now?). Nihon Hōsō Shuppan Kyōkai.

Yoshida, Tomoya 1989, *Datsu konpyūtaa kanri shakai* (Transcending a society manipulated by computers). Gijutu to Ningensha.

Yoshihiro, Kiyoko 1987, *Hikon Jidai* (The age of singles). Sanseidō.

Yoshihiro, Kiyoko 1988, *Otoko-tachi no hikon jidai* (The age of male singles). Sanseidō.

Yoshino, Kosaku 1992, *Cultural Nationalism in Contemporary Japan: A Sociological Enquiry*. London: Routledge.

Yoshitani, Izumi 1992, *Nippon no chūshō kigyō* (Medium-sized and small-scale enterprises in Japan). Shin-Nippon Shuppansha.

Yuzawa, Yasuhiko 1987a, *Zusetsu gendai Nihon no kazoku mondai* (Illustrated accounts of family problems in contemporary Japan). Nihon Hōsō Shuppan Kyōkai.

Yuzawa, Yasuhiko 1987b, *Atarashii kazokugaku* (New family studies). Kōseikan.

Yuzawa, Yasuhiko 1995, *Zusetsu kazoku mondai no genzai* (Illustrated accounts of family problems today). Nihon Hōsō Shuppan Kyōkai.

Index